Values, Education and the Human World

ST ANDREWS STUDIES IN
PHILOSOPHY AND PUBLIC AFFAIRS

Founding and General Editor:
John Haldane
University of St Andrews

Volume 1:
Values, Education and the Human World
edited by John Haldane

Volume 2:
Philosophy and its Public Role
edited by William Aiken and John Haldane

Volume 3:
Relativism and the Foundations of Liberalism
by Graham Long

Volume 4:
Human Life, Action and Ethics:
Essays by G.E.M. Anscombe
edited by Mary Geach and Luke Gormally

Volume 5:
The Institution of Intellectual Values:
Realism and Idealism in Higher Education
by Gordon Graham

Values, Education and the Human World

Essays on Education, Culture, Politics, Religion and Science

Edited and Introduced by
John Haldane

St Andrews
Studies in
Philosophy and
Public Affairs

ia

IMPRINT ACADEMIC

Published in the UK by Imprint Academic
PO Box 200, Exeter EX5 5YX, UK

Published in the USA by Imprint Academic
Philosophy Documentation Center
PO Box 7147, Charlottesville, VA 22906-7147, USA

ISBN 1 84540 000 3

A CIP catalogue record for this book is available from the
British Library and US Library of Congress

Cover Photograph:
St Salvator's Quadrangle, St Andrews by Peter Adamson
from the University of St Andrews collection

Contents

Notes on the Contributors vi
Introduction viii

VALUES EDUCATION
John Haldane
1: The Nature of Values 1
David Carr
2: Problems of Values Education 14

CULTURE
Anthony Quinton
3: A Cultural Crisis: The Devaluation of Values 33
4: A Revaluation of Values: Keeping Politics in its Place . . . 50
Anthony O'Hear
5: Education, Value and the Sense of Awe 68
6: The Pursuit of Excellence 85

THE STATE
Richard Pring
7: The Aim of Education 103
8: The Context of Education 121
Mary Warnock
9: Meeting Educational Needs 140
10: Good Teaching. 155

RELIGION
Jonathan Sacks
11: Political Society, Civil Society 173
12: Languages of Morals 182
Stewart Sutherland
13: Values, Religion and Education: Diagnosis 191
14: Values, Religion and Education: Prognosis? Cure? . . . 205

SCIENCE
Mary Midgley
15: Science and Poetry 219
16: Atoms, Memes and Individuals 234
Bryan Appleyard
17: The Threat of Scientism 250
18: The New Marx 259
References 268
Index 272

Notes on the Contributors

Bryan Appleyard has been a columnist on *The Times* and *The Independent* and currently writes for *The Sunday Times*. In 1986 he was 'Feature Writer of the Year' and in 1992 he was 'Commended Feature Writer'. His many books include *The Culture Club* (1984), *The Pleasures of Peace* (1989), *Understanding the Present – Science and the Soul of Modern Man* (1992) and *Brave New Worlds: Staying Human in the Genetic Future* (1998).

David Carr is Professor of Philosophy of Education in the University of Edinburgh. He is the author of *Educating the Virtues* (1991), *Professionalism and Ethical Issues in Teaching* (2000) and *Making Sense of Education* (2003). He is also editor of *Education, Knowledge and Truth* (1998) and co-editor of *Virtue, Ethics and Moral Education* (1999) and (with John Haldane) of *Spirituality, Philosophy and Education* (2003).

John Haldane is Professor of Philosophy in the University of St Andrews where he is also Director of the Centre for Ethics, Philosophy and Public Affairs. He has also held positions at other universities, including the Royden Davis Chair of Humanities at Georgetown University, DC. He is the author (with J.J.C. Smart) of *Atheism and Theism, Second Edition* (2003), *An Intelligent Person's Guide to Religion* (2003), *Faithful Reason* (2004), and editor of *Philosophy and Public Affairs* (2000) and other volumes.

Mary Midgley was a member of the philosophy department at the University of Newcastle but she is best known as a columnist and broadcaster and as the author of a number of books on various moral questions, including *Heart and Mind* (1981), *Evolution as a Religion* (1985), *Wisdom, Information and Wonder* (1989), *Science as Salvation* (1992), *Utopias, Dolphins and Computers* (1994), *Animals and Why They Matter* (1998) and *The Myths We Live By* (2003). The arguments presented in her Cook lectures are further developed in *Science and Poetry* (2001).

Anthony O'Hear was formerly Professor of Philosophy in the University of Bradford and is currently Weston Professor of Philosophy in the University of Buckingham. He is Director of the Royal Institute of Philosophy and editor of its journal *Philosophy*. His many books include *The Element of Fire: Science, Art and the Human World* (1988), *Introduction to the Philosophy of Science* (1989), *Beyond Evolution: Human Nature and the Limits of Evolutionary Explanation* (1997), *After Progress* (1999) and *Philosophy in the New Century* (2001).

Richard Pring is a Fellow of Green College and former Professor of Educational Studies and Director of the Department of Educational Studies, in the University of Oxford. He has also been editor of the *British Journal of Educational Studies*. His publications include the following: *Closing the Gap: Liberal Education and Vocational Preparation* (1995), *Knowledge and Schooling* (1976), *The New Curriculum* (1989), *Knowledge and Schooling* (1996), *Philosophy of Educational Research* (2000) and *The Philosophy of Education* (2004).

Anthony Quinton (Baron Quinton of Holywell) was a fellow of All Souls and New College before becoming President of Trinity College, Oxford. He has also been Chairman of the British Library. His many publications include *Utilitarian Ethics* (1974), *The Nature of Things* (1978), *The Politics of Imperfection* (1982), *Thoughts and Thinkers* (1982), *Hume* (1997) and *From Wodehouse to Wittgenstein* (1998).

Jonathan Sacks was the first holder of the Chair in Modern Jewish Thought at Jews College, London and subsequently became Principal of the College. In 1991 he was appointed Chief Rabbi of the United Hebrew Congregations of the Commonwealth. In 1990 he delivered the Reith Lectures on the theme of The Persistence of Faith. The arguments presented in his Cook lectures are further developed in *The Politics of Hope* (1997). His other books include *The Dignity of Difference: How to Avoid the Clash of Civilisations* (2002) and *From Optimism to Hope* (2004).

Stewart Sutherland (Lord Sutherland of Houndwood) has been Principal of King's College London, Vice-Chancellor of London University, HM Chief Inspector of Schools, and Principal and Vice-Chancellor of the University of Edinburgh. He is also President of the Royal Society of Edinburgh and Chairman of the Council of the Royal Institute of Philosophy. He was formerly editor of *Religious Studies* and co-edited *The Philosophical Frontiers of Christian Theology* (1982). His own publications include *Atheism and the Rejection of God* (1977), *Faith and Ambiguity* (1984), and *God, Jesus and Belief: The Legacy of Theism* (1984),

Mary Warnock (Baroness Warnock of Weeke in the City of Winchester) was formerly Mistress of Girton College, Cambridge and Headmistress of Oxford High School. Her many publications include *Ethics Since 1900* (1960), *Sartre* (1963), *Existentialist Ethics* (1966), *Existentialism* (1970), *Imagination* (1976), *Schools of Thought* (1977), *Memory* (1987), *A Common Policy for Education* (1988), *Universities* (1989), *The Uses of Philosophy* (1992), *An Intelligent Person's Guide to Ethics* (1988), *Is There a Right to Have Children?* (2002) and *Nature and Morality* (2003).

Introduction

The chapters that follow were all written under the patronage of the Gordon Cook Foundation to which thanks and appreciation are due. Apart from the first two essays, which address very general issues about the nature of values and about the possibility of education in them, the chapters consist of revised versions of Victor Cook Memorial Lectures delivered in the universities of St Andrews, London (Kings College), Cambridge, Aberdeen, Oxford, Glasgow and Leeds.

Victor Cook died in his ninety-third year on 15th March 1990. He was born in the autumn of 1897 to a family associated with a successful engineering company in Aberdeen in the North East of Scotland. From an early age he wished to be a teacher, but the premature death of his father put an end to this ambition as it fell to him to carry on in the family business. He never married and in due course sold his interest in the firm and devoted the remainder of his life to promoting the cause of his intellectual child, *values education*. In 1974 he established an educational charity — *The Gordon Cook Foundation* — bearing the name of a brother who predeceased him. This creation has survived its founder's own death and continues the task of promoting values education.

Victor Cook's personal contribution to the aim of education in the field with which he was most concerned took two main forms: first, producing classroom material for young children in which values, particularly moral ones, might be developed; and second, lobbying politicians, administrators and educationalists in order to have programmes of this sort adopted within schools in Scotland and beyond. Unlike some recent theoretical approaches to the subject, Cook's idea of linking values and education was not that of purportedly uncommitted analysis.

There has been an interest within educational theory and schooling (originating in North America) in the practice of drawing children's attention to the evaluative presuppositions of what they say and do. This activity of 'values clarification' is related to the post-enlightenment ideals of autonomy, positive freedom and empowerment. The assumption is that it is good, in some formal sense, to know what values you are committed to; but this does not extend to the claim that certain substantive values are good, or that some are better than others. Victor Cook, by contrast, clearly did think that some ways of going on are better than alternatives. Furthermore he believed that those whom society charges with the education of its children have a duty (not a mere permission) to introduce pupils into these ways of going on. In other words he favoured teaching *in* and *of* values rather than an agnostic study *about* them. Clearly a large number of conceptual and normative questions arise at this point, and it is to the credit of the trustees of the Foundation that Cook founded that they recognise the need for research into these questions and have been willing to support it.

The first two of the following chapters are intended to provide a general theoretical framework to which subsequent issues might be related. They derive from the suggestion made by Dr. William Gatherer, former Chairman of the Gordon Cook Foundation, that the authors write on basic philosophical aspects of values and values education in a style suitable for an interested public, be they educationalists, teachers, students or general readers. In 'The Nature of Values' it is argued that the widespread assumption that talk of values in no more than the expression of personal preferences reveals the influence of a philosophical perspective that is neither obligatory nor even compelling. On the contrary, a plausible view of the world and of the place of humankind within it shows values to be implicit in the natures of things. In 'Problems of Values Education' something of this defence of objectivity is assumed, and starting from the distinction between *instrumental* and *intrinsic* value various educational philosophies are expounded and evaluated. Central to this latter discussion is the question of liberalism, and it is made clear that a range of possible positions exists within a broad understanding of the liberal tradition, not all of which are equally viable.

The authors of these opening chapters (Haldane and Carr) share the same broad philosophical outlook so far as concerns the status of values and the possibility of grounding educational policy decisions in the evaluative facts of human nature. They do not suppose, however, that this makes the task of thinking clearly about educational aims an easy one. On the contrary the conclusion that there are rele-

vant facts about values imposes a discipline upon practical delibera-
tions that is lacking if values are conceived of as no more than
expressions of subjective preference.

The issues and arguments addressed by the various distinguished
authors whose revised lecture texts comprise the remaining chapters will be more or less familiar to different readers. Philosophers,
political and cultural theorists, historians of ideas, art critics, educationalists, and practitioners of other academic and cultural disciplines will all find things of interest and significance to them. But it is
equally important that the general educated reader should engage
with these discussions and they have been written with that purpose
very much in mind. The lecturers selected their own topics for study,
offered their analyses and made their cases. One could, therefore,
read the several chapters independently. However, they also exhibit
continuity of general theme and of broad outlook, as well as involving a movement in the direction of increasing specificity, which
gives them a unity and an order.

Lord Quinton is concerned with 'radical' challenges to high culture as these direct themselves against the literary canon, the traditional intellectual values of enquiry and expression, and the idea of
objective truth, and he considers the implications of this attack for
education, before offering a robust defence of culture and its values.
Following this, Anthony O'Hear takes up the central question for all
philosophical discussions of value, asking whether something is
good because we desire or approve of it or whether the assumption
of the objectivity of goodness is necessary in order to make sense of
our valuing anything. He then connects the idea that value tran-
scends our preferences with a need for education to create a sense of
the good and the true in advance of promoting critical and sceptical
attitudes. From this conclusion he proceeds to consider the structure
of education and the place within this of culture and tradition. In one
sense, therefore, the discussion comes full circle but since O'Hear
turns the direction of his argument towards specifics of current educational policy and practice one may better say that the movement is
a spiralling one.

Lady Warnock and Richard Pring refer back to some of the issues
and arguments of the previous lectures and continue the examination of educational thought and practice, now directing attention to
the specifics of schooling. Each has things to say about the history of
UK government policy in the last thirty years; and each finds failings
in the underlying social and educational philosophy, and inadequa-

cies in the organisation of education and teacher training. Both write from a background of practice in schools and universities, and as philosophers interested in educational theory. Thus as well as learning a good deal about the history of educational policy, readers will find themselves drawn into philosophical reflections about the nature of education and the adequacy of the liberal/vocational contrast and about ideas of educational needs and of good teaching.

The issues addressed by Jonathan Sacks and Stewart Sutherland are intellectually challenging and clearly important for the future of cultural thought in general and for educational policy and practice in particular. Dr Sacks is an academic and, as Chief Rabbi, a religious leader. Lord Sutherland is also an academic and an academic leader. Between them they bring to bear a good deal of thought and experience about questions of value and education. Nonetheless, they are frank in giving emphasis in their lectures to the difficulties facing us as members of societies that are generally pluralistic, often atomised, and frequently sceptical.

Jonathan Sacks observes a contrast between political society and civil society. Drawing on the myth of Genesis he makes the point that from earliest times it has been clear that mankind cannot live alone but equally finds it difficult to live together. The tradition of modern political thought has made much of the idea of the social contract but, as Sacks points out, this tends to assume competitive relationships and to reduce sociality to mutual self-interest. In contrast, there is the originally Jewish notion of *covenant* in which individuals are bound together through moral relationships into forms of community. The problem for us today is that community seems ever more necessary, yet without common religious or moral commitments ever more difficult to achieve; at the same time, however, people feel uncertain about the very idea of moral and religious values.

This general theme is picked up in the first of Sutherland's lectures, which is concerned with diagnosing the problems we face in trying to relate to each other the concepts of education, values and religion. He stresses the importance of the fact that educational practice rests upon educational philosophy — however unreflective and fragmentary the latter may be. The task, then, is to offer something better to those charged with the education of our children. While Sacks begins in the past and looks from there forward, Sutherland starts with a description of the twentieth century as one of 'upheaval, disruption and uncertainty in its deepest social and intellectual foundations'. He then seeks the sources of this and traces them

xii   *Introduction*

to three features or trends: cultural pluralism, the fragmentation of knowledge, and moral atomisation.

Lord Sutherland notes that educational philosophies have typically rested on accounts of human nature. The question is whether anything of this sort can be fashioned nowadays. He explores in somewhat greater detail lines of ethical thought mentioned by Jonathan Sacks and then proceeds to argue for an account of mankind as essentially reflective and self-interpreting. This introduces the prospect of a form of humanistic spirituality and, in that broad sense, he offers a reworking of the idea that the aim of education is the development of the soul.

The issues addressed by Mary Midgley and Bryan Appleyard are of equally profound importance, concerning nothing less than our understanding of human nature and of how our knowledge of the material world bears upon our historical conception of ourselves as free subjects guided in part by judgments of value. The general significance and contemporary relevance of such issues needs no comment, but they have particular importance when we consider the aims of education and the relative importance of scientific knowledge and humane understanding.

Mary Midgley is a philosopher of renown who has spent a lifetime reflecting upon the relationship between our sense of values and our animal nature. Bryan Appleyard is a prominent journalist and social commentator who combines a lively appreciation of what is current with a considered view of what has been achieved by, and is of lasting worth, in the thought and practice of the past. Between them Midgley and Appleyard offer an interesting combination of ideas about the assumptions and implications of styles of thought that do not just draw from science but assume that science is the only credible approach to understanding human life.

It was noted that the lectures gathered here were first given at various leading British universities. More precisely, each set began in St Andrews and then travelled to other locations. The idea of the series was conceived by the Centre for Philosophy and Public Affairs (expanded in title in 2001 to include explicit reference to *Ethics*) and then implemented by it. The Centre was established by the University of St Andrews in 1984 with the twin purposes of promoting the place of philosophy in the examination of issues of public importance and of supporting research into those branches of philosophy that are concerned directly and indirectly with questions of value and action.

Although the Centre has been involved in a variety of activities it has to this point developed two main vehicles for the pursuit of its aims: first, a visiting fellowship scheme which has brought academics from many parts of the world to St Andrews to engage in research; and second, a public lecture and seminar programme. There is a special reason why a centre dedicated to the aims of ethics, philosophy and public affairs, located within an ancient Scottish university, should be an appropriate setting for public lectures of this sort, for there is within Scotland a tradition of publicly debating issues of great importance for moral and civic life; a tradition which is made possible by, and contributes to, the continuing existence of an educated public.

Speaking in another lecture series, in acknowledgement of the work of the most important post-war British philosopher of education, *viz.* Richard Peters, Alasdair MacIntyre observed the following:

> It is in the eighteenth century that the modern concept of an educated public first finds application; and the example of such a public which has most and immediate relevance to our own concerns is that of the public created by the remaking of the Scottish Universities in the first half of that century. (MacIntyre (1987), pp. 17–18)

MacIntyre subsequently went on to extend his treatment of the theme in his Edinburgh Gifford Lectures *Three Rival Versions of Moral Inquiry* (MacIntyre, 1990). In the original lecture he poses the question 'What conditions are required for the existence of such a public' and answers that these are of three kinds, of which the first and most important is that there

> be a tolerably large body of individuals, educated both into the habit and the opportunity of active rational debate, to whose verdict the intellectual protagonists are making appeal. These individuals must understand the questions being debated as having practical import for generally important aspects of their shared social existence. And in their communication with one another they must recognise themselves as constituting a public.

The aim of addressing such a public is what lay behind the creation of the Centre's public lectures series; and it became clear to me as Director of the Centre that one way in which Victor Cook's educational interests might be recognized and advanced, and in which a suitable tribute to him could be offered would be through a series of public lectures on various themes gathered under the general heading of *Values and Education*.

The idea of holding such lectures in Scotland's oldest university. in which the history of disputing 'questions' of philosophical import goes back to the beginning of the fifteenth century, added a fitting dimension which I hope would have been pleasing to Victor Cook. But the primary aim was not to construct a well-situated and elegant memorial, so much as to have values in relation to education discussed in a spirit of which Cook would have approved, even if the discussion might sometimes be couched in unfamiliar terms. Those terms would be broadly philosophical ones, but in order to ensure a high quality of discussion, intelligible and appealing to an educated public, it was important to have well-qualified lecturers to whom the issues mattered, and to increase the opportunity for members of that public, as well as academics, to receive and respond to the lectures. The latter aim led to the practice of delivering the lectures in second and third venues, and to the Centre's producing the original texts in booklet form. With the publication of this volume the ideas first set forth in lecture halls may be received by a yet wider audience.

It is fitting that this volume also marks the launch of the series *St Andrews Studies in Philosophy and Public Affairs*, and also fitting that this series should begin at a point when the Centre embarks on its twenty-first year. Whatever developments lie ahead, one may be sure that ethical and philosophical questions will not diminish or fade from interest and it is equally certain that issues of education will remain prominent among the concerns not only of academics but also of the public generally.

It is very much to be hoped that readers will take up, from whatever standpoint, the matters discussed below and make their own contributions to the ongoing debate about values and education. In once again thanking the Foundation for supporting the idea of the lectures and its implementation and for granting permission for the publication of these texts I must emphasise that the views expressed in the are not necessarily those of the Trustees of the Gordon Cook Foundation.[1]

John Haldane

St Andrews, Autumn 2004

---

[1] Some of the authors have incorporated material from their lectures in books, in particular Jonathan Sacks (1997) and Mary Midgley (2001). Their wish to do this has been pleasing to the Centre and the Foundation in as much as it tends to confirm the latter's estimate of the aptness of encouraging enquiry in the field of values and education. In bringing together all sixteen lectures the present volume highlights some of the central issues in that field and we hope this may encourage further examination of them.

Part 1:

VALUES AND
VALUES EDUCATION

John Haldane

The Nature of
Values

Introduction

Philosophers sometimes complain of not being heeded by others who, they believe, should be interested in their reflections, for example scientists, theologians, sociologists, art and literary theorists and policy makers; and they occasionally add that the trouble lies with the fact that most people are not philosophically minded. There is some truth in this. Philosophers are generally very good at detecting fallacies and marking relevant distinctions; whereas non-philosophers are liable to confuse important differences: for example, between grounding, motivating and justifying reasons, i.e. confusing what might be *evidence* for a claim with someone's personal *motivation* in making it, or confusing what might *explain* an action with what might, or might not, *justify* it.

If philosophy has a vocation to go beyond conceptual clarification and to help people think their way to the truth about fundamental matters, part of its task may not be to provide an education in new philosophical doctrines so much as a re-education out of old ones, or out of the versions of these that have taken shape, as ideas have trickled down through the culture. I say this because it has come to seem even more clear that current ways of thinking about morality, and about values more generally, are the products of philosophical ideas developed by writers in the eighteenth, nineteenth and twentieth centuries. Of course, the ideas in question are much older than this, going back in fact to the earliest stages of philosophy; but in the last two centuries they have become part and parcel of what now seems to many educated people to be a body of established truths about the nature of reality. In what follows, then, I want to dismantle some of the main elements of this orthodoxy and to do so in order to show

how questions about values are connected with other aspects of our thought.

Some Preliminary Distinctions

What are the 'questions about values' and what is the modern orthodoxy? True to the methods of philosophy we need to begin by making some distinctions, in this case ones between different *perspectives* and between different *levels*. Some questions about values are psychological and sociological. For example, biographers and historians are often interested in the ideals that motivated people; and periodically there are surveys of social attitudes designed to keep track of changes in morality, i.e. in people's thoughts about certain kinds of behaviour and in the behaviour itself. These are empirical questions to be investigated and answered by various means including very sophisticated social scientific methods. But, however successful these means may be, all they can tell us about are people's attitudes and behaviour. They cannot settle the many particular questions that people ask about what is good and bad, right and wrong; nor can they settle the more abstract question: what is it for something to be good or bad?

Leaving psychology and sociology behind, therefore, we now move into the area of values themselves and this quickly gives rise to the *philosophy of value* (sometimes referred to as 'axiology'). First, however, a distinction of levels needs to be made. Consider the most elementary questions of values such as: Is friendship good? Is football better than opera? Is honesty always the best policy? Is human life inviolable? Is marital fidelity necessarily good? Is justice more important than liberty? These are *ground-floor* questions. They are the sorts of issues that are often discussed in the press and on television, and they are ones that exercise the minds of most thoughtful people, at least from time to time.

Some questions of these sorts are felt to be easily answered, but most are judged to be difficult. Indeed the ones to which the answers seem obvious are for that reason generally not even posed. For example, it sounds odd to ask if torturing animals for pleasure is permissible, because virtually everyone to whom this question might be posed would answer that it is not and would be repelled by the thought that anyone could believe otherwise. Still the question can be asked, and as soon as it is a further question suggests itself. If torturing animals is wrong then why is it wrong? Attempts to answer this sort of question about the basis and content of value judgments moves us up from ground floor moralising to *first-floor* theorising.

As we make this ascent, however, it is important to bear in mind that the majority of people may not be moved to ask why something is good or bad, nonetheless they will certainly be concerned with what they judge to be of value. The last point needs to be understood correctly. I am not claiming that people go around all the time, or even part of it, asking 'is this good or bad? is that worth doing? should this be avoided?' and so on. Many do, of course, but the general claim is not about what people consciously say or think, but about what is presupposed by their behaviour.

Consider for a moment the question what is the difference between a mere bodily movement and an action? Shelves full of philosophy books have been written about the nature of action, but one thing is generally agreed and that is that action is intentional, i.e. aimed at some end. When someone acts there is something he or she is trying to achieve. One can always ask why they did it with the assurance that some goal, however humble, was intended. This being so we can also say that from the point of view of the agent at least the end in question was conceived of as desirable. This is not to claim that he or she consciously thought 'this is a worthwhile goal'; and even less is it to suggest that the goal is question was 'objectively' good. The point rather is that inasmuch as an agent has performed an action, he or she has an attitude of approval to that which the action was intended to realise. Certainly we can do things that we regret, even as we are doing them; but to the extent that we are acting intentionally there is some respect in which the result is viewed as desirable. It is in this sense that everyone who acts is concerned with values.

Conscious of our own fallibility, and curious as we are, reflection normally leads to questioning about what others regard as good and bad; and further reflection drives the mind upwards to the more abstract level of first-floor theorising, where we ask what, if anything, makes things good (or bad)? Otherwise expressed the question is: what do good things have in common? Historically a wide range of answers has been proposed, but most of these can be fitted into three broad categories. First, the *theological*: something is good if God approves of it and bad if He disapproves of it — limiting cases of His approval being a command and of His disapproval a prohibition. Obviously views of this sort rest upon claims even more controversial than those likely to be made about particular values and, as I shall indicate later, there are problems with this approach to values even for the theist.

The second broad category is that of the *deontological*. Theories of this sort hold that certain characteristics, actions and states of affairs are good (or bad) in and of themselves. Our way of expressing views of this kind is by saying that they 'value-classify' things at the level of *types*. For example deontological ethical theories sometimes hold that lying is always morally wrong. Here the emphasis is on the *type* of behaviour not on individual actions. Of course in condemning the type one is condemning its instances, but the essence of this view resides in the fact that what is wrong with an episode of lying is not features of the individual case but rather the fact that, whatever the particularities, it is an instance of a *kind* of action that is always wrong.

So far, however, nothing has been said about why lying is prohibited or more generally about what, for the deontologist, makes things good or bad, right or wrong. There is no universally agreed deontological theory. However since the eighteenth century, and mostly under the influence of Kant, deontologists have usually related values to the fundamental right of *respect*. For Kant himself respect was owing to rational beings only; indeed one might say that respect was owing principally to *rationality* as such and to human beings in so far as they are repositories of it. Later thinkers, however, have sought to extend the constituency of value beyond rational beings to sentient creatures, and, more recently (in the West at least), to all living things. Some even go so far as to claim a fundamental 'existential' value which is possessed by each and every thing, from micro-physical particles to planets and galaxies, and which is deserving of respect.

The third broad category of value theory is perhaps the most widely supported in advanced industrial societies and is certainly that which people tend to find least puzzling. This is *consequentialist* axiology, according to which something is good to the extent that it promotes or constitutes states of affairs held to be good on their own account. Relatedly an action is right insofar as it results in good consequences. Notice that on the issue of whether a *type* of action is right or wrong the consequentialist has to look first to the instances and on this basis try to construct an answer to the general question. Unlike the deontologist, he regards rightness and wrongness as properly speaking a property of individual actions relating to their actual or probable results. Any account of the value of types, therefore, can only be based on the pattern of individual consequences.

Having ascended to the level of theory the reflective mind is liable to be struck by a further question. Is anything *really* good, i.e. objectively so? We begin in innocence presupposing the desirability of this or that goal, and then ask explicitly what things have value? This stimulates the appetite for generality, provoking the question: what, (if anything) links together the variety of worthwhile goals? Now there arises the issue of whether deontological and consequentialist theories are merely accounts of the underlying patterns of our thoughts and attitudes about values, or whether they describe an independent order of objective goods and requirements. In asking whether these are 'real' we move to the *second and highest floor* in the structure of thinking about values: the 'metatheory' of axiology. Note that since most interest is in the area of morality and first-floor ethical theory, it is more common to find writers discussing 'metaethics'. Nonetheless similar issues arise in respect of other fields such as aesthetics and politics and, although it is important to bear in mind the possibility that different accounts may be appropriate for different areas, there are clear similarities in the arguments for and against objectivism and subjectivism in respect of moral, political, aesthetic and other values.

Two Philosophical Perspectives

Having distinguished between empirical questions about people's attitudes, and philosophical questions about the content of those attitudes; and then distinguished within the latter three levels — those of (i) particular valuations, (ii) general structures of valuation and (iii) the metaphysical status of values, i.e. their place in the scheme of things, we arrive at the issue which most exercises the philosophical conscience: *are values objective?* Earlier I suggested that at this level of thought about morality and other spheres of value and requirement there is an established opinion and that it is related to a more general view about the nature of reality. For want of a more engaging title let me just call this the 'empiricist orthodoxy'. In doing so, however, I need to issue a couple of disclaimers. First, although some of the views I shall be discussing are associated with particular authors such as David Hume and John Stuart Mill, I am not here in the business of determining intellectual provenances. Second, there are significant disputes among empiricists about the structure of reality and our knowledge of it and about the right account to give of our ideas of values. Nonetheless, there are sufficient points of agreement, particularly in essentials, as to allow for generalisation. Remember also that what I am discussing is not restricted to the pure doctrines of philosophers but encompasses the diluted and contaminated versions of these that are the result of the trickle-down process.

To understand the power of empiricism it is helpful to appreciate something of the history of ideas out of which it developed and to much of which it was a deliberate reaction. In his work, subsequently titled the *Metaphysics*, Aristotle tells us that philosophy began with leisure. Only when they had established the conditions for secure and stable life did men have the opportunity to distance themselves from immediate practical concerns and reflect upon the nature of the world — the *Kosmos*. Whatever the social history of philosophy it is clear from the earliest fragments recording the ideas of philosophers prior to Socrates — the 'pre-Socratics' — that their principal concern was with such questions as: how can the world be thought about in a systematic way? Here the concern was as much with the possible structure of the world as with the powers of human understanding. For in order that there might be general truths about the nature and behaviour of the cosmos it must have some order. This thought led in due course to an idea about the natures of things that is expressed in a Pythagorean formula: limit (*peras*) imposed upon the unlimited (*apeiron*) producing the limited (*peperasmenon*). Further refined this became the doctrine of 'hylomorphism': the principle that every thing can be analysed in terms of a medium (*hyle*) and an organisational form (*morphe*). So a wooden ball is so much matter having spherical form; a horse, so much flesh and bones arranged in a certain living form; a galaxy, stars and planets in a certain configuration.

Clearly this ancient philosophical analysis is a powerful one and it remained the central doctrine of philosophical thought through the Middle Ages, only beginning to weaken in the fifteenth century. The reasons for its demise, which accelerated in the sixteenth century and seemed complete by the end of the seventeenth, are complex but the central force in its displacement was the rise of new analytical schemes associated with a particular method of enquiry: metaphysically unburdened empirical investigation conducted through controlled experiment — in short, the rise of modern natural science.

It is, in fact, a moot point the extent to which the 'new' knowledge was metaphysics-free. Its account of the fundamental structure of the world involved a version of an ideal propounded by some of the presocratic cosmologists, the claim that material objects are compounded out of imperceptibly small particles *'atomoi'*. The modern version of atomism *viz.* 'corpuscularism' was importantly different, however, inasmuch as it progressively dispensed with the idea of governing forms or natures and substituted for these geometrical arrangements and mechanical causation. This process which the phenomenologist Husserl was later to describe as 'the mathematisation of nature' effected a radical change in the way the world was seen. For Aristotle and his medieval followers the natural world is a hierarchical order of species. Each thing has a governing nature which makes it to be a thing of that kind and determines the characteristic patterns of its development and behaviour. Although plants and animals are composed out of matter it is not their matter but their organising specific forms that explain their distinctive natures. Of course matter has properties of its own such as the liability to fall downwards and that, for the Aristotelian, explains the universal behaviour of natural things in this respect, but it does not explain the different structure and properties which quantities of matter possess when they are informed by specific principles of organisation and activity.

One important aspect of the difference between Aristotelian and modern science consequent upon the substitution of mechanics for organic activity is the way in which explanation and understanding no longer invoked purposes and functions. In the older view one understands the behaviour of organisms and of their parts in terms of teleologies or directed activities. These link together various sub-organic processes and the different stages in the history of an organism. A fruit is a seed carrier; a seed is in process of developing into a sapling which is on the way to becoming a tree; the tree puts out blossoms and in due course fruits which are for the sake of propagating the species. On it goes: the parts and functions of living things contributing to larger processes themselves regulated by governing forms or natures. Now notice two features of this view of the natural order: first, it is *non-reductive*; and second, it is *normative*. It is non-reductive because it does not think that the structure and behaviour of whole entities is a function or 'upward-generated' consequence of its basic material elements. It is normative because it implies that certain states and processes are good or bad inasmuch as they contribute to or inhibit natural processes of developments. Given, for example, that the heart has the function of pumping blood, and that the circulation of the blood is necessary for the distribution of minerals and other nutrients throughout the body, and for the clearing of other substances out of it, it follows that damage to the heart is *ipso facto* bad. This feature, which I shall call the 'normativity of nature', is quite general. If it makes sense to describe objects in terms of functions and events in terms of processes then questions of efficiency, harm and benefit arise.

In rejecting the teleological view of nature and replacing it with the idea that the ultimate reality is one of mechanically interacting particles and that all the rest is just a complication of this, a matter of quantitative not qualitative differences, the modern view created a problem of the relationship between *facts*, the domain of science, and *values*, the domain of who knows what? In an age of religious belief it seemed that theology might take care of the issue: the world provides the facts and God dictates the values. But there were two problems with this. First, the science that dispensed with purposes also seemed to remove one basis for belief in God, i.e. that He was the designer of nature and the inventor of purposes. Second, even if one believes in God there are problems with the idea that His commands are the sole basis of values.

The most familiar of these problems is usually presented in terms of the 'Euthyphro Dilemma' (a title deriving from Plato's dialogue *Euthyphro*, in which a version of it features). Consider the question: Is something valuable because God commands it? Or does God command it because it is valuable? To favour the first seems to make value inexplicable and arbitrary. If God were to have commanded the ritual torture of infants it would on this account thereby be valuable, but that strikes most people as absurd. However, if one favours the second option the implication is that things are valuable independently of God's commanding them. Support for this view comes from a further consideration that undermines the claims of theology to provide a general account of values generally. Individuals and groups have made all sorts of claims about what God commands. In trying to determine whether these are, or even could be, authentic revelations, religious believers assess the content of the purportedly Divine commandments. If, as in some cases, the claim is that God orders the ritual slaughter of those who are not believers, this is generally taken to be evidence against the authenticity of the 'revelation'; the grounds being that a good God would not command evil acts. But this, of course, suggests that there is some criterion of what constitutes good and evil independently of the claims of revelation.

It might be replied that the source of this is prior revelation; but if one is willing to apply a non-revealed moral standard at some stage in history then one cannot claim that God's revealed will is the source of *all* values.

Nature having been reconceived in atomistic/mechanical/ mathematical terms and thereby no longer being seen as a repository of teleological norms, and the effort to provide a theological basis for values seeming to be ineffective, some writers tried to work out accounts of objective value based on reason and/or conscience. Although these have their interest, however, they were confronted with a series of objections from David Hume which, in the following two centuries, came to be widely regarded as destructive of the possibility of any kind of value objectivism.

Hume's theory of knowledge is in the tradition associated with the modern scientific worldview. As in the rest of nature, changes in us, such as the acquisition of new beliefs, are to be explained by reference to interactions within and between objects. So far as our knowledge of the world is concerned these originate in the impact of the environment on the sense organs. Generalising, therefore, the empiricist maintains that knowledge of how things are is a function of (and probably reduces to) the content of sensory experience. Combining this with an atomistic metaphysics the conclusion is arrived at that all we can be aware of are the motions of material objects and study of these fails to show us any values: good, bad, right and wrong. Nothing in the world, or in our experience of it, provides grounds for belief in objective values.

This, in brief, is the basis of the proclaimed 'fact/value gap'. No observed facts reveal or entail any values. Additional to this claim is another one, equally important in the empiricist argument against moral objectivity and suggestive of a subjectivist account of moral thinking. Hume observes that in his reading of theologians and moralists he found that they move from propositions about what *is* the case to claims about what *ought* or *ought not* to be done; but this he professes (ironically) to find surprising. On the basis of these remarks Hume is generally credited with having established a further logical gap: that between *is* and *ought*. Of course, we may argue from observed facts, such as that a man is starving, to a prescriptive conclusion, e.g. that he ought to be fed. But of itself this is no refutation of the Humean thesis, since the response is that the conclusion only follows when a further premise is added, *viz.* that starving men ought to be fed. Once more, and generalising, the empiricist claim is that no 'ought' proposition follows from a set of premises unless this includes an 'ought' statement.

Part of the interest and power of Hume's view is that it suggests an alternative basis for moral values and requirements, a naturalistic and empirical account of the source of our thoughts that some things are good and others bad, some actions right and others wrong. Instead of looking to facts in the world around us we should attend to attitudes and sentiments within ourselves. In short judgments of value and requirements are expressions or projections of our subjective desires and preferences. The approach has received a variety of refining treatments producing a range of 'expressivist', 'emotivist' and 'projectivist' theories. But the subtle differences between these are of less significance than the unifying thesis that values are subjective.

Before responding to this empiricist orthodoxy it is necessary to observe two points about the subjectivist theory of values. First, it need not hold, and Hume himself did not maintain, that all values are simply expressions of individual preference. Rather it can allow that many values are socially constituted out of commonly held attitudes and preferences. The importance of this is that it provides a reply to one kind of objection to crude subjectivism, namely that we think that individuals can be in error in their evaluations. For example, we simply do not suppose that it is a matter of personal attitude whether torturing animals is wrong, and we would regard anyone who approved such conduct as morally wicked. This might seem to constitute strong evidence against a subjectivist theory until one appreciates that it is open to such a theory to identify wrongness with *general* disapprobation. Thus while it may not be a matter of fact but of feeling that torture is wrong, someone who did not share this feeling, or possessed contrary ones, might still be held to be 'mistaken' inasmuch as his response is at variance with the social norm in such matters.

The second point to note is that subjectivism is a *metatheory*. Unlike consequentialist and deontological theories of value it is not concerned with the content or justification of moral and other valuations but with their 'metaphysical standing' i.e. as factual or not factual, truth-bearing or non truth-bearing. It is, in other words, an account appropriate to the *second floor* of our structure. That being so, a question remains open for the subjectivist, namely which if any sort of first-floor moral theory should he or she adopt? Largely for reasons that are easy to work out the empiricist tradition has strongly favoured consequentialism. If values are just preferences then it is natural to think of moral theory, say, almost as a branch of social psychology. And asking the question what do we approve of? writers in the empiricist tradition, most famously Jeremy Bentham and John Stuart Mill, have responded in terms of such notions as utility and happiness. Happiness is what we want and approve of, unhappiness what we shun; and we approve and disapprove of other things to the extent that we judge them to be conducive to, or to constitute, such end states.

Thus the passage from a pre-modern view of nature as a system of formally-structured living substances and of values as objective features pertaining to proper functioning and natural well-being, to a modern conception of reality as constituted of basic physical units and forces and of values as projections of the states of some objects (human beings) on to other objects and situations. 'Post-modern' ideas on these matters are more or less radical extensions of value-subjectivism but often combine this with similar views about every other domain of human thought and practice — including science itself!

Back to the Future: Natures and Values

Where then does this leave us? Ironically one consequence of the intellectual development that led to Hume's fact/value gap might be the adoption of forms of 'post-modern' thought in which that gap is itself transcended. If everything is subjective then there are no 'hard facts' to be contrasted with 'soft attitudes'. At most one might find reasons (i.e. attitudes) to distinguish between 'harder' and 'softer' attitudes; less and more locally-subjective phenomena. This way of responding to the problem of values certainly finds support among contemporary philosophers both in the English-speaking world and in continental Europe. However it rests on claims hardly less controversial than theological ones and is not likely to be found attractive by those whose concern is with whether a place for values can be found in an objectivist worldview.

Clearly the question: are there objective values? will continue to stimulate controversy, and it would be absurd to try and resolve it conclusively here. This said, however, those inclined to subjectivism need to consider very seriously whether it is consistent to hold this as the truth about values while continuing to treat issues of personal behaviour and social policy as if they concerned objective matters of fact. Indeed this raises the question of whether a general subjectivism about all values is not self-undermining. In arguing about these issues, parties on both sides of the dispute tend to assume the objective validity of cognitive and rational values. That is to say, even 'subjectivists' tend to be objectivists about the values of evidential weight, rational cogency, argumentative rigour, coherence, intelligibility and truth. They do not suppose that the determination to be guided in one's thought by such values is no more than a matter of preferences. On the contrary they share the objectivist assumption that we seek cogency, coherence and intelligibility because they are rational goods, and do not assume that they are goods because we seek them.

If this line of thought proves unsettling for the subjectivist it also prompts the question how can one be an objectivist given the modern empiricist world view? The challenge is appropriate; but I suggest that rather than try to reconcile moral and other axiological objectivisms with orthodox empiricism one reconsiders the opposition between the latter and the Aristotelian worldview. A very considerable merit of that view is that it permits the objectivity of values without forcing them in to an occult immaterial realm. Otherwise expressed, it offers the prospect of combining an objectivist metatheory of values with a naturalistic metaphysics. In saying this, however, it is important to recall that the older naturalism insists upon the non-reducibility of the forms and teleologies of living things. Indeed it is precisely because it discerns holistic patterns of growth, development and flourishing that it sees norms in nature.

The challenge of the new science was that these hylomorphic and teleological way of thinking are misconceived and fail to grasp the fundamental structure of reality which resides below the level of living things, and has no place for organic functions and goal-related processes. Undoubtedly post-Aristotelian science has vastly extended our knowledge of the world and no-one could seriously doubt the physical basis of organic entities. But in urging the truth of the earlier view one need not deny these facts. Organic forms and natural teleologies are compatible with microphysical particles and electromagnetic radiation. The empiricist mistake has been to insist upon the exclusivity of the reality of entities of the latter sort and to require that all other descriptions be reduced or rejected. The truth of the matter is that not every truth is a truth about matter. There are forms, principles of organisation and activity, by which things live and by which, in favourable circumstances, they flourish.

So much for the general objectivity of natural norms. This leaves a great deal to be done in developing an account of human values. But the aim of the foregoing has been to argue that philosophy does not exclude the possibility of an objectivist account of these and to suggest the general character of such an approach. As in the case of other natural beings we have natures by which our lives are structured and directed. But, of course, human natures are not only very complex they also include aspects that are certainly rare in nature and may be unique — such as rational psychologies. Furthermore, while our natures may prescribe the general course of our lives they do not exhaustively determine it. It is part of the human form of life to deliberate and act in accord with reasons. In other words our rationality extends the possible range of directions in which we might develop. The task of education is to contribute to this development, and that of values education is to show how reflection can provide reasons for choosing some routes and not others.

2

David Carr

Problems of Values Education

If, then, there is some end of the things we do, which we desire for its own sake (everything else being desired for the sake of this) and if we do not choose everything for the sake of something else (for at that rate the process would go on to infinity so that our desire would be empty and vain), clearly this must be the good and the chief good. Will not the knowledge of it, then, have a great influence on life? (Aristotle: *Nicomachean Ethics*, Book I, Part 2)

Introduction

John Haldane concluded with the suggestion that values education might well be regarded as concerned with rational reflection on the goals and purposes of human life. Whether or not this is so, however, rather depends upon the answers one is inclined to give to the sort of questions previously considered about the nature of values as such. In short, different views about the nature of values must issue in diverse conceptions of the way in which the processes of education are implicated in their communication or transmission — a question to which we now turn.

Briefly, there are two main ways in which the content of education — the knowledge and dispositions transmitted through teaching — can be regarded as worthwhile in human affairs. First, the knowledge and dispositions in question can be seen as of instrumental or *extrinsic* value as a means to the achievement or satisfaction of certain further independently specifiable human ends or goals; secondly, they can be viewed as of *intrinsic* value or as worthwhile for their own sake. However, as one might expect, there are also important connections between these views of the value of educational activities and the different forms of ethical theorising aired in part one: utilitarian and other forms of ethical consequentialism, for example, incline to an extrinsic or instrumental view of the value of educational activities and we have also seen how the subjectivism

inherent in empiricist perspectives on values reinforces consequentialism at the *first floor* of ethical theorising.

Indeed, it seems more than likely that as a result of what has been
called the 'trickle-down process' a certain popular subjectivism
about the nature of values is largely responsible for the predominantly instrumental turn which public thought about education in
moral and social values has recently taken. It seems to have been
widely assumed during recent outbreaks of moral panic about the
apparent breakdown of law and order and discipline among the
young, for example, that the problem of moral and social education
is precisely that of discerning *means* by which current social ills and
discontents might be remedied. Moral and social education, then, is
nowadays widely regarded as a quasi-causal process whose main
significance lies in the production of generally acceptable standards
of social conduct.

Whilst not wishing to underestimate the gravity of contemporary
social problems, or belittle public concern about them, however, it is
by no means clear that an instrumental or consequentialist perspective is either the only or the best one to adopt with regard to moral
and social education. Of course, since morality is a matter of urgent
practical concern in human affairs, the way in which a given moral
code influences the behaviour of individuals for good or ill is liable
to loom large in the evaluation of any programme of moral instruction which is based upon it; but this is not to say that it is proper to
evaluate such a programme *exclusively* in these terms — for certain
outcomes widely held to be socially desirable might well be achiev-
able in the last resort only by policies or strategies more likely to
lower than raise the general moral climate of a civilised society.

How otherwise, then, might we approach the question of how best
to educate individuals in moral and social values? Precisely, we
might rather ask — in a non-instrumental way — what qualities or
dispositions most clearly or readily conduce to the moral improvement or enhancement of human life in real terms; what qualities, in
short, is it worthwhile for human beings to possess for *their own sake*
or *in themselves* — irrespective of the salutary consequences for public order or social control which might also follow from widespread
possession of them. A list of candidates for inclusion among such
qualities would doubtless comprehend those personal and interpersonal dispositions traditionally called moral *virtues* — honesty,
self-control, courage, justice, charity, compassion and so on — and
exclude such other evidently undesirable characteristics or *vices*

such as dishonesty, intemperance, spite and selfishness. The crucial point is, however, that — as past philosophers have insisted — virtue is its *own* reward; the possession of such qualities in and of themselves is of benefit to the possessor — regardless of any other consequences for good public order.

Educational Traditionalism and its Critics

The idea that education might generally be construed as the promotion of certain intrinsically valuable states or dispositions of knowledge and virtue is to a large extent, associated with the perspective known as educational *traditionalism*. Indeed a defining feature of traditionalism is that it regards education as a matter of transmission from one human generation to the next of all that is generally thought to be worth preserving in a given culture. We may be misled about this because traditionalism has sometimes been interpreted — particularly in sociological accounts — as valuing the potential for social cohesion of culture transmission more than the intrinsic worth of what is liable to be transmitted; so-called consensus or structural-functional analyses have inclined to instrumental interpretations of educational traditionalism as a process crucial for the preservation of social identity and continuity. But the sociological account of traditionalism probably rests on a familiar confusion between a sociological or descriptive sense of culture, as used to refer to the customs and practices constitutive of a given social order, and a normative or evaluative sense intended to identify rather what is of greatest value or highest achievement within a given society. The more familiar justification of educational traditionalism, however, rests on the evaluative notion of culture as the flower of human aspiration and achievement to date — in a well-known formulation 'the best that has been thought and said in the world' — and it maintains that this requires educational transmission from one generation to another precisely *because* it is good or valuable in its own right. Thus, we should not ask for what purpose we initiate young people into culture so construed, or whether some further good might be the real point of such initiation; such a question merely misses the Aristotelian point that all instrumental justifications must end somewhere in something that is good without qualification — precisely with that which is worthwhile for its own sake.

On the traditionalist view, however, what is of ultimate worth in human life is to know the truth, to love what is good and to do what is right and honourable in the light of decency and justice, and it is the purpose of education to guide the individual towards this. Hence, it is common for traditionalists to draw a fairly sharp distinction between *education*, construed as a concern with what is valuable for its own sake and *training*, as concerned rather with the acquisition of certain instrumentally-conceived skills by which we earn our daily bread; for although such skills are of some significance in securing the basic material conditions for any worthwhile human existence there is nevertheless a clear sense in which such conditions are subsidiary to the purpose of life — whatever makes life worth living — itself. On this view, then, values education should not be construed as an aspect or *part* of education, for an initiation into positive values is simply what a good education *is*; it concerns, precisely, the acquisition of those intrinsically worthwhile forms of rational knowledge and moral goodness in terms of which real quality of life requires to be construed.

But, in that case, how is the *intrinsic* value of these states of knowledge and goodness to be apprehended or affirmed? In fact, rather different answers to this question are available in different versions of traditionalism; ultimate truths and values may be regarded as founded on the authority of religious revelation, charismatic leadership, moral intuition, rational enquiry or as even legitimated by reference to tradition or custom itself. Indeed, the ultimate test of what is valuable about a given social custom or cultural practice may be seen as residing simply in the fact that things have always been done a certain way and that what has sustained and given meaning to the lives of our ancestors should be regarded as having actual or potential value for generations to come.

It should be reasonably evident, then, that social and educational traditionalism, howsoever grounded, is an essentially *conservative* perspective in which filial piety — proper reverence and respect for custom and tradition and the wisdom of elders and ancestors — is regarded as a cardinal virtue. It also thereby inclines, however, to a generally paternalist approach to the transmission of values from one generation to another — to a view that it is the right or duty of some, by virtue of their superior insight, wisdom and knowledge, to decide what is good for others, even to override the natural desires and interests of others in their alleged best interests. This paternalism is most conspicuous, for example, in the social and educational philosophy of Plato whose influence on the subsequent development of traditionalist conceptions of education was of no small significance. In the *Republic* and elsewhere, Plato drew up a blueprint

for the rational construction of a just social order on the basis of certain ethical principles which he claimed to be accessible only to those
of sufficient wisdom or intelligence; the large majority of others in
his ideal society, would be *required* to live and abide by these principles which they would grasp at the level of myth and custom rather
than informed reason. Plato's hard realist or objectivist ethics, then,
readily translates into a conservative and paternalist conception of
social order and justice that is also profoundly anti-democratic.

To be a traditionalist, however, *is* to be committed to the view that
some of the values internal to a given form of life are worth handing
on to others because they have intrinsic value or are worthwhile for
their own sake and this would also appear to imply some sort of ethical *objectivism* or *absolutism*. It is hardly possible to base traditionalism on ethical subjectivism because the view that something is of
value only because I desire it is tantamount to a denial that it *has
intrinsic* value. Even a relativist traditionalism of the sort defended
by social theorists such as Durkheim seems of dubious coherence
since it is hard to insist that what should be regarded as of value in
this social context is of *enduring* worth whilst conceding that it is neither better nor worse than some alternative or contrary view held
elsewhere. For a genuine traditionalist, then, at least some forms of
knowledge, truth, conduct or enquiry must be valued in a way that is
not readily reducible to considerations of individual or social perspective or preference. It is precisely on these grounds, however,
that a traditionalist account may be considered questionable from a
variety of other educational and social perspectives.

The principal opposition to traditionalist educational views has
come from so-called progressive or radical theories of education.
What is common to all the different brands of anti-traditionalist critique is a deep suspicion of the conservative idea that human culture
as received does represent 'the best that has been thought and said'
— some repository of fixed and final truths of the sort which religious fundamentalists have claimed to find in the Christian Bible,
perhaps, or Plato claimed that his Guardians would be able to discern via exercise of the mode of ratiocination he called *dialectic*.
Whilst the various critics of traditionalism are by no means all
subjectivists or relativists about truth and value they do agree that
the accumulated wisdom of the past is deeply questionable from a
variety of perspectives — that it is therefore mistaken, even dangerous, to identify what is of human value with such knowledge and
downright mischievous to teach it, in the manner of Gradgrind, as

permanent or incorrigible. The case against traditionalism takes three main forms — two kinds of *progressivism* and what is often referred to as *radicalism*.

First, what we can call classical or *libertarian* progressivism is generally associated with the enlightenment philosophy of Jean-Jacques Rousseau. In *Emile*, Rousseau mounted a powerful and audacious critique of the conventional traditionalism of his day in the name of an extreme asocial form of education, focused on child-centred experiment and discovery learning, which was designed to enable individual reason to develop unhindered or unimpeded by any sort of adverse social influence. The usual criticism of Rousseau's radical educational proposals is that it is difficult to see how they might ever be seriously implemented in practice but in fact something very true to the spirit of his views has been attempted in certain famous progressive educational experiments of the twentieth century — although these have not acknowledged any explicit debt to Rousseau himself. Be that as it may, however, it is clear that Rousseau's work provokes very large and important questions about the nature of authority and freedom in education and about the effects of social influence on the formation of capacities for open-mindedness which raise considerable problems for educational traditionalism.

A second, more recent, progressive development (also foreshadowed by Rousseau) which can be called *epistemological* or pragmatic progressivism is associated primarily with the name of John Dewey. This perspective raises questions about the epistemological rather than the socio-political dimensions of traditionalism and it strikes at the very heart of the idea that knowledge as traditionally conceived does or could enshrine objective or absolute truths of the sort in which realists about knowledge from Plato onwards have believed. For Deweyans and other pragmatists knowledge has a distinctly provisional character and is better regarded as a tool for the practical control of human circumstances than as a God's eye view of how the world actually is, beyond human interest and experience. Whilst Dewey by no means rejects the significance of traditional modes of human enquiry, his radical reinterpretation of knowledge as primarily of instrumental value for the solution of human problems raises large questions about the objectivity of truth and it is no straightforward matter to make sense of a traditionalist idea of the intrinsic value of knowledge in Deweyan terms. Moreover, progressive ideas of a Deweyan kind have exercised considerable influence over the development of primary education in this country and elsewhere during the post-war period in a manner than has recently been interpreted by some as posing a threat to traditional values.

Educational *radicalism,* however, goes beyond these two forms of progressivism by combining both sorts of scepticism about knowledge and about authority in a single perspective. The principal intellectual ancestor of radicalism would appear to be Karl Marx, who is commonly held to have regarded knowledge as a social construct which is exploited by some social groups to wield power and control over others. The Marxist perspective has influenced generations of social and educational theorists, especially via the writings of the sociologists of knowledge and, just as the different forms of progressivism have had practical effects on the public and private sectors of education, so radicalism, through the writings of such so-called *deschoolers* as Illich, Goodman and Reimer, has also influenced educational practice through the ideas of 'free schools' and community education. Radicalism is highly antipathetic to any idea that knowledge might have intrinsic value and is profoundly and uncompromisingly instrumentalist in outlook; the real value of knowledge is to equip individuals with power to control their own affairs and so-called intrinsically worthwhile knowledge — invariably another name for the sort of academic enquiry which is intellectually inaccessible to certain social classes — is simply a ploy for depriving many people of that control.

In short, instrumentality about the value of knowledge and enquiry is what all these critiques of traditionalism have in common. Whereas the traditionalist holds that there are certain forms of knowledge, character and conduct which are of absolute human value in their own right regardless of their possible pay-off in practical or instrumental terms, progressives and radicals doubt whether any forms of knowledge or preference can be exalted in such terms without due regard to the protean nature of human needs and interests, and they are deeply suspicious of the motives of those who wish to argue to the contrary.

Liberal Education — A Middle Way?

Clearly, however, it is not just scepticism about knowledge or authority which lies behind these anti-traditionalist critiques — they are also driven by a significant moral motive; each position seeks to avoid or reduce the potential for *indoctrination* which is ever present in conventional or traditional approaches to education. All are critical in their more or less extreme ways of approaches to the initiation of young people into received wisdom which focus too strongly on the *received* — on what is inherited or assumed largely without question — and which neglect to develop or engage the critical powers and capacities of the human intellect. From Rousseau to A.S. Neill, traditionalism has been tried and found wanting on the grounds that it all too readily produces the uncritical conformist whose mind is hardly more than a clutter of useless and outworn information — rather than the individual who can engage in the critical, flexible and creative re-evaluation of values in response to new needs and changing circumstances.

But, equally clearly, the answer to an educational approach which is excessively deferential to tradition and which too rigidly adheres to past doctrines and dogmas is hardly an approach which emphasises freedom, innovation and instrumentality to the point of complete irreverence for, or neglect of, what might be considered of lasting or rather more than transient value about past human achievements; if a rigidly conservative traditionalism is unacceptable on grounds of actual or potential indoctrination, the various forms of progressivism and radicalism are equally problematic in their reductive instrumentalism and relativism. If all knowledge, preference and conduct is of merely instrumental value then everything in human affairs is undertaken for the sake of something else and nothing for its own sake; but then, in the words of Aristotle, life becomes empty and vain — a meaningless treadmill.

What all this suggests, of course, is that it might be more sensible to seek some sort of *via media* between the extremes of traditionalism and progressivism — some position of compromise which combines a healthy reverence for bygone wisdom and past accomplishment with a proper recognition that past achievements are not the last word on any matter but are precisely susceptible of criticism, development and transcendence in the light of fresh insights and new discoveries concerning what is true, right and good in human affairs. And, in recent times, it appears to have been widely accepted that the sought-for middle way is to be found in the idea of *liberal traditionalism* — essentially in the reinterpretation of a traditionalist culture initiation view of education in terms of something like liberal-democratic ideals and principles of open enquiry and freedom of thought and opinion.

Liberal theory is, of course, the chief legacy of enlightenment thought — of precisely the sort of philosophical reflection which produced the educational progressivism of Rousseau's *Emile*. In the

classical nineteenth-century form which it assumes in the social philosophy of J.S. Mill, however, it aims more modestly than any progressivism or radicalism at the defence of an individual's basic right
to liberty of thought and action without undue coercion or interference from others. In *On Liberty*, Mill observes that:

> the sole end for which mankind are warranted individually or collec-
> tively in interfering with the liberty of action of any of their number is
> self-protection. (Mill, 1859, 1991, Ch. 1).

Primarily, of course, liberalism is a theory of how in an open society human relations are to be ordered in social or political terms —
rather than a moral theory as such; but it is a theory with clear moral
implications. The basic aim of liberalism is to maximise individual
human freedom — and freedom, as Mill also observes, *consists in
doing what one desires.* But to avoid the possible anti-social consequences of certain individual desires liberalism leans heavily on a
distinction between what can be regarded as ethically permissible to
think and do from a *procedural* point of view and what is acceptable
in more *substantial* terms of moral attitude and belief. At the level of
substantive moral perspectives, opinions and judgments, of course,
almost anything is permissible; individuals are perfectly entitled, for
example, to endorse such expressions of strong moral evaluation as
'child murderers should be given the death penalty' or 'contracep-
tion is a sin against the Holy Spirit'. What they are *not* entitled to do is
to try to force those who do not agree to think or act in accordance
with such sentiments. So although liberalism conceived as a regulative principle of social conduct is inclined to give the benefit of the
doubt to any and every kind of thought or opinion, it takes a firm
stand on at least one principle of moral substance — defence of the
rights and liberties of individuals and minorities from various kinds
of non-liberal interference. From this perspective, some really quite
objectionable or repellent social attitudes — such as racism — are, in
a sense, to be tolerated; what is not tolerable is any attempt to deny or
violate the rights of other people by racist behaviour.

The liberal, then, defends the individual's right to freedom of
thought and opinion — but unlike many libertarian progressives or
radicals he is prepared to acknowledge that independent thought
cannot operate in an intellectual vacuum; serious critical thought
depends on some body of knowledge or values on which to go to
work. Thus, in general, educationalists who are also liberals incline
to a traditionalist initiation model of education as the *sine qua non* of
any serious open human enquiry. But like epistemological progres-

sives — though not necessarily sympathetic to their thoroughgoing pragmatism — they are generally antipathetic to any view of education as a matter of once and for all initiation into fixed or unchangeable values.

Consequently liberals understand 'the best that has been thought and said' — as, indeed, did Matthew Arnold himself — to refer not just to so many conclusive or unalterable truths but rather to certain currently unsurpassed standards of nevertheless evolving modes of human enquiry and conduct. Understanding the world more clearly or making some sort of progress in personal moral terms are indeed to be construed as worthwhile for their own sake by reference to objective goals of truth and goodness; but the education which assists us towards these goals should be viewed more as engagement in a process — of travelling with a new view — than in terms of arriving at some fixed destination.

The error of the strict traditionalist, then, is to view education as a sort of indoctrination in incontrovertible truths rather than as an initiation into established but evolving forms of open enquiry — whereas the mistake of the radical or progressivist is to regard it as a matter of open critical enquiry operating in abstraction from the sort of epistemological contexts which are clearly required to give such criticism any real role or purchase. To borrow from Kant — in a not dissimilar context — one might say that for the liberal traditionalist whereas content without enquiry is blind, enquiry without content is empty. Thus, it may seem that liberal traditionalism offers the perfect answer to the educational theoretical dichotomy of traditionalism and progressivism by retaining the idea that education is an initiation into what is worthwhile for its own sake whilst accommodating the point that what human beings consider to be worthwhile is liable to evolution in the course of further rational enquiry. The solution proposed by liberal traditionalism to the problem of values education is that what is ultimately of intrinsic value are certain forms of liberal rational enquiry into what is good and true. But is this solution satisfactory?

First, we need to recall that central to the concerns of those who are interested in questions of values education as distinct from education in general are, of course, not *any* sorts of human enquiry which might be pursued for their own sake but, in particular, those forms of enquiry or understanding focused on the pursuit of the *good life* — on what it is right for human beings to *be* or to *do* in moral and social terms. Indeed, as we observed at the outset, the current concern about values education is motivated less by an anxiety about the cranky or eccentric scientific theories people might be inclined to hold and more by worries about whether they are, from a moral viewpoint, living positively or negatively, socially or antisocially, benefiting or harming themselves or others.

From this perspective, however, the application of liberal theory to educational issues and concerns is deeply and inherently problematic precisely because liberalism is itself heir to the kinds of scepticism about the objectivity of moral and social values which were examined in the first part of this work. Liberalism is itself predicated on a certain set of assumptions to the general effect that moral and social disputes and conflicts are not susceptible to objective resolution in the allegedly straightforward manner of natural scientific disputes. Moreover, this seems not to be simply an accidental or contingent feature of liberal theory but an inherent or constitutive one; the very origins of liberal theory lie in the efforts of enlightenment philosophers to discover a route to the rational arbitration of those moral and social divisions and differences that had threatened to tear Christendom apart during bitter conflicts which followed the Reformation. The precise social philosophical problem to which liberalism proposes a solution is that of providing a successful strategy for the peaceful coexistence of different and apparently irreconcilable moral, religious and social beliefs — some way of entitling individuals to their own points of view.

But there is, of course, more than a hint of philosophical ambiguity about this strategy. On the one hand, it appears that it often does embody a profound scepticism about the very possibility of deciding on rational grounds between different moral and social perspectives; for if moral and social evaluations are *no more than* expressions of individual and social attitude and preference they can have little objective basis and the matter of their truth and falsity can hardly arise. On the other hand, however, even if the liberal steadfastly declines to endorse this sort of radical scepticism about the objectivity of particular value judgments and insists on the truth of some and the falsity of others he is still committed to a certain attitude or stance of *neutrality* with respect to beliefs he regards as false or even repugnant; at the very least, particularly if he has any sort of responsibility for public administration, he is bound to tolerate or extend the right to freedom of expression of views he may well deplore or despise.

But this presents quite serious difficulties for any liberal reworking of educational traditionalism; it creates intolerable tension between the traditionalist idea of education as initiation into forms of inherently normative or evaluative discourse with respect to which a teacher is expected, indeed logically required, to have a critical and informed view and the liberal requirement to observe neutrality, on pain of illiberal constraint or indoctrination, with regard to the free development of individual attitudes and preferences. In short, from the perspective of liberal traditionalism, a teacher is supposed to guide and direct the child towards what he takes to be the highest possible goals of human wisdom, character and conduct whilst simultaneously ensuring that the moral, social and other evaluative judgments and preferences of the child or young person are not unduly influenced or constrained in one way or another. It is small wonder that this rather paradoxical position has over the years spawned a vast and complex literature on the topics of rational autonomy and indoctrination much of which has been focused on a peculiarly liberal but also rather far-fetched conception of the *neutral* teacher who is able to foster or promote rational enquiry into moral and social issues without unduly influencing the views of young people in this way or that.

Enquiry into Values and Liberal Neutrality

Whatever the merits of liberalism for the construction of a just, orderly and civilised society — and these have been hotly contested in recent times — it would seem that any attempt to reconstruct educational traditionalism in the light of liberal principles is deeply problematic. It certainly cannot be doubted that the recent large-scale attempt to do so in contemporary social conditions of cultural pluralism, widespread secularism and post-industrial market economics has led to the emergence of quite different conceptions of education and teaching from those which prevailed in this country and elsewhere well up to the middle of the twentieth century. A general liberal disquiet about the rational foundations and status of moral and social values in modern social and economic circumstances has gradually issued in a marked shift away from older conceptions of education as a matter of initiation into the best that has been thought and said and of teaching as a *vocation* to form the choices, preferences, character and conduct of young people in the light of some ideal or vision of the good, to a newer, more precisely defined, but at the same time more restricted, conception of education as a *profession* according to which it is the role of the teacher to provide a contractually-grounded service — the delivery of certain useful academic and vocational skills — to consumers or customers.

On the older vocational view, then, the teacher was someone charged with a sacred mission to mould young people in the light of certain high ideals of truth and goodness and to a considerable degree this also required the personal life of the teacher to be continuous with his occupational role — in areas and aspects of life other than the professional he was expected to uphold a range of decent and civilised virtues and values and to personify them to children both within and beyond school; on the more recent professional conception as long as a teacher observes certain contractually-defined commitments and obligations, he is not just permitted but encouraged to give a wide berth to the positive exemplification of values on pain of *indoctrination* — of the undue influence of his own values on impressionable young minds — and his personal values and private conduct are, by the same token, largely his own affair.

Clearly, of course, both these views have serious shortcomings. No doubt the older vocational view of the teacher was too closely tied to paternalist demands that the teacher should conform to a particular dogmatic or monolithic conception of what is true and good in human affairs; but, arguably, the more recent professional view is equally mistaken in attempting to separate the private or personal and the public or professional with respect to the ethical or moral aspects of education and teaching in a way which seriously underrates the significance of teacher example for the effective communication of positive values.

At the heart of the problem of education in moral and other values — and what, more than likely, accounts for the dilemma we have just noticed about the role of the teacher with regard to values education — is the complex confusion of several rather different issues and distinctions. The principal difficulty, of course, is that of how to understand education in general as initiation into rational enquiry and values education in particular as initiation into enquiry with regard to diverse evaluative perspectives, in social, cultural and political circumstances in which people are obviously very deeply divided about what they believe. It is clear that liberal principles and considerations have become entangled in this problem because, besides promising the possibility of free and open enquiry, they also enable one to adopt a neutral stance on contested ground.

The trouble is, however, that whether or not it is proper to adopt this standpoint of liberal neutrality in relation to issues and circumstances of wider public and social policy it seems hardly appropriate for a teacher to do so during the conduct of any sort of education. For such *neutrality* — especially when combined with the subjectivism which, via the trickle-down process, has infected popular notions of the status of moral discourse — is all too readily transformed in the context of education into something which is virtually indistinguishable from a general *agnosticism* about the very possibility of any sort of rational grounding of moral and other evaluations. But once such agnosticism takes a serious hold, and moral and social values are treated as unsusceptible of rational appraisal, the end of genuine rational enquiry with respect to them — and hence of moral and social *education* as such — hoves into view. In the event such education thereby reduces either to social and moral *training* at the traditional end of the spectrum, or the mere elaboration or articulation of my own preferences or prejudices on the liberal subjectivist side.

In short, genuine *education* in moral and social values can only remain a possibility if values continue to be viewed as potentially true or false in some substantial or objective sense. With specific regard to the teaching of values, then, the introduction of principles of liberal neutrality into education as traditionally conceived simply issues in a confusion of the perfectly unexceptionable ethical point that everyone has a right to his or her own opinion with the much more dubious epistemological view that one moral or social opinion is as true or good as any other; but no coherent theory of moral and social education — let alone a traditionalist theory — could be constructed on this latter perspective.

The propensity of liberal neutrality to collapse into general epistemological agnosticism when introduced into some educational contexts, however, has — especially when reinforced by the trickle down of philosophical subjectivism — significantly influenced certain crucial areas of the liberal traditionalist curriculum. A currently fashionable approach to the conduct of rational enquiry in the context of religious and moral education which focuses on the idea of 'personal search', for example, is quite evidently predicated on subjectivist and relativist views of the nature of religious and other value judgments — on the idea that there is ultimately no truth of the matter to be discovered with respect to most, if not all, expressions of strong moral and religious value and commitment. With particular regard to religion, pupils are to be encouraged to recognise that there *are* no rights and wrongs, truths or falsehoods, in matters of religious opinion; that the choice of one belief is as good as any other and, above all, that no-one has any right to try to impress his or her own religious commitments or preferences too vigorously on anyone else.

But however commendable this last liberal sentiment may be and whatever the merits of personal exploration of the different evaluative options with respect to religious faith — helping children to become clearer or better informed about the various world religions there are — the complete agnosticism which is here implied about the possibility of religious truth must call seriously into question the very possibility of genuine religious enquiry and hence render the idea of religious education inherently problematic, if not actually null and void. In short, the agnosticism which follows from the introduction of liberal neutrality into education in religious, moral and other values inclines to a further confusion of values *education* with values *clarification* — a confusion which appears to have seriously vitiated contemporary discussions of religious education.

But if an education in moral, social and other values has to be conceived as at least *in part* a matter of serious enquiry into the *truth* of different value judgments — rather than as a simple matter of acquiring information about what people believe or of examining or articulating our own inclinations or preferences — where and how are such truths to be found and why do we not have the same sort of certainty and consensus in the realm of moral values as we do, for example, in the area of scientific knowledge and judgments?

As so-called post-empiricist philosophers of science are nowadays inclined to argue, this familiar contrast of the scientific and the evaluative is highly misleading since there are no more (but perhaps no less) certainties in the field of scientific enquiry than there are in the realms of moral and other sorts of evaluative discourse; indeed scientific theories and hypotheses, so we are told, are provisional, liable to perennial overhaul and shot through with value assumptions. Of course, as the first part of this work indicated, this line of argument needs handling with some caution since there is an ever-present danger, if it is taken too far, of throwing out the baby of scientific *objectivity* with the bath water of scientific *certainty*.

However, it is certainly hard to see how any serious conception of human knowledge as a product of rational enquiry and of education as the process of initiation into knowledge so construed might *dispense* completely with the notion of objective truth as a significant regulative norm or principle of enquiry; all genuine reflection with regard to any significant realm of human enquiry, theoretical or practical, must proceed in some degree of confidence that the exercise of human reason can actually get us somewhere by way of progress in our knowledge of how things are or should be in a world which exists *outside* our own heads — otherwise we might just as well think what we like or not bother to think at all. But regarding truth as a goal of enquiry does not mean we can ever be sure, in our epistemologically fallen state, that we have finally grasped it. In *I Corinthians* we are told by the Apostle that at present we see through a glass darkly; only then face to face. But though we may lack present certainty, and remain bound from a human perspective to see only indistinctly, we should not thereby conclude that we cannot, via our best efforts of reason and observation, ever come to see at all — or that by even greater application we might come to see, if not face to face, nevertheless still better.

But seeing better or more truly is a matter of seeing things for what they *are* rather than of seeing through a fog of subjective self-interest or self-delusion — and this is what our moral values and virtues are concerned with no less than our scientific theories and hypotheses. Our basic moral evaluations are precisely concerned with arriving at a true view of ourselves and our relations with others unclouded by the prejudice, delusion, self-deception, vanity, self-interest, weakness of character and so on which invariably prevent us from becoming all that we should be in moral terms — honest, loyal, self-controlled, charitable, courageous, rather than dishonest, treacherous, spiteful, backsliding and cruel.

From this perspective, however, a further confusion is discernible on the part of the moral subjectivist and that is the tendency to regard values as epistemologically *ersatz* forms of judgment or belief — as mere *opinions* unsusceptible of empirical proof or rational demonstration. But although judgments are certainly possible concerning the truth or falsity, goodness or badness, of values; values are not, as such, primarily beliefs but rather rational *dispositions* or principled preferences which are plumbed into practical human affairs and therefore apt for appraisal in terms of the practical rather than the theoretical goals of human life; hence, values are tested differently from beliefs in the fires of human experience; but they *are* tested by reference to whether or not they ultimately conduce to certain rationally-defensible goals of human flourishing.

But what are these goals? How may we determine the proper direction for our best moral efforts and aspirations when everything in the realm of ethical values seems to be so fiercely contested? Once again the objection would seem to rest upon certain dubious assumptions and confusions — for example, on the doubtful subjectivist assumption that moral values are no more than personal opinions or commitments and on the confusion of a social or ethical principle concerning the right to my own opinion with a moral or epistemological issue about whether my opinion should be accorded equal weight with any other. But it is also possible to detect in all of this a rather over-simple conception of the general way in which moral development or progress needs to be understood in human affairs.

For the higher stages of moral development cannot be understood simply in terms of the possession of more true than false moral beliefs. Moreover, even if the citizens of Plato's *Republic* were more likely under the direction of his Guardians to act justly than the citizens of a democracy this would clearly not mean that they were better morally educated than the latter. The moral development at which education aims, then, is clearly as much a matter of complexity and particularity of *understanding* as of correctness, sincerity or commitment — and understanding may be deeper or shallower, more or less sensitive. It is this, of course, which accounts for the only seemingly paradoxical circumstance that we may sometimes entertain higher moral respect and regard for the thought and conduct of those whose views we do not share than for those whose views, it may sometimes be embarrassing to acknowledge, we do.

Basically, however, moral enquiry is no different in this respect from any other sort of human enquiry and we should certainly not be misled by this consideration into holding that in moral affairs some other quality — sincerity or casuistry perhaps — matters more than whether what we believe and do is correct, right or good. So although it must remain a matter for further dispute and discussion whether we treat women in general in our society or the young people in our schools as justly as we should, it seems inconceivable on the basis of any serious moral reflection that any society in which women are physically mutilated for ritual purposes or young people are subjected to institutionalised violence for disobeying school rules should be regarded as operating in a better moral climate than one in which such customs are deplored as indefensible. In the course of further moral and evaluative enquiry it may well become clear that we are still very far from seeing face to face, but we need not thereby despair of having made *any* progress or of the power of educated reflection to take us yet further.

Part 2:

**EDUCATION, VALUES
AND CULTURE**

3

Anthony Quinton

A Cultural Crisis: The Devaluation of Values

Introduction

The subject of these first two lectures in the Victor Cook Memorial Series is not the three abstractions that feature in their general title on their own, apart from a brief preliminary canter around them. What they are really concerned with is a crisis in contemporary culture in our part of the world, which has first made itself felt in the domain of education and which consists essentially in the repudiation of values that have been usually accepted. I believe that if this revolution against familiar values prevails there will be a break in the continuity of our culture, larger even than that which constituted the Renaissance, and is really more comparable to that which accompanied the fall of the Roman empire and its replacement by the barbarian kingdoms.

A Cultural Crisis

With the Renaissance the focus of cultural interest moved from heaven and the soul's eternal destiny to the earth and to the embodied life of human beings upon it. Educationally it led attention away from the abstract studies of logic, metaphysics and theology to rhetoric, from dog-Latin to the style of Cicero, from the fathers of the church and the commentators on the Sentences to the poets and orators of Greece and Rome. The idea that the classical imaginative literature of Greece and Rome was the ideal and total completion of the educational process turned out to be remarkably durable. It prevailed in all but the most humble and rudimentary schools until well into my early life.

The current revolution directs itself against the values incorporated in the literary canon, in the first instance, that is, against the generally accepted, if constantly revised, list of masterpieces of literature. That canon defines what one ought to have read and understood, at least in reasonably large part, if one is to count as an educated person. Loosely associated with this attack, and conceived in much the same spirit, is a less coherent assault on the values of the intellect. I mean in talking of these to refer to the values implicit in the ideas of speaking rightly and thinking rightly, of conformity to the rules of language and the rules of logic and method.

The prophetic figures of the Renaissance saw themselves as leading a march back to a glorious past, to the more golden passages of the histories of Greece and Rome. The current revolution seems to go back much further, to the primitive, to what may be described as natural or barbarous, according to taste. Barbarous rather than savage, in terms of Collingwood's distinction between them, since where the savage is untouched by civilisation, the barbarian is determined to destroy it.

A brief parade of symptoms of the crisis may help to make it more vivid and concrete. There is the scene of the Rev. Jesse Jackson leading a crowd of 500 students at Stanford University, the major private university of California, as they chanted 'Hey, hey, ho, ho, Western culture's got to go'. There is the widely used formula, purporting to describe the authors of the books making up the canon: Dead White Males. There is the project of replacing the familiar style of study of English or other literature with something called 'cultural studies', a pseudo-sociological pursuit of alleged political content in imaginative literature, the arts (fine but preferably popular) and mass entertainment. There is the censoring by local government library committees of ideologically unacceptable works from the shelves. At a more basic level there is the failure in primary education to develop literacy, or, where that is achieved, to encourage reading. In its place there are intruded collective activities or 'projects', which seek to make the classroom and the playground as much like each other as possible. Emphasis is laid on self-expression, which, in the case of those too young to have much in the way of selves to express, has to be valued more for its simple noisiness or amplitude than for anything it may objectively achieve.

The same kind of indulgent antinomianism prevails in the teaching of the English language. The perfectly reasonable view that dictionaries should not be anachronistically prescriptive, should not lay down as correct senses of words which have largely fallen out of colloquial use, is blown up into the doctrine that there is no distinction between correct and incorrect at all. Grammar is similarly seen as oppressive, an attempt to destroy the self-esteem, and even identity, of the working class by imposing middle-class habits of speech on them.

The assault on rationality is a many-faceted one and less explicit than the corresponding attacks on literature and language. To a considerable extent it is a matter of exemplary practice rather than of conscious theory. When Heidegger and Sartre entered the British field of consciousness after 1945 they astonished those who read or heard about them by their lack of intellectual decorum. Their successors in the leadership of intellectual fashion on the continent of Europe have kept up the bad work: Habermas, Foucault, Derrida. The gratuitous obscurity which is offered as a challenge and a reproach to the naive lucidity and pedestrian argumentativeness of Anglo-Saxon empiricism more or less guarantees that what is said will be misunderstood, or, in the face of criticism, be held to have been misunderstood.

There are, however, some bodies of explicit anti-rational theory about. At a fairly manageable distance from the conventional intellectual tradition there are objectors to the supposedly supreme objectivity of natural science, moderate in the case of Kuhn's theory of successive paradigms, wildly extreme in Feyerabend's doctrine that anything goes. The assumption that there is such a thing as objective truth and an objective reality for it to be true of has been undermined from various directions, by anti-realism and by Rorty's dismissal of the pretensions of philosophy to be some kind of intellectual judge or referee. If this is the persuasion of the intellectual elite, it will soon filter down to the classroom and encourage the belief that thought is simply the expression of what one feels, that it does not have to submit to any controls of logic and method.

Before setting out to expound these cultural forays in greater detail there are two other preliminary matters to be dealt with. First, I shall consider the relations between culture, education and values in general, not so much to vindicate my choice of a title for these lectures as to focus definitely on what is at issue, which is, briefly, not culture in its most inclusive sense, but high culture. Secondly, I shall seek to put our present situation in some sort of comparative context by outlining an extremely short and selective history of education. This will, I believe, show that our crisis is unique in its destructive potential.

Culture, Education and Values

These three features are intimately connected. Culture is what is transmitted from one generation to another by education. The rest is biological inheritance. Values are central to, although not wholly constitutive of, education. Therefore values occupy a central position in culture. That culture is what is handed on by education would not be disputed, I imagine, so long as some appropriate qualifications are made. I shall force myself not to linger over these since they are needed only to prevent misunderstanding. First of all, the education that conveys culture is very far from being all formal, that is to say carried on in some kind of school. Much of it will come from parents and other adults or contemporaries whose activities may be observed and imitated. Furthermore education need not be intentional or, if you feel that it must be, learning does not presuppose an intentional educator. One can learn from someone who has no idea that one is watching him.

What are the main kinds of cultural items that are learnt? Above all they are items of practical knowledge or skills: how to speak meaningfully and grammatically and the associated arts of reading and writing, how to reason, investigate and criticise one's own beliefs and those of others, how to get the most out of things, for example by attention. Values have a double application to skill or practical knowledge. In the first place, the fact that they are intentionally taught, if they are, shows that somebody thinks they are worth learning or, at any rate, teaching. That is an external value, one might say, of a taught and learnt capacity. But a skill also has an internal value, since to have acquired the skill is, to some extent at least, to have mastered the right way to do the thing in question and to have come to know what that right way is, even if one has not yet fully mastered it. These internal and external values are not wholly distinct. In the standard case, that of sincere or committed teaching, it is just because the teacher thinks that what the skill defines as right is right that he thinks it worth imparting.

Everyone who thinks at all about education nowadays is so conditioned to denying that to be merely informed, to know a lot of facts, is to be educated that it is worth saying that, if not the central element in education, information or knowledge is still essential to it. In part that is because the more theoretical or cognitive skills need information to work on. To speak and write, to reason and investigate you need some raw material of fact. A kitchen is not a larder, but it is no use without one. But to admit that is not to deny the primacy of skill or know-how.

All cultures teach the prevailing language, approved and customary modes of behaviour and how to do things that need to be done and that people know how to do. None of that requires formal education, which comes in with literacy, the first schools in the original river-valley civilisations having been schools for scribes. Once there is writing the range of cultural achievement is much increased. There is great oral poetry, some oral law and aphoristic wisdom, simple crafts do not need writing. But science, mathematics, articulated philosophy, history that is not legend or memorised chronicle, the novel — all have to be written down. It is largely from these that a conception of culture altogether narrower than the comprehensive anthropological one under consideration so far develops, that is to say Matthew Arnold's conception of culture as high culture.

He defined it, in effect, as 'the best that has been thought and said in the world' and thought that to pursue it is to pursue human perfection. I propose to modify Arnold's formula and define high culture as what has *been best thought and best said*, in other words as the greatest intellectual and literary achievements or, if culture be thought of as a characteristic of an individual and not as an objective body of work, as familiarity with those achievements. That is close to T.S. Eliot's list of the ingredients of high culture: first learning, then 'philosophy in the widest sense', as he puts it, 'an interest in, and some ability to manipulate, abstract ideas', and next the arts — literature in the first place, no doubt — but also painting and music. A fourth ingredient for Eliot, urbanity or civility, I shall ignore as really being nothing like and having nothing at all to do with the others. It is high culture, understood as the summit of intellectual achievement, measured by established intellectual and literary values, that is currently in danger.

I turn to my threatened very short outline history of education to show that in literate communities high culture is identifiable at an early stage of their development. It is most readily seen in education where it forms the curriculum of the most highly-esteemed and most ardently-sought teaching.

A Short History of Education

In archaic Greece serious formal education was much the same thing as the study of Homer, with his lessons in knightly honour, appropriate to a warrior society. In due course Euripides and Menander as well as orators, philosophers and historians were added to the canon. There emerged an oscillation between stress on cognitive rationality, as in Plato and Aristotle, and stress on style and eloquence, nourished by rhetoric rather than logic, as in the sophists and Isocrates, that was to persist until modern times. The Roman emphasis was on rhetoric, as befits the greatest nation of legal thinkers and practitioners. In taking over the Greek canon they made it a condition of being truly educated that one should know Greek. The Greeks had seen no point in knowing any language but Greek.

Monastic and cathedral schools kept education going after a fashion. The difficulty of incorporating pagan literature into the education of Christians was gradually overcome. Greek had died away. The literacy required for reading the Bible became the defining characteristic of the clergy. Around the twelfth century the large part of Aristotle's works which had until then not been available in the West came in from the Arabs and were translated. Universities emerged for Aristotle's logic, metaphysics and physics to be taught in and applied to the exposition of church doctrine. Medieval higher education was strongly cognitive or logical in emphasis. Vocationally considered, its aim was to turn out administrators for partially-literate feudal kings and nobles. There was nothing much of a literary side to it.

With the Renaissance rhetoric replaced logic, purity of style replaced validity of reasoning. Yet the revised and enlarged classical canon had a marked cognitive element. It called for translation from, and into, classical languages and so inspired a sense for exact meaning and conscious adherence to the rules of grammar. The Renaissance curriculum prevailed in the teaching of the upper classes until very recent times. Other fields of study were introduced and took some time away from Greek and Latin — science and history and modern languages — but the classics retained their leading place. And the medieval, Aristotelian tradition was not obliterated. It continued to dominate the universities, despite the exasperated criticism of major thinkers like Bacon, Hobbes and Locke. It was, indeed, an aspect of the general decline of the universities after the Renaissance, reaching its nadir in the eighteenth century.

At a lower social level much-increased literacy understandably coincided with the mass production of books by the printing press and the appearance of vernacular Bibles to allow for the cultivation of Protestant religious self-reliance. Vocational teaching became available for more of the general mass of the population.

In the nineteenth century economic requirements encouraged vocational pressure on the curriculum of the more exclusive schools, but the classical canon preserved its status. In the twentieth century more and more people have received higher education, so more and more schools have had to prepare pupils for it. That has led to the introduction of useful subjects, such as engineering, and widely accessible ones, such as English. The canon these lectures are concerned with is largely a combination of the Greek and Roman classics with the acknowledged classics of English literature, with some European supplements. The modern part of this compound was not invented to serve the needs of newly-created English departments. It was an established tradition, something that every educated person had previously been expected to get up on his own. Such works as Johnson's *Lives of the Poets* helped to form it. So our canon is not new. It is continuous with what was picked out as the best by Greeks and Romans, as revived at the Renaissance, and has been added to and otherwise varied in composition ever since.

Such a canon is not peculiar to the West. The most notable canon is that of the Chinese classics. Assembled partly by and in the lifetime of Confucius, they later became the crucial examination subject used to select mandarins, surviving the energetic attempts of an emperor to suppress them. The Chinese canon, like that of the West, goes back more than two and a half thousand years. The Chinese arrived at the novel, however, three hundred years before we did.

The history of formal education can be looked at from two points of view, one concerned with what is taught, the other with whom it is taught to. The second factor does not have to affect the first. If what has hitherto been taught only to a few is the best there is, why should it not be made available, as numbers expand, to a larger number? In the nineteenth century, when literacy became pretty well universal in Britain, there was a vigorous movement for self-education in the lower ranks of society. They were not to be satisfied with any watered-down version of the literary canon. They wanted the real thing and Ernest Rhys was there to supply it, with his Everyman's Library. In what follows that should be kept in mind.

I have slightly adjusted Arnold's definition of culture, in the narrow sense of high culture, to read: what has been best thought and best said. That covers both sides of the long oscillation I have recounted between the primarily intellectual and the primarily literary content of the highest kind of education. Intellectual higher education is now more a matter of studying a subject in its current process of development than of mastering a set of classic texts. The older way of doing things still prevails in ancient history and in philosophy, but not very much in modern history, hardly at all in economics and the social sciences and only vestigially in the natural sciences.

Examining the Challenges

The three challenges I am going to consider to high culture are directed against what, following Arnold, I see as its two main ingredients — and, in the third place, against the seriousness about language, about speaking and writing, which is required for effective study of either of the other two. The challenges in question are distinct. The rejection of the canon is vocal, explicit and clearly identifiable. The war against language and the intellect is more diffuse, more embedded in practice than polemically articulate. But they have some common elements which can be mentioned at the outset.

Both are, to start with, essentially political. The forms of culture attacked are seen as the possessions of a minority — it would be more accurate to say: several minorities. Since that is so it is assumed that they must be instruments serving the interests of the minority or minorities involved. To impose them on people outside the minority is, therefore, oppressive: it ignores the needs and experience of the outsiders or it causes them to think of the world and human society in a way that confirms their domination by the minority.

The excluded majority is divided into a now familiar number of categories: women, sexual deviants, blacks, non-Westerners generally, sometimes the young. There are various apparent ideas about to what extent and in what way ordinary high culture should be handled. Should it be allowed to continue in a suitably humbled form, like a former aristocrat in a communist country, acting as caretaker of the museum that was once his palace? That is what the establishment of university departments of women's, black or gay studies would seem to point to. Should the canon simply be augmented with works by authors from the groups said to be inadequately represented? Or should some disciplines be altogether given up in favour of others: literary criticism replaced by 'cultural studies', philosophy by conversation in the manner of Richard Rorty? The votaries of high culture, it is believed, are on to a good thing, to the extent that it helps to protect their dominant social status and, in the interests of justice, they must be expropriated.

Let me turn to the sharp leading edge of the attack on high culture: the rejection of the canon. It has been much more evident and has gone much further in the United States than here. One reason for that is that the idea of the canon is very obtrusive in American education, where it is usual in universities to offer a 'required' or compulsory course on Western civilisation. The heart of these courses is a list of selected readings from 'great books': Plato, Augustine, Erasmus, Pascal, etc. Their purpose is to make up for the deficiencies of American high schools in acquainting their students with anything that could count as knowledge of their cultural inheritance.

The critics point out that these lists of great books are of writings by dead white males and are put together by white males, who are ordinarily alive, but much under the influence of their dead predecessors. It may be added that both the selected and their selectors are for the most part bourgeois and straight. It should be admitted that this observation is broadly correct. There are a few women in the canon (many more than in the parallel canons of painting and music, but, of course, in nothing like their proportion in the population at large). There are no blacks at all. That there are no Chinese, Indian, Arab or Persian representatives, a defender of the canon would say, is not from lack of merit but because of linguistic remoteness. It is not a perfect answer. But works of these four great literatures are available, indeed in cheap, canon–sustaining series like Everyman's Library on Penguin Classics. The gay have no real statistical cause for complaint. Five canonical poets in English were homosexual: Marlowe, Gray, Hopkins, Whitman and Auden (six, if Housman is reckoned great). Nearly all canonical writers were middleclass, although an occasional Villon or Burns breaks through.

There are obvious explanations of the fact that the contents of the canon should be largely by, and even more largely selected by, white, middle-class males. It is selected by literary intellectuals, like Johnson, Coleridge and Arnold, or, more recently, by university teachers. These are occupations into which women have only recently made their way. The poor have had neither the conditions of life, nor in many cases the literacy, for serious reading and writing. But do these limitations on those selected and their selectors undermine the claim that the works in the canon are of conspicuous excellence?

The critics of the canon do not really engage with it on that level. What they do first is to attack the credentials of those who select the canon and then proceed to their main business which is the alleged bad consequences of canonisation. One way of seeking to undermine credentials is the familiar manoeuvre of scepticism about value judgments. In this case it relies on the distinguishing marks of the selectors to prove that their shared interests must underlie their valuations. For that to be effective the critic would have to show that there is a connection between the two. And that is usually just assumed. The thought that the selectors prefer works written by people like themselves over works written by other kinds of people which *are of equal or greater merit* is not available to the sceptic about value. In fact something like it is to be found in polemically feminist writing about literature, because in their case there really is a body of arguably undervalued work to appeal to. But that recourse is not available to blacks or the poor.

What are supposed to be the bad consequences of canonisation? Accounts of these are sometimes positive or direct, sometimes negative or indirect. The positive view is that teaching the canon forces on the oppressed outsider a white male middle-class way of viewing the world which falsifies his experience and obliterates his own view of the world. That, it is argued, manipulates him into putting up with the subordinate role which outsiders are held properly to occupy in the dominant viewpoint, as a Victorian family servant might say 'we go to Menton every winter.' A milder variant of this position says that a canon made up of books by white, middle-class males obstructs the development of imaginative sympathy with those outside the privileged circle. Thus in Shakespeare the poor serve the purpose of light relief; the rustic actors of *Pyramus and Thisbe* in *Midsummer Night's Dream* for example or Dogberry and his colleagues in *Much Ado About Nothing*. The same could be said of Hardy's peasants — and he was one himself, as Shakespeare was not.

The indirect bad consequences alleged are somewhat easier to grasp. Essentially they are that the literature of the canon diverts attention from the clamorous and crisis-ridden present either to timeless beauties and eternal verities or an idealised, imaginary past. To put the point more forcefully; it does not merely divert attention that could be better placed: it acts as a palliative to social evils, provides a bogus substitute satisfaction for real needs. Even more indirectly, high culture is criticised for its failure to be primarily directed towards the emancipation of the oppressed. That is reminiscent of Tolstoy's doctrine that the excellence of a work of literature is determined by the contribution it makes to the brotherhood of mankind. Acting on that principle he judged *Uncle Tom's Cabin* to be supremely good.

These conclusions about the bad consequences of the canon lead to proposals of reform which are of various degrees of vehemence. The most moderate is that of enlarging the canon, or revising it, so as to include works by authors from the oppressed groups. Thus Frantz Fanon joins John Stuart Mill, or replaces him. But that is really at best a practical makeshift, like the participation of totalitarian parties in parliamentary government. In so far as it is believed that all valuation is irremediably biased and subjective, anything that claims to be a canon will be no more than an expression of the preferences of an individual or group.

Consistent with that is the extreme conclusion that evaluative literary criticism should be abandoned. It should be replaced by the new discipline of 'cultural studies' in which literature and other broadly comparable things like films, television shows, videos and comic strips should be examined to determine their political significance, their contribution to or their impairment of the interests of the oppressed. By that stage, quite evidently, no other characteristics of a literary work make it worth study apart from its political bearing. Mere revision of the canon still allows for a significant difference between literature and other objects of cultural study.

The attack on intellectual values is many-pronged. To be complete it needs to be, since they are numerous and varied. Some, like those of clarity, simplicity and unambiguity, are comparatively informal, although they can, of course, be formally taught. But this aspect of rhetoric is not a systematic discipline. It is like good manners, in that while some broad rules of thumb can be laid down, the skill involved is not a technique, but a capacity to adjust behaviour in the light of its effect on the sensitivities of others. In the case of these informal values of discourse, consideration for the reader is the governing factor.

These values have not, I think, been directly challenged. But the pursuit of them has been abandoned by a large number of vocal and admired thinkers. Much German philosophy has been evilly written since Kant's unfortunate example. But Cartesian clarity persisted in France up to Bergson's stylish communication of his elusive message. Sartre, importing Heidegger, initiated a catastrophic rout of the French intellect which reached a high point with Foucault and Derrida. The German critical theorists, from Horkeimer and Adorno to Marcuse and Habermas wrote in a mixture of the styles of Hegel and Marx.

Degeneration of style has been accompanied by degeneration of structure. Terms indicative of logical organisation abound in the writings of the unmasking thinkers of contemporary Europe: *thus* and *so*, *therefore* and *it follows*, *contradictory* and *incompatible*. But, when examined, these prove to be a kind of ornamentation. Where an effort is made to extract an intelligible line of argument it turns out to be absurdly fallacious. John Ellis has painstakingly reconstructed the way in which Derrida recommends to the reader his paradoxical conclusion that writing is prior to speech (see Ellis, 1989). What Derrida does is to progressively redefine 'speech' so that it means 'writing' and 'writing' so that it means 'speech'. His technique is to pronounce some amazing but fairly intelligible thesis — for example, that there is nothing outside the text — and then surround it with a tissue of highly obscure and not discernibly relevant matter so as to intimidate the reader into swallowing the amazing thesis.

To show that this is not just casual abuse, I shall consider an example.

> A written sign is proffered in the absence of the receiver. How to style this absence? One could say that at the moment when I am writing, the receiver may be absent from my field of present perception. But is not this absence merely a distant presence, one which is delayed or which, in one form or another, is idealized in its representation? This does not seem to be the case, or at least this distance, divergence, delay, this deferral must be capable of being carried to a certain absoluteness of absence if the structure of writing, assuming that writing exists, is to constitute itself. It is at that point that the *difference* as writing could no longer be an ontological modification of presence. (Derrida, 1988, p. 7).

That starts intelligibly enough. Something written need not have an audience which is present at the time and place of writing. The audience may be somewhere else. The suspicion is voiced that he is not just a distant presence, i.e. presumably present somewhere else, but is capable of absolute absence, i.e., presumably, of not existing at all. All this to express the truism that something can be a piece of writing even if nobody ever reads it. But why dramatise that by saying that the possibility of a piece of writing's being unread is necessary if it is to constitute itself as writing? It gives a wholly superfluous air of menace to the concealed truism. To say that something does not have to be read to be a piece of writing is not to say that it *must* be capable of being not read, only that it is capable of being not read. Another truism lurks in the final sentence, namely that what makes a cluster of marks into a piece of writing is not present where and when the marks are. For one thing there is the intention of the writer: another, more important item is the set of social conventions about the making of such marks which endows them with meaning and so enables the writer to carry out his intention to communicate. But nothing in the passage about unread writing has any bearing on this second truism at all.

Derrida is the most extreme and, in his curious way, distinguished of stylistic debauchees. He is further down the road of self-indulgence than Sartre or even Foucault. But he is not alone. He has many imitators in American academic life and some in Britain. Here is a ripe specimen of this new form of discourse. It comes from an essay about the Turin Shroud.

> What we need is a concept of figurative *Aufhebung*. We would have to consider the dichotomy of its field and its means, and how they employ a dialectical mimesis as initiation of absolute knowledge: how it attempts to transform sensible space and so begin a movement (Hegel would have said automovement) in the direction of a certitude, figural certitude. An absolute seeing that would transcend the scansion of seeing and knowing . . . (see Didi-Huberman, 1987).

If Derrida hides truisms, and falsisms, in his prose and serves them up with an illusion of logical connectedness, that last quotation is simply babble, a sort of verbal delirium. Those who write like that, and also the somewhat overlapping group of those who repudiate the canon, share a common assumption that there is no such thing as objective truth, that all systems of belief reflect interest and bias and that there is no fixed and solid reality for our beliefs to be true about. It follows that the beliefs which we dignify with the title of knowledge in the light of the methods by which they were arrived at, methods dignified in their turn by being labelled rational or scientific, have no objective validity, but are relative, or even subjective, and the associated methods are too.

Scepticism is almost as old as philosophy, but traditional scepticism was based on supposed limitations of human intellectual power rather than on the emptiness of the goals pursued by the credulous believers whom sceptics were criticising. In the current view there were three great masters of deception or unmaskers of illusion in the nineteenth century: Marx, Freud and Nietzsche. For contemporary relativists the greatest of these was Nietzsche. It took time for the European mind to be prepared for the heart of his message. Marx's theory of the superstructure and Freud's of the unconscious emotional determinants of conscious mental life were needed to prepare the way for acknowledgment of Nietzsche's conception of beliefs as instruments in the service of the will to power. All our experience of the world is from some perspective or other and a perspective is a way of imposing order or form on a reality which in itself has none.

In Foucault's work there is an attempt to identify a sequence of such perspectives, which he calls *epistèmes*, in the history of European thought. He closely followed Nietzsche's notion of what we call knowledge being really in the service of our will to power by examining the ideologically-driven variations in prevailing conceptions of what it is to be mad, ill, criminal or sexually deviant. In the case of each of these social rejections allegedly objective science is used to force a set of people to the margins of society. There is a parallel between this and Thomas Kuhn's account of the history of science as a succession of periods in each of which a certain paradigm or standard, acceptable form of theorisation prevailed to the exclusion of all others until a scientific revolution replaced it with a new paradigm.

Less farouche than Foucault and less confined in scope than Kuhn is Richard Rorty. His principal target is epistemology, the theory of knowledge, to the extent that it supposes itself qualified to bestow certificates of cognitive respectability on other disciplines, or, as he might put it, other bodies of participants in the cultural conversation. The mistake of epistemology is to suppose that it is possible to compare the world in itself (nature) with the ways in which we represent it to ourselves (the mirror) to see if those representations correspond to what they refer to and are, therefore, true. The unsatisfactoriness of that account of the way in which we ascertain the cognitive value of our beliefs is familiar as a legacy of nineteenth-century absolute idealism as well as of Viennese logical positivism, at least until Tarski came and, supposedly, removed the scales from the eyes of the critics of correspondence. What is new is Rorty's adoption of a rather sedentary version of pragmatism in which the representatives of different disciplines converse with each other on equal terms.

Another American opponent of the alleged illusions of objectivism is Stanley Fish, formerly Professor of Literature and of Law at Duke University and more recently dean of the College of Liberal Arts and Sciences at University of Illinois, Chicago, and generally assumed to be the original of Morris Zapp in David Lodge's novel *Small World*. Inspired by Marx rather than Nietzsche, his argument against objectivism is short and simple. The factors which relativise our beliefs to our biases and interests are just as calculated to affect any principles or criteria of truth or justification or rationality to which we might appeal to modify our beliefs. So, for Fish, any such principles have no more authority than 'mere belief and unexamined practice'.

Foucault, Rorty and Fish may be described as undiscriminating relativists. They do not apply their relativism to any particular body of beliefs, but spread it around in a wholesale fashion. Nietzsche came to that position eventually. But earlier in his career he excepted science from invalidation and confined his perspectivist doctrine to religion, metaphysics, art and morality. In that he was at one with the more militant and orthodox positivists, who took religion and metaphysics to be empty and took moral and other value-judgments to be no more than expressions of emotion.

Nietzsche based his perspectivism on the idea that interpretation is always from a point of view. He extended the doctrine to science on the ground that science is as much an interpretation of experience as metaphysics or poetry. Two other factors have, I believed, encouraged thinkers of the present day to follow him in this respect. One is ideological hostility to science. It is seen not merely as an intellectual precondition of such deplored developments as nuclear warfare, industrial pollution and genetic engineering, but as somehow in favour of them. A little more cautiously, it has been held that scientism, the view that scientific knowledge is the best or the only real kind of knowledge, is implicitly propaganda for the application of science-based technology. The other is the curious hold on philosophers of science who take science to be the best kind of knowledge, of non-realistic accounts of scientific theory, which regard such theories as useful fictions, readily replaceable instruments of prediction.

If science, the last stronghold, is given up, then rationality, objectivity, disinterestedness in general are exploded, revealed to be devices, at best unconscious, for the pursuit of group or personal interests and the achievement of power over others. What practical implications it is sensible to see revelation as having is a complicated matter. Perhaps it need have no practical effect. A reflective scientist might simply carry on as before. For, even if his chosen pursuit is, he is now persuaded, inevitably biased and perspectival, it is no more or less so than anything else. But many, perhaps, will be persuaded by this line of thought that, since it is only a kind of sophisticated fairy-tale, it is not worthwhile going through the efforts involved in qualifying oneself to do it and in carrying it on in a professionally recognised way.

The attack on the intellect, or on its pretensions to rationality and disinterestedness in the most elevated fields of its application, bears on it as it is to be found in the domain of higher education. But any encouragement it gives to the indulgence of subjective whim and impulse there will make itself felt at the more primary levels of the educational system. And there have been reverberations. Relativism is in a naturally sympathetic relation to the development of multicultural studies. Equally the denial of objectivity, Derrida's view that interpretation, the essential work of the intellect, is play or Rorty's that it should take the form of social conversation — all these ideas are in tune with educational practices which reject disciplined processes of learning in favour of exploratory self-expression.

Literacy

I am not going to pursue the topic of elementary educational changes in general. But I want to consider the changes that have taken place in the teaching of language, since linguistic capacity — the ability to read with understanding, to speak and write with lucidity and order — is an indispensable requirement for effective literary study of the canon and for work in the fields in which the highest achievements of the intellect have been made.

The aspect of change with which I am particularly concerned is that which opposes the notion of language as being governed by rules. It sees the idea that an adequate capacity for speech requires the internalisation of these rules as constraining and elitist. They are taken to stunt or obstruct the free self-expression of speakers, on the one hand, and either to confirm the position of the elite by excluding the masses who do not speak as they do or, alternatively and conflictingly, by imposing an artificial manner of speech on them which cuts them off from their roots. The apparent conflict between exclusion and admission can be eliminated by distinguishing those who qualify for admission to the elite by learning effectively to speak as the elite do and the large remainder, the excluded, whose non-elite status is audibly marked by their failure to learn.

The matter is complicated, in England at any rate, by the way in which accents are distinctive of social classes. But that is not the kind of 'speaking properly' that is at issue here. What is in dispute are the requirements that a competent speaker should have a large vocabulary of words which he can use in their established meanings and that he should be able to assemble them in discourse in accordance with the rules of grammar. A teacher primarily concerned with expressiveness will give little or no attention to these things. That indifference may be solidified into hostility by the ideas that dictionaries should not be prescriptive and that grammar, like the operative meaning of words, is constantly changing.

It is persuasively argued that language is a natural, evolving phenomenon and that the function of dictionaries and grammars is simply to record how it is actually used. The way it is now is the outcome (to a large extent, for there are also neologisms to take account of), of individual deviations from what was, at the time, the prevailing practice. If most people use 'disinterested' as a synonym for 'uninterested' or say 'they invited Mother and I' rather than 'they invited Mother and me' that is all that the newer way of speaking requires for correctness.

Education is the transmitter of culture and the inculcation of values is at the centre of education. Traditionally, high culture, as embodied in the canon and the more theoretical academic disciplines and made possible by developed linguistic capacity, has been assumed to be the supremely valuable part of education. Hitherto those who wished to extend education from the few to the many aimed to enlarge the constituency for high culture. But now, by those who would unmask it as an elitist device, it is under the threefold attack I have described. In my second lecture I shall address myself to the cogency of this attack.

4

Anthony Quinton

A Revaluation of Values: Keeping Politics in its Place

Introduction

In the previous lecture I described various directions from which the high-culture component of the traditional content of education is under attack. The canon of supposedly supreme works of literature, the intellectual values that are most concentratedly pursued in the higher theoretical disciplines, the linguistic skills needed for effective study of the canon and the higher disciplines are all repudiated from the point of view of a militant egalitarianism which seeks to undermine their respective claims to superiority as compared with rock videos, women's or gay studies and the 'discourse' of Derrida, Dave Spart or Raymond Williams.

Before taking a critical look at the objections raised against high culture I shall briefly do two other things. First of all, it might be interesting to reflect on possible explanations for this violent cultural insurrection. Secondly, I want to consider, in bare outline form, what might be the consequences, for education and for culture and, therefore, for the community at large, of the revolution's success. Early in the first lecture I hinted darkly that it is a kind of incursion of the barbarians and that thought needs to be substantiated.

Considering the Revolution

The denial of objective truth, of real knowledge and of a real world to be known is, perhaps, an understandable, if delayed reaction to the uninterrupted diminution of anything like literal religious belief among the more reflective and thoughtful. It is not surprising that Nietzsche, who took the death of God seriously, should be the inspiration of those who seek to unmask the pretensions to objectivity of the Western mind. More fundamentally than in the role of an authoriser of morality, God served to guarantee the orderliness and intelligibility of the world. A world created by an intelligence in essence like that of human beings, even if infinitely more powerful, ought to be intelligible to them. But, of course, the absence of a cosmic guarantee of order and intelligibility is not a proof, or even much of a reason to believe, that they are not to be found in the world, but are arbitrarily imposed on it.

An entirely humdrum and respectable conviction that the canon is a fairly parochial affair could be excited by enhanced communication and travel. As things are *The Thousand and One Nights*, *The Dream of the Red Chamber*, *The Tale of Genji* are, so to speak, already associate members although they are not exactly required reading There have always been a few Europeans interested in non-European literature: Sir William Jones, Goethe, Edward Fitzgerald, Arthur Waley. Through their translations they have supplied narrow glimpses of other canons than our own. It must be an anachronism to imagine that a canon composed exclusively of European works is comprehensive. But to arrange greatly enlarged membership of the canon is quite another thing from dismantling it altogether. Nor would the need for such an enlargement call for the degree of passion that the very idea of a canon excites in its current critics.

It is plain that the chief force behind the attack on high culture is a vehement and comprehensive egalitarianism. The question is: why should Western intellectuals and academics — particularly French and American ones — have embraced it with so much enthusiasm? They would reply, no doubt, that it is an entirely intelligible response to the evils of contemporary capitalism: nuclear weaponry, industrial pollution, neo-colonial exploitation. But these offences are hardly specific to capitalism, unless somehow China and the former Soviet Union can be made out to be really capitalist societies. The Vietnam war had a very disturbing effect on the American university scene. Students were first made guilty, and then angry, by exemption. Opposition to the war, for which there were anyway good reasons, was exacerbated by the fact that others were fighting it for one. That accounts for the unattractive flavour of the following description of the war, many years after, by a left-wing feminist. 'It was', she says, 'fought for the most part by ghetto residents commanded by elements of the southern lower-middle-class'. The word 'elements' for some disliked class of human beings, as Orwell pointed out, is often to be found in the vocabulary of totalitarians. Observers of the present cultural crisis as it has taken form in America at the moment have noted that its instigators are those who were rebellious students of 1968. They are now at the height of their professional careers. Their conception of theory and literature as of pre-eminently political significance is combined with a corresponding determination to control the centres of power in the university and in what were once scholarly organisations. In line with their unembarrassed assumption that the life of learning is a political struggle, they ensure that appointments and promotions go to people of their way of thinking.

The launching of *Sputnik* in 1957 awoke a feeling in the United States that the country was falling behind its main adversary in intellectual competitiveness. The outcome was a great increase in government support for universities and an associated shift from the conception of them as ivory towers set in elite playgrounds to one which took them to be a vital component of the nation's strength. The humanities benefited from the new prosperity, but not gratefully, perhaps because it was not really intended for them. The events of 1968 saw a large reversal in the public perception of universities, which recent disclosures of misapplications of public funds within them can only have intensified. In an unsympathetic public environment, dissidents within them have made effective use of the autonomy of universities, which was designed to protect them from political pressures, to turn them into citadels of political revolt in cultural clothing. That is not going to enhance public esteem for them.

What will happen if the kind of domination of intellectual life the dissidents have secured in some of the most prominent and sophisticated universities in the US becomes general? What will be the effect of the abandonment of disciplined, rule-observing speech and writing in schools? No great penetration is needed to answer these questions, but, in order to develop an organised and reflective response to what is going on, it is necessary to set the probable results out in an explicit way.

The canon will be expelled as an elitist imposition. In its place 'cultural studies' of a special kind will reign. The simple mental fare served up by the entertainment industry in a large sense of the word will be scrutinised for its political content. The productions of members of oppressed or unprivileged groups will be required for study, to the extent, at any rate, that they bear a politically correct intention on their faces. Oral poetry and folk art that is calculated to function in the style of a rock concert in obliterating individuality in a kind of communal ecstasy will be encouraged. The ideal graduate of the new-style university is already approximated to by the kind of semi-literate partisan that infests television, the world of documentary photography and a good deal of journalism.

The assault on intellectual values will assimilate the study of the older humanities — philosophy, history, literature — on the one hand to the delirious obscurity and incoherence which pervades their practice in France and also to the unapologetic tendentiousness of certain kinds of 'committed' social science. What might happen in the natural sciences is more shadowy in outline. On the one hand equal status will be accorded to beliefs and techniques that are currently regarded as unscientific, an evaluation which dissidents regard as mere elitist prejudice. All sorts of alternative medicine will be accommodated alongside what we now think of as scientific medicine; not just acupuncture and homeopathy, but diagnosis from spots of blood or pieces of hair, the use of spells, anything that any culture has used to identify and treat illness. On the other hand, certain established fields of scientific inquiry will be run down as contributory to such evils as nuclear warfare and environmental pollution: space exploration and industrial chemistry, for example. In an egalitarian spirit, alchemy and astrology might well be brought in from the cold and rehabilitated.

That scenario for the natural sciences is perhaps a bit hyperbolic. It is hard to imagine that any substantial progress along the road indicated would not evoke a powerful counter-reaction, not just from directly threatened groups like the medical profession and the existing scientific community, but also from their clients, from government, in the first place, and beyond that from the rational part of the general population.

But a dissolution of the humanities into a compound of political indoctrination and self-expressive, antinomian play is far from inconceivable. Even that, it could reasonably be supposed, would not be likely to last for very long, provided that the dissidents did not secure control of the state as well as the university. Public and private finance would dry up. Doctors, engineers and other needed professionals could be taught in straightforward professional schools. In fields where hard research is possible it could go on in specialized research institutes. The university could simply fade away, as it nearly did in in eighteenth century England. The humanities and literature could be kept going in an informal way as they were then.

But, even if complete success for the revolution seems unlikely because of reaction against it or simple self-destruction, there are intermediate positions which are not attractive. An example is the weird division of the Philosophy Department at Sydney, Australia, post-1968, one bit being standard, the other ideological. A larger one was the coexistence in the universities of the Soviet Union and its satellites of sumptuously provided instruction in the gibberish of Marxism–Leninism, as defined for the time being by Stalin and Suslov or whoever, and perfectly rational work in mathematics, physics and logic.

The effect, finally, of the abandonment of disciplined language teaching would be that those touched by it would be unequipped to study the canon or the higher theoretical subjects anyway. That is easier to foresee since the process is already so far advanced. In their anxiety not to subject their pupils to any kind of constraint some primary schools do not try to improve their speech but let it pour forth in all its semi–articulate disorder. To do that and to fail to teach effective reading or promote the reading of any but the most pictorial and colloquial books is to make grammatical and verbally-rich discourse, spoken or written, unintelligible to the victims of the process.

The Canon and its Critics

I turn now to a critical examination of the way in which the displacement of the canon is recommended. Despite the professed disdain of the displacers for ordinary rational argument, it is impossible, or at any rate unsatisfactory, for them to demand its removal as a blank imperative. Facts, or alleged facts, about the content and the motives for the composition of the canon are stated and are implied to be reasons of some kind for getting rid of it. The first of these facts really is a fact, as has already been conceded. This is that the canon is parochial, or, more precisely, Eurocentric. It could be said, as well, that the canon in any particular European country is top-heavy in its representation of that country's language.

The circumscription involved is not altogether unreasonable. Not many students or readers, even students studying the canon in higher education, can be expected to know more than one or two languages other than their own well enough to read effectively in them. So, if they are to read outside that narrow linguistic area, they must rely on translations. There is a tiresome puristic doctrine which regards translation of imaginative literature as acceptable only as an aid to limited capacity to read the original, as in bilingual editions, or as a kind of literary exercise on ready-prepared literary raw material for autonomous imaginative writers like Dryden and Ezra Pound. A kind of answer to this purism is provided by the Authorised Version of the Bible, which is at once a supreme ingredient of the canon in English and, as a translation, the work of a fairly anonymous group of no independent literary standing. One could ask the question: is it not better to read Homer and Virgil in translation rather than a minor work of Dickens or Thackeray — *Barnaby Rudge* or *The Newcomes*, for example — or rather than not read them at all?

But the extent to which the canon, as acknowledged in any particular country, is confined to writing in the language of that country should not be exaggerated. In Everyman's Library or the *Editions de la Pléiade*, which may serve as rough institutional realisations of the English and French canons, a large proportion of the books included was originally written in neither English nor French. Each contains substantial representation of the literature of the other and also works from other major European literatures: Russian, German, Italian and Spanish. Everyman has also contained, and may contain again, the Bible (described as Ancient Hebrew Literature), Persian Poems, the Koran, Hindu Scriptures and Chinese Philosophy in Classical times. Non-European literature, from the *Epic of Gilgamesh* onwards, is even better represented in the Penguin classics series.

The canon is not the fixed repertoire of works in Greek and Latin it was four or five hundred years ago. It is constantly under revision and, in particular, is constantly being extended. Even those like Leavis, who interpret it in the most exclusive, little–Englandish form, do not deny the existence of literature of the highest value outside the restricted range of what they suppose it to be practicable to teach.

Other allegedly excluded groups are also present to an even more defensible extent. Certainly women are not to be found in it in direct proportion to their numbers in the population, except perhaps in fiction. If there are unfairly kept out women, who, as it is said, express a genuinely feminine point of view in a way that Sappho, Jane Austen, Emily Bronte and Virginia Woolf do not, let them be brought forth for consideration. Homosexuals probably do have a proportionate presence, although not as campaigners for gay rights. Gide's *Corydon* and Forster's *Maurice* are passed over in favour of *Les Faux Monnayeurs* and *A Passage to India*, for literary reasons, not as a piece of homophobic repression. Societies of the Third World that are minimally, and only very recently, literate are absent on the same grounds. Stories about animal tricksters, orally conveyed, are part of the childhood of mankind and, apart from anthropologists, are principally of interest to children.

Opponents of the canon draw critical attention to the social type of its selectors as much as to the writers whose work is included in it. These canonisers too are 'dead white males'. The first thing to notice about them is that although, inevitably, educated, they are not from the social and political elite. Johnson was the son of a man who ran a market bookstall and was desperately poor for much of his life. Coleridge went to a charity school, Christ's Hospital, and spent most of his life dependent on charity. Arnold, better born than they, no doubt, worked at the full-time drudgery of school inspection; Eliot for many years held a minor position in a bank. Leavis, son of a man who had a piano shop, did not get a decent university appointment until late in life, and lived on his meagre college income. Certainly they were not subsistence farmers in the tropics, but subsistence farmers have no literary opinions, although it would be a fine thing if they did.

Women have contributed to the canon much more than they have managed to define it. No doubt they were discouraged from thinking they could do so by way of a conception, imposed on them by men, of what their proper role was. The assumptions and institutional barriers which brought this about have now been largely dismantled. If Mrs. Leavis is to be believed, she, rather than her husband, was the driving force behind the most resolute canon-defining and canon-preserving movement of the twentieth century.

It is not, of course, the bare fact that the authors of the canon and the critics who select them for it come from a particular and limited social domain that is the fundamentally objectionable thing about it. It is rather the kind of writing written and preferred by such people which is seen as defective. White, male, middle-class and mostly straight, they impose a view of the world determined by those characteristics on those who are educationally subjected to the canon.

At the superficial level of subject-matter there is something in this, so far as the non-white are concerned. *Huckleberry Finn, A Passage to India* and *Burmese Days* are exceptional books. But, since so much imaginative literature is about romantic love between the sexes, women are abundantly present, at any rate, and by no means universally represented in a meek and subservient light. Some major male novelists are more memorable for their accounts of women than for their accounts of men: Tolstoy and Hardy are examples.

Nor do fictional characters at the lower end of the social scale always figure in a more or less ornamental way as light relief. In Scott's novels, what may be called the vernacular characters are always more solid and vital than the rather pallid representatives of the ruling class, unless the latter are villainous like Balfour of Burley in *Old Mortality* or the character who gives his name to *Redgauntlet*.

The thought implied by the opponents' claims of bias in the canon is that it serves the interests of the ruling class. Not much of it indeed is outright revolutionary propaganda, although some is, much of the poetry of Shelley, for example. But then nor is much of it reactionary propaganda, either. Even as conformist a writer as Galsworthy is critical, in a limp, high-minded way, of the established order. Evelyn Waugh, explicitly reactionary in his political views, hardly glorifies the most socially elevated and powerful of his characters. For the most part, where it is not politically indifferent, the canon is hostile to the status quo. That is why there was resolute opposition to state support for public libraries in the mid-nineteenth century.

But references to such things as the somewhat unorganised reforming impulse in much of Dickens will not placate the opponents of the canon. At one level, the fault of the works that make it up is that the criticism they make or imply of the status quo is largely confined to the realm of individual morality. In its concentration on particular people it fails to address the grand collective issue of emancipation. The great bourgeois novelists of the beginning of the century all take the general structure of the social system for granted. When they do cast an eye on those with truly revolutionary sentiments it is a violently hostile one, as in *The Possessed*, *Princess Casamassima* and *Under Western Eyes*. Even where not directly engaged in the defence of things as they are, they suggest, it is alleged, that the ideal form of life is that of the rich, cultivated bourgeoisie, sustained by the exploitation of others.

That is really a somewhat ridiculous anachronism. The novels of James and Proust are now historical fiction, no more recommending an immediate return to the social conditions they describe than *Ivanhoe* proposes a revival of the feudal system. Those few who are rich enough now to live as well as Swann or Milly Theale pursue the pleasures of the Marquesses of Bristol and of Blandford or of Lord White and Sir Ralph Halpern. But even a vanished world can have a bad effect in the critics' view. Its essential fault is that it does something other than excite impulses directed towards the emancipation of the oppressed, diverts attention from the overwhelming primacy of that political purpose. That is the one standard by which everything is to be judged.

Is the dismantling of the canon really going to do anything for the great cause? Is it not part of the point of emancipation that it should enable many more people to have effective access to the canon and other ingredients of high culture than they have now? If furthering emancipation of the oppressed is the over-riding purpose why concentrate on high culture as something not totally committed to it any more than on ice-skating or mountain-climbing? The critics of the canon are simply repeating in a modernised form the message of Tolstoy's *What Is Art*, that the entire and exclusive value of art resides in its enhancement of emotions of human fraternity. One could perfectly well sympathise with emancipation or fraternity without taking them to be so uniquely and overridingly important that nothing is of any value except in relation to them. If one believed that, then all but the most primordially self-preservative things people do would have to be abandoned or transformed out of recognition. That would make the question — emancipation for what? — unanswerable. It would lead to the misuse of things that are of independent value in themselves to make some minute contribution to the primary aim, as revolutionary soldiers might burn some Raphaels to keep warm.

Critics of the canon, however, would dispute the independent extra-political value of the works that compose it. There can be no formal disproof of that claim. What can be said is that the high estimation of the canon is the result of a convergence over a long period of the judgment of those who have attended most closely to the items in question. That is really all the answer that is needed for value scepticism that rests on the fact that opinions differ. What more could be asked for? Does anyone seriously question the principle of convergence of experienced judgment in the evaluation of cricket players or opera singers or holiday beaches? There are many different kinds of thing in which people have an interest or which they want, many different kinds of thing are sources of satisfaction, enjoyment or fulfilment. Some of them can be enjoyed directly, without preparation. To enjoy others we need some kind of training. To the extent that we are untrained or unprepared it is only sensible to follow the guidance of the initiated.

Furthermore, the supreme value exalted by the opponents of the canon is inevitably a secondary, derivative one. Redistribution has a point only if there are things other than the form of the redistribution aimed at which are of value in themselves. The politically obsessed confine these goods in themselves to power, first of all, and to wealth and status after that. But these too are all primarily means to ends. The possession of power, wealth and status is, of course, pleasant to contemplate if one has it. But the main point of power is its exercise and of wealth its expenditure. Their charm as objects of contemplation is entirely derived from the possible uses to which they can be put. Cultural revolutionaries, by sanctifying emancipation, deprive it of purpose. If their seizure of cultural and educational power were to succeed it would ensure that people generally were unequipped to enjoy a large range of available satisfactions.

It must, then, be admitted that the canon is limited. But it is not closed: its membership is perpetually changing. Its limits, furthermore, although they skew it in a Western direction, are not such as to exclude non-Western writing, and, in view of the difficulties of translation, which increase with cultural remoteness, they are not unreasonable. The selectors are not members of the ruling elite. The canon selected does not deal much with the people of the non-Western world and their experiences, but women and sexual deviants are well represented both as subject-matter and authors. Far from being apologetic or propaganda for the status quo, much of the canon is, in Lionel Trilling's phrase, adversarial, particularly since a large reading public replaced princes as the ultimate dispensers of literary patronage. Its value does not lie in any directly emancipatory purpose it may serve. But unless it had its proper, literary, value an important part of the purpose of emancipation would disappear.

Knowledge and its Critics

So much for the canon. I turn now to the attack on intellectual values, based on the belief that there is no such a thing as objective truth or objective rationality or justification. The obvious and repeated objection to that is that it is self-refuting. There are several ways in which the point can be made. One is that it is absolutely self-refuting, in other words, a straightforward self-contradiction, since 'there are no objective truths' is logically equivalent to 'it is an objective truth that there are no objective truths'. The relativist could reply that he does not deny that 'p' and 'it is true that p' are equivalent, only that 'p' and 'it is objectively true that p' are.

The objectivist can respond in a number of ways. First, he can ask if it is objectively, or only relatively, true that all truth is relative. The first option is self-refuting. The second prompts further interrogation. What does it mean to say that something is relatively true? Is it to say anything more than that something is believed by some person or group? It is hardly news that the beliefs of different people and groups are often in conflict. But when this is forced on their attention they ordinarily try to do something about it, to find out which belief is correct and then persuade the incorrect of their incorrectness.

A further question arises at this point. Is believing something intelligible without the notion of objective truth? Is to believe something not to take it to be objectively true? One could even go further along that line of criticism by asking whether the idea of meaning is not necessarily tied up with that of objective truth. To understand the meaning of a sentence is to know what circumstances license its affirmation, as constituting to everyone the conditions of its truth, at least in fairly elementary cases, but, perhaps, in more complex ones, the conditions of its justification. The meaning we attach to the utterances of someone else is a matter of what in the circumstances of utterance makes them true. That is most obvious in the anthropological case of working out what is meant by utterances in a wholly unfamiliar language. We effect an entrance into it by picking out some commonly uttered sentences — 'it is raining', 'that is a dog' and things of that sort — whose circumstances of utterance have something evidently in common, and work up to less context-bound remarks from there. There is no difference in principle between the anthropologist's situation and that of an English speaker who hears someone emitting sounds that form part of his own familiar vocabulary. But, in practice, just because he already has an elaborate, if inarticulate, theory about a language that has that vocabulary, he assumes that the meaning attached to the sentences emitted by others made up of that vocabulary is the same as he attaches to them. And, of course, he is usually, although not quite always, entirely right to do so.

The point of the inescapability of truth can be made in a more concrete and straightforward way by considering what someone might be doing by uttering an indicative sentence like 'it is raining' or 'people in the Third World are exploited' or 'there is no such thing as objective truth'. One can use it to assert something, to make a statement. One can alternatively use it to pretend to assert something, as in telling a story. One can use it, again, to test a microphone or to supply evidence to the appropriate sort of specialist about the state of one's throat or the quality of one's pronunciation. What distinguishes its use as an assertion is that it is uttered as true, or, at any rate, as something there is reason to think is true. A claim to truth, even if tentative, is essentially involved in an act of assertion. To assert something is to invite or encourage one's hearer to believe what one is saying, to take it to be true, whether or not it is true and whether or not one believes it oneself.

For the most part relativists simply ignore these objections. But, since relativists do not, for the most part, just blankly assert their relativist doctrine, but offer reasons in support of it, they really ought not to ignore them. They contend that their opponents do objectively believe certain things which are inconsistent — really inconsistent — with things they themselves believe and that these errors can be explained, really, objectively explained, by the biasing circumstances of the misled believers.

The sociologist Mannheim tried to preserve the consistency of his position by claiming that some people, of whom he was one, were a 'free-floating intelligentsia', epistemically privileged and above the strife of contending relative truths. Current relativists repudiate this unplausible claim to a unique privilege and, like Rorty, admit that their own beliefs are on the same relative level as the beliefs of their opponents. To do that is to assimilate what they are saying to story-telling. Derrida talks of the *play* of interpretation. Rorty says discussion should be understood as conversation, free contributions to a pool of discourse, offered in a spirit of take it or leave it.

There are two objections to that. In the first place it is, self-refutingly, to claim that it is objectively true, on objectively true grounds, that there is nothing better than this, no such thing as real, serious disagreement. Secondly, and more important, the idea that communication is the exchange of utterances which the participants in a conversation find it agreeable to believe raises the question of what it is that they are playing at. Nonassertive uses of indicative sentences are parasitic on their assertive use. To understand a story one has to have an understanding of what the sentences that compose it mean, of what they could be used to assert, even though they are not being so used in the storytelling. In a more down-to-earth idiom, one has to know what it would really be like if the story were true. Without real assertion there can be no pretence of assertion.

All this anti-relativist argumentation, it might be held, is to make unnecessarily heavy weather of what is going on. When someone utters something which would, taken at its face value, be self-refuting it is surely natural, tolerant and constructive to reinterpret

what they are saying. The difficulty in this case is that the self-refuta-
tion is so fundamental, not just a local blur or piece of noise in a generally intelligible context, that the whole communicative project is
undermined. What can be admitted is that there are certain considerations which lend a little colour to the relativist doctrine, even if they
do not in fact justify it.

Much of what we now believe was not believed before. Much was
believed which is now disbelieved. We may conclude that our own
beliefs will be lavishly revised in the course of time (sometimes
wrongly, perhaps). But that does not show that those of our beliefs
that will be correctly abandoned in the future will be shown by that
fact to have been only relatively true. What will be shown is that they
were not true, but only believed. And a great deal of what we believe
has always been believed and always will be: that human beings feel
pain, while stones do not; that water quenches fire; that apples are
edible; that sea-water tastes salty.

All beliefs are, indeed, first arrived at from a particular point of
view. Often the falsity of a belief can be accounted for by some pecu-
liarities of the point of view of the believer. But must the fact that all
beliefs are in this way perspectival universally invalidate or
relativise them? Are not some perspectives epistemically superior to
others: daylight to darkness, calm to excitement, curiosity to anger?
What is more, if beliefs originate from a particular point of view they
are not locked into it. The believer can consider the matter from other
perspectives and can incorporate the perspectives of others by critical interchange with them.

An important and generally-ignored case of apparent disagreement which is not genuine inconsistency is the selective operation of
our interests. For example, two people may disagree about the cause
of increasing crime, one attributing it to social deprivation, the other
to an insufficiently strong police force. But both may be right, not, of
course, in believing that their respective diagnoses give *the unique*
cause of rising crime for there is none, but that both are parts of the
complex cause of the phenomenon. Either of the suggested policies
for reducing or containing crime could have the desired effect, but
the costs of the two policies may well be differently viewed.

The same selective factor is at work in what might be called competing descriptions of a given thing. I am an Englishman, a male, a
human being, a mammal, a living organism. It is objectively correct
to describe me in any of these ways, but in different contexts different descriptions may be appropriate. This fact is the basis of a famil-

iar kind of joke, like that of the tailor who measured Stalin for a suit and, when asked what the tyrant was like, replied 'he was a short 42'. Not all truth is interesting or important, in fact very little of it is. To assert something is to suggest, outside the smallest small talk, that what is said is of some interest and that is often disputable. But to be uninteresting is not to lack objective truth.

Confronted by the self-destructiveness of intellectual nihilism it is possible to question the sincerity of those who propound it. If Derrida, who takes a notably possessive attitude to his writings, were to bring a case against someone for plagiarising him, would he look tolerantly on a judge who deconstructed the statement that the plagiarist had copied his work, interpreting it the other way round as meaning that Derrida had somehow prospectively copied the work of the alleged plagiarist, along the lines of his own thought that writing is prior to speech? Would he not feel indignant about a chemist who had deconstructed a doctor's prescription for a bilious ailment from which he was suffering?

The lavishness of his claims about the unconstrained freedom of interpretation invites pedestrian, one might even say insensitively philistine, comments of this kind. Are we then to suppose that the claims carry a hidden rider to the effect that they cover only theoretical discourse? It should be noted in passing that, being part of theoretical discourse themselves, they would still be self-undermining. The main point is that this would be to trivialise theoretical discourse by segregating it from rational control.

An entertaining example of this kind of implicit limitation of scope is provided by the unfavourable remarks of Stanley Fish about the practice of peer review of work submitted for publication in scholarly periodicals, which are presented to reviewers without their author's names on them. He says he should be exempted from this kind of equal treatment because, as he puts it, he 'has paid his dues': what he puts in should be accepted simply because he is an academic star. That is possessive individualism in its purest form. It resonantly affirms the bourgeois principle that justice rests on desert, not on need.

Meaning and its Critics

The third and final element of the assault is its egalitarian/libertarian view about language. The oppressed masses, it is held, are kept in subjection by having prescriptive dictionaries, the rules of grammar and Fowler-like principles of style imposed on them. Children should be encouraged to express themselves freely and impulsively, in whatever way comes naturally to them, and not be fettered in the bonds of bourgeois utterance.

There is, indeed, a case to be made against rigidly prescriptive dictionaries, grammar books and manuals of style. Language is constantly evolving. To be rigidly prescriptive about it is not to give useful instruction but to imprison learners in a kind of semantic museum. A dictionary that beside the entry for 'discover' put only 'reveal' or beside 'nice' 'exact' would be like a twenty-year-old copy of the *Good Food Guide*: a recipe for disappointment.

But if meanings and rules of grammar change over the long run they must have a fair degree of fixity at any given moment for effective communication to be possible. The gravitational pull of idle, careless speech and writing is constant. Educational insistence on the rules is needed to counteract it, quite as much as the discipline of hygiene is needed to stem the easy solicitations of dirtiness. The fact that it is needed means that there are conflicting practices. It may be that a new practice, originated by ignorant neglect of a distinction, like the assimilation of 'disinterested' to 'uninterested', will eventually become too widespread to rule out. There are, after all, other words near enough in meaning to 'disinterested' in its traditional sense to serve as approximate substitutes for it, 'impartial', 'objective', 'fair-minded'. What is unfortunate about the assimilation is that it suggests that the only way of being impartial is to be indifferent to the matter in hand or emotionally uninvolved with it. A change of usage is powered here by a false belief with bad practical consequences.

The alternative to the kind of temporary fixity and definiteness of meaning I have called for is a kind of generalised floating ambiguity. Ambiguity is not always to be deplored. It is economical, using one thing to do two jobs, like stirring soup with a tyre lever. But that is only really safe where one word is used for two very different purposes, such as Mill's favourite 'bank', or when used for two related but syntactically distinct purposes as in 'drop', used of what is dropping and of the space through which something is dropped. In these cases there are clearly demarcated boundaries of application.

But in what I have called 'floating' ambiguity, users of the words infected by it will confuse themselves and confuse others. A few years ago politically enthusiastic people often said that bad housing is violence. It is, of course, nothing of the sort. Like violence, it is deplorable. Unlike violence, however, it is not intentional, although it can be remedied by human action. Furthermore it avoidable by its victims in a way that violence, which is ordinarily peremptory, is not. And the kind of harm it does is slow and cumulative; no sudden, painful and disabling shock is administered to the victim. What this loose way of speaking objectionably suggests is that since bad housing is violence it is appropriate to respond to it with violence in its standard meaning in virtue of an underlying principle of an eye for an eye.

A less clear-cut, but more obviously floating, example of ambiguity, one which has floated to the outermost limits of vagueness, is 'society', as in such formulae as 'it's not the criminal's fault, society is to blame'. It is not at all clear, either to speaker or hearer, what is being referred to. Is it everyone else or some particular group of people? At the back of the speaker's mind, perhaps, is the idea of the ruling class, the people who are supposed to dominate society. The implausibility of this is concealed by the loose reference which takes in the more obvious fault-sharers, the criminal's parents and associates, but loses them in the crowd.

In the affairs of practical life there is too much immediately at stake for linguistic corruption to get much of a hold. People are still going to be saying the same things when they say that a sparking plug is damp or that a piece of fish has gone off. But at a more general level there is no such practical limit set to the looseness of speech. Disputants will be at cross-purposes with those they dispute with and even with themselves; sometimes in supposing something to be relevant to the matter in hand when it is not (as with the two aspects of the passage from Derrida I looked at in the first lecture), sometimes in supposing that they have actually asserted anything at all.

Language is an instrument for articulating our awareness of the world and ourselves and for communicating that awareness to others. The reality it works in is hard stuff, not indefinitely malleable. To cope with it the instruments of articulation need to be kept in good order, which in their case is a matter of preserving their common currency and of preserving the distinctiveness of their individual uses. At the far end of linguistic anarchism lies the reduction of communication to the expression of feeling, like the gruntings and chirpings of beasts and birds. That would be the final erosion of the most distinctively human thing about human beings.

The celebrated Third World thinker Confucius, when asked what counsel he would give were he appointed adviser to Prince Mei, said he would ask, first of all, for the rectification of language. In what we may see as a too-prescriptive spirit he said that things should be called by their right names, as if the name of a thing were something fixed eternally, once for all. Convinced, with the author of *Genesis*, that names are man-made, we admit that meanings depend on convention. But a convention is nullified if it is not generally observed.

I have been arguing against the relaxation of several large bodies of cultural constraints. The canon constrains by laying down that some books are supremely worthy of being read. The principles of rationality constrain us to sift our beliefs critically and in an orderly way and to make them as accessible as possible to this treatment by stating and arguing for them clearly and simply. Linguistic discipline constrains us not to take the easiest way out in discourse. It is always pleasant to relax constraints and, therefore, kindly to relax their application to others. But the pleasure and kindness involved here are shortlived and lead to pain in the long run. The achievements of the human species have been brought about by active effort to master ourselves and our environment. Culture, in its most inclusive sense, is the accumulated capital that has emerged through that effort. High culture is the most demanding and self-critical part of the general cultural accumulation in which the best, the most systematic and penetrating, knowledge of ourselves and the world is developed. It is a certain good. The emancipatory triumph to which its destruction is supposed, by it attackers, to contribute, is only a remotely possible outcome of its destruction.

In fact, its destruction is no more likely a result of the cultural revolution I have been considering than general emancipation is of the trashing of high culture. If the revolutionaries succeed in capturing power in the universities, it will be the universities that will be transformed, not the community at large. Universities do not sustain themselves, they have to be paid for by governments — and, therefore, in the end taxpayers — and by private benefactors. They will not go on indefinitely supporting centres of intellectual and aesthetic carnival. Who ever heard of a successful revolution that began by seizing the university, rather than the central telephone exchange or the main repository of arms? But the oldest medieval institution still in recognisably the same sort of working order as it originally was, which, in its eight hundred-year history, has often served high culture well, even if at times it has slept, is, in our present world, its principal citadel. If the university is undermined high culture will have to regroup itself elsewhere and it may be badly damaged in the process.

In these lectures I have said nothing directly about moral values, but some moral values are involved in the activities I have been talking about. The most important is honesty. It is important to realise that it is not the same thing as sincerity, although they are related. The most full-heartedly sincere expression of belief falls short of honesty if the belief in question is inadequately formulated and inadequately examined. Part of honest communication is putting what you are trying to get across so that what you actually mean is apprehended by your hearer.

Conclusion

I do not want to end either on a despondent or on a merely edifying note. As to despondency, I believe that the revolution can be contained, if it is recognised and resisted, not meekly submitted to from fear of unpopularity or of simply being out of the fashion. The roots of the revolution are fairly shallow. It is loosely anchored in the various groups of the really or apparently oppressed it purports to speak for. The passive multitude its exponents rather condescendingly wish to emancipate should not be satisfied with the disembowelled substitute for high culture their emancipators are preparing for them and there are signs that they will not accept it, such as parents' revolts against playful schooling and the falling numbers of applicants for humanities courses in the United States.

As for edification, looking back on what I have said it reminds me uncomfortably of elderly persons in my own youth going on about the decay of standards and, in particular, of the slightly risible figure of C.E.M. Joad. He settled down in later life to the production at regular intervals of books with such titles as *Return to Philosophy* or *Philosophy for our Time* in which the absolute values of truth, goodness and beauty were defended in a dilutedly Platonic manner. In holding that truth is not relative, but that only belief is, I have not assumed that truth, knowledge or the literary merit of the canon is an absolute value. I think these values are rooted in human nature, not part of the eternal architecture of the world. But I still think them really valuable, not least as stepping-stones on the way to more comprehensive knowledge and a more inclusive canon, understood as a possession of the human species in general and not just of some biased and self-interested group of exploitative power seekers.[1]

---

[1]   I want to acknowledge my heavy dependence on Roger Kimball's *Tenured Radicals* for illustrative material from the United States (see Kimball, (1990)).

5

Anthony O'Hear

Education, Value and the Sense of Awe

Human beings are undoubtedly part of nature. Our existence is dependent in many complex ways on the balance of nature, obviously on conditions on our planet, perhaps less obviously on the state of the sun and the solar system, and doubtless too, on things which happened right at the start of the universe.

We can look in detail at aspects of our make-up and experience. We can, for example, examine just how our perception of colour works, showing how a coincidence between certain wavelengths of light and properties of our sense organs yields us this experience. We can also tell stories about the survival value of our having colour vision. Colour vision allowed our remote ancestors to pick out berries, fruits, predators, etc., better than their competitors in the struggle for existence, which is why we have it now. In principle, it seems that a combination of the physiological and the evolutionary could give explanations of much of our physical and mental make-up, showing us to be products of nature and part of nature.

It is true that human beings, unlike other species in nature, are not purely Darwinian in their mode of development. Human parents can and do systematically transmit what they have learned in life to their offspring. In Darwinian natural selection the gene is the means by which parents transmit faculties, abilities and dispositions to their offspring. The key point about the genetic transmission of characteristics is that the experience of parents normally has no effect on their genes, and so can't be genetically handed on. A man might have acquired a calloused hand in decades of hard manual work, but this has no bearing on the likelihood of his son being born more horny handed than had the father not laboured.

Unlike other animals, however, we have developed symbol systems, of which language is the most important. In learning their native language, children pick up all sorts of habits of thought and behaviour, way beyond their genetic inheritance. They learn classifications, meanings and evaluations, many of which could hardly be envisaged in the absence of a community and some of which are peculiar to a particular community. Without language a creature would be hard put to distinguish shame from guilt, let us say, or either emotion from a whole range of other negative feelings and reactions. And as we learn from anthropology and literature, the precise meaning of shame is rather different in England now from the associated emotion in Homeric Greece or modern Japan.

In learning a language, we learn a form of life, as Wittgenstein emphasized. And in so doing, we learn in all sorts of ways from the *experience* not just of our parents, but also of other forebears both close and remote. Does anything follow from the Lamarckian nature of human culture about why cultural forms, our forms of knowledge and our forms of life, survive and develop in the way they do?

Let us suppose for a moment that the Cartesian project of refuting scepticism about our most basic beliefs and values is adjudged a failure; and that it proves impossible to base what we know and believe on any foundation unassailable by sceptical doubt. We might then explain the persistence of our basic beliefs and customs in terms of their usefulness to our survival — in Darwinian terms, that is — rather than in terms of their rationality. We believe, say, that most of us have never been on the moon, that the world has existed for a long time, that I have a hand in front of me, or that causing wanton injury is wrong, not because, without begging the question, we can prove any of these things to be true, but rather because these are beliefs and values presupposed in our form of life, a form of life which has proved its mettle in assuring the success and survival of those who are part of it. In this way there is a form of natural selection operating on beliefs and values: those which belong to successful groups and (perhaps) help their survival are thus selected for in so far as the group itself survives.

Naturalistic accounts of the survival of beliefs and values are not without some plausibility; nevertheless there is no difficulty in envisaging that a society or group might derive its very success from its adherence to a *false* belief or a *distorted* value. Precisely because a false belief or distorted value is likely to distinguish the group which possesses it from other groups, it forms the focus around which the group identifies itself, and from which it gains its cohesion and strength in face of what it sees as infidels. Few non-Muslims, for example, would regard the central claim of the Koran to be true or approve of the Muslim treatment of women; yet in the early centuries of Islam and arguably again today, it is from their adherence to the — at best — questionable claim about Allah, Mohammed, the Koran and the associated ethos, that the followers of Islam derive their power (and an Islamic anthropologist might well make similar remarks about Christ being the Second Person of the Blessed Trinity and Christian attitudes to sexuality).

Thus, even though we can give naturalistic accounts of our faculties and beliefs, we can also raise questions about the truth and epistemological status of what they tell us. The naturalistic analysis of colour perception to which I referred earlier does pose for us the question as to whether something (colour) which *seems* to be a fundamental property of the universe really *is* so. In other words, even while giving a naturalistic account of a part of our experience, we are led to question the validity of certain initially unquestioned beliefs or attitudes associated with that experience.

What I conclude from this ability we have to question and think about our genetic and cultural inheritance is that as human beings we are not simply passive elements in a wider, more inclusive process of nature, subject only to the pushes and pulls exerted on us by those processes. At the very least we are capable of standing back from our engagement in what Newman called the flow of life. One potential result of this reflectiveness is that people disengage from their existing perceptions and practices, regarding them as products of physiological or social factors which may lead to distorted or partial perspectives on the whole of which they are a part. (So colours are not part of the stuff of reality; one's natural adherence to the values of the culture in which one is brought up owes as much to one's upbringing as to any strongly grounded sense that they are right.)

Because of our possession of symbol systems, particularly language, we do not just act, feel and react in the world. We are able to formulate for ourselves beliefs about the principles on which we act, to theorise about them and to criticise and improve them, and also imaginatively to construct new ones. Our Lamarckian nature is not just a matter of our being able to transmit information nongenetically. What makes that possible also makes possible our ability to reflect on and, as a result, modify our beliefs and values. A world of meanings, then, of explicitly formulated beliefs and attitudes and other cultural products stands between us human beings and the world of raw, uninterpreted fact.

In reflecting on particular beliefs and values we hold, we can, as I have said, view them naturalistically, as the result of various causal factors, natural and social. Looking at them in this way, we may regard them as what might be called projections of aspects of our make-up on to the world. Thus, our sense that the world is coloured, along with our sense of some actions being right and others wrong, comes to be seen as a matter of neurophysiological activities and emotional feelings, which have their origins within us, being diffused over a world in which there are really no colours, no moral properties. Hume, who held this view both of colour and of morality, also held that seeing an object as beautiful or deformed is a matter of 'gilding' or 'staining' it with the colours borrowed from internal sentiment (see Hume, 1751, 1951, Appendix 1).

Without denying that aspects of our perception, and many of our beliefs and our attributions of value, both moral and aesthetic, are due in part to features of our own make up, I now want to suggest that in the case of judgments of truth and value, it is impossible for us to regard our best considered efforts as simply projections. In the case of our beliefs about the surrounding world and its contents, it is — as I have shown — possible to discount some, seeing them as products of an idiosyncratic interaction with reality. But the reason we can do this is because we regard the larger story — the causal story — as sufficiently true for the purpose. In telling this larger story, we are assuming, and have to assume, that at certain points our beliefs *are* attuned to the world.

Indeed, it is hard to see how we could do otherwise while continuing to act and make our way through the world. A thoroughgoing scepticism on our part regarding beliefs about the world is not possible so long as we continue to act in the world; part of our acting indeed involves discriminating between true and false beliefs, and acting on those we believe to be *true*; beliefs we take to be true we cannot see as simply an effect of some idiosyncratic interaction of ours with the world which leads us to project on to the world features which it does not really possess.

For analogous reasons which have been elaborated by Charles Taylor (1989) it is equally hard to see our value judgments as simply projections of feeling, as just some gilding and staining of the world on our part, or as manifestations of a Nietzschean will-to-power. As part of being what Taylor calls a 'functioning self', deliberating, judging and acting in the world, we cannot help but have recourse to notions like courage, generosity, kindness, dignity, fairness and their opposites. We need such concepts to make sense of our own lives, and to understand the lives of others. The use of evaluative notions such as the ones I have mentioned in a life-guiding way presupposes that the user accepts these terms as indicative of virtues which are good in themselves, and good not simply because they serve certain interests of his. Maybe the virtues do serve human interests in a general sense, but to do a generous or a noble or a courageous act implies that the agent is seeing what he is doing as generous, noble or courageous — and hence as good in itself — and good not just because it serves certain interests, individual or collective.

The Nietzschean or other moral sceptic may claim that all we ever do in our valuing is to serve self-interest, more or less openly, more or less widely conceived. But this is to overlook the obvious fact that even in seeking our own interest or self-fulfilment, we have to regard some things as worth being interested in, as worthwhile in themselves, as goods in themselves in which the self might find fulfilment. And, in practice, even the most thoroughgoing proponents of reductive views of value usually end up advocating some value as ultimately worthwhile in itself, as we see in various ways in the cases of Nietzsche himself (will-to-power), E.O. Wilson (knowledge) and Michel Foucault (liberation). And, as Lord Quinton pointed out in his second lecture, for most of us power and liberation, at least, are valued as means to the attainment of other ends which are valuable in themselves and to which they are but means. ('Cultural revolutionaries, by sanctifying emancipation, deprive it of purpose.' (p. 59))

Reflectiveness, then, which might at an earlier stage in our argument have seemed to be on the point of destroying morality, by interpreting our morality naturalistically, may now come to the aid of morality, when we begin to think about the actual fabric of our moral life. For if someone were to say that the only things worth being interested in for themselves — the only constitutive goods for us — were selfish pleasure and riches, we could remind him of the saying in the Gospels about the profit of gaining the whole world when one suffers the loss of one's own soul, or of the Socratic adage that the good man cannot be harmed. That on some level we all understand these and similar sayings, as well as everyday talk about such virtues as compassion, courage, kindness and justice, and that we feel ourselves bound unconditionally by some of what is implied in such talk shows that untempered hedonism is not in practice the only value in our lives (and similar objections could also be made to the monistic re-valuations of Nietzsche, Wilson and Foucault).

As Taylor puts it, moral scepticism of a Humean or a Nietzschean type thinking that 'we do not speak from a moral orientation which we take to be right' is 'a form of self-delusion'

> incompatible with the way we cannot but understand ourselves in the actual practices which constitute holding that (orientation): our delibera-tions, our serious assessments of ourselves and others. They are not con-structs you could actually make of your life while living it . . . [but are] only kept aloft by a certain lack of self-lucidity, which keeps the relevant meta-construal from connecting with the terms in which we cannot but live our actual moral experience. (Taylor, 1989, pp. 99–100).

Scepticism about truth and about value, particularly scepticism motivated by naturalistic accounts of our perceptions, beliefs and practices, involves detaching ourselves from our actual existence as agents, as believers, as participants in a world natural and social. Our reflectiveness can lead to a sort of moral and epistemological disengagement, disembodiment even, given that our existence as agents is intimately connected with our being embodied in a world; but this stance is at odds with our experience and participation in our practices — scientific, moral and aesthetic. Reflectiveness about our beliefs and values can straightforwardly improve them, as when one realises that some apparently bent sticks are not bent, or per-haps, more complicatedly, that a prevalent conception of justice is fuelled more by resentment for some of one's fellows rather than by genuine concern for others. But at another level, reflectiveness ceases to improve and begins to undermine. The two examples I have just given have historically been powerful in setting thinkers off in the direction of scepticism about *all* appearances, about *all* val-ues. But then further reflection can reveal that global scepticism itself is unsustainable, at least as a doctrine to live by: that as reflec-tive agents we are creatures with a natural orientation to the true and to the good, and that as we conceive it in our lives, the good is some-thing more than individual self-interest.

In saying that we have an orientation to the good and the true, am I also claiming that there is anything outside of us to which this orien-tation is directed? In the case of truth, we can, of course, say that the world itself forms the objective correlate of our drive to truth. Some would doubtless follow C.S. Peirce in seeing the sometimes uncer-tain harmony between our theories and the world underwritten by both us and the world being moved by the love of God. But perhaps we do not need any metaphysical claim of this sort to make sense of our need to distinguish between what is and is not true, the need being something built into our self-consciousness and its object and immediate satisfier being the world itself.

Things, though, get more difficult when we come to consider what I am calling our orientation to the good. Although the structure of our experience as self-conscious agents is the basis of our ability to make a distinction between what is good and what is merely useful to us individually or collectively, the problem is to know what the object might be to which our orientation to the good is directed. What, in other words, can we regard as the source of our moral goods, goods which have the command they have over us because we do not see them simply in terms of projections of human desires or needs? What we see as *just* a projection of our desires or needs, individual or collective, can, in virtue of that very fact, equally be seen as provisional, cancellable, dispensable; replaceable by some new willing of mine, as against the willing of the rest. This, at least, is what I learn from Nietzsche. But from my own experience and from what I see of life around me, I learn that, for example, the imperatives against wanton cruelty or in favour of certain types of moral and physical courage are not provisional, cancellable or dispensable. I learn this particularly on the occasions when I see that I and others do dispense with them, and when it is forcefully borne in on me that a form of human life without such values would be a bad form of life. I can say this even while admitting that my precise conception of the good life and its virtues may be mistaken. What, in the light of any valuations and the role that they play in my life, I cannot admit is that the whole conception is wrong, and that there could be a good form of human life which did not in some large measure contain virtues continuous with and intelligible in the light of my conception.

There is doubtless a considerable embarrassment today in saying *anything* about objective values, or about the background needed for such talk. As Iris Murdoch put it in her essay 'Against Dryness':

> We no longer see man against a background of values, of realities which transcend him. We picture man as a brave naked well surrounded by an easily comprehended empirical world. For the hard idea of truth, we have substituted a facile idea of sincerity. What we have never had, of course, is a satisfactory Liberal theory of personality, a theory of man as free and separate and related to a rich and complicated world from which, as a moral being, he has much to learn. We have bought the Liberal theory as it stands, because we have wished to encourage people to think of themselves as free, at the cost of surrendering the background. (Murdoch, 1961, p. 18).

The problem I have been skirting round is the question as to whether that orientation to the good — which I find embedded in our form of life and moral discourse — can survive an ethic based on some notion of human choice, sincere or not. My conclusion has been that it cannot. We have to see ourselves as subservient to a good which cannot, as things stand, be seen as reducible to human choice, individual or collective. The good and the virtuous are what we *ought* to choose, they are not constituted as such by our choices. That in the absence of a shared symbolic order, such as was at one time provided by dogmatic religion, it may be hard to justify this sense, or, in the face of a certain type of questioning, to keep it alive, is true, but not necessarily an occasion for despair. After all, not everything about dogmatic religion was or is conducive to human flourishing, or even to the exercise of a reasonably generous conception of the virtues. In any case, apart from our lived sense of the sacredness of human life and of something approaching awe in matters to do with the creation, beginning, nurturing, and ending of specifically human life, we do have other non-religious intimations of the transcendent:

> Good art, thought of as symbolic force rather than statement, provides a stirring image of a pure transcendent value, a steadily visible enduring higher good, and perhaps provides for many people, in an unreligious age without prayer or sacraments, their clearest *experience* of something grasped as separate and precious and beneficial and held quietly and unpossessively in the attention. (Murdoch, 1977, pp. 76–7).

One thinks in this context of such emblematic figures in twentieth century art as Proust, Cézanne, Rilke and Henry Moore: Proust, with his painstaking *récherche* of experience, and the sense that our lives and hopes and experiences can be redeemed when they are expressed, contemplated and articulated aesthetically; Cézanne painting Mont Sainte-Victoire for the three dozenth time, and proclaiming '*le paysage se pense en moi et j'en suis la conscience*'; Henry Moore embarking on a similar exploration of the complex correspondences between landscape and human form; and Rilke's enterprise in his *Neue Gedichte* of bringing the unexpressed to expression, of transforming what is outer and visible into inwardness and feeling, an enterprise encapsulated in his letter of November 13th 1925:

> our task is to impress this preliminary, transient earth upon ourselves with so much suffering and so passionately that its nature rises up again 'invisibly' within us. We are the bees of the invisible.
> We drink ceaselessly the honey of the visible, so as to gather it into the great golden beehive of the invisible. (Rilke, 1936, p. 355).[1]

---

[1] This letter is extensively discussed in Heidegger's essay 'What Are Poets For?' (Heiddeger, 1971). I have to say that the poet's expression of his vision is superior to the philosophical commentary, linguistically, humanly and morally.

And again in the words of the *Ninth Duino Elegy*:

Are we perhaps *here* to say: House,
Bridge, Fountain, Gate, Jug, Fruit Tree, Window —
possible Pillar, Tower . . . but to *say* — do you see —
oh to say in such a way, as the things themselves never
within intended to be?

There is then a task, a value that comes to be only in and through human existence, including human desire and choice, but once the task and the value exist, they are entitled to command desire and choice.

I find it significant that it is hard to think about our moral experience without being drawn to think of the transcendent, particularly when I contemplate the work of the artists I have mentioned, and I am sympathetic to the attempt to provide some such context for human life. Nevertheless my argument up to this point strictly speaking requires only that what Taylor calls the best account of our lives and moral experience rests on the recognition of value sources regarded as independent of and, as things stand, as irreducible to our desires, individual or collective. On pain of distorting our understanding of value and of our lives, we cannot see our values as projections of our desires or as no more than devices for the smooth running of society. Whether that sense of the autonomy of moral value reflects something metaphysical about us, or whether it is a feature of human life which — like language and self-consciousness — has emerged during the course of our evolution, or whether both are true, can be left open for my current purpose. For that it is sufficient to assert that there are values, including moral values, which spring into existence (along with human desire, passion and choice), but that once the values exist, they are entitled to command our desires, passions and choices.

As I believe that the nurturing of this sense of the objectivity of value is a crucial part of civilised life, and essential to the order which sustains civilised life, I now want to consider how best children might be brought up or educated to possess it. In one sense, of course, the question is easy to answer. They should be brought up to use the concepts and make the judgments whose pervasive role in our form of life founds the basis of the sense that value is objective. Nevertheless, something more interesting should be said, if only because there are currents of educational thinking which are likely to undermine that sense of awe on which any idea of the objectivity and transcendence of value depends.

The characteristic terms of our moral vocabulary are terms such as generosity, honour, honesty, dignity, kindness, justice and compassion. Endowed with virtues such as these, individuals come to act in a de-centred way, and to regard the world and their fellows as they are, rather than as means to one's own ends. To have these attitudes and virtues is to be imbued with respect for others and a sense of awe towards the imperatives thus incumbent on us.

By contrast, in his essay 'Inside the Whale', George Orwell wrote

> Patriotism, religion, the Empire, the family, the sanctity of marriage, the Old School Tie, birth, breeding, honour, discipline — anyone of ordinary education could turn the whole lot of them inside out in three minutes (Orwell, 1940, part 2).

It does not, of course, follow from this that 'anyone of ordinary education' would be right to do this; my concern, though, is that there might be something about 'ordinary education' which disposes young people to engage in superficial re-valuations of the sort Orwell mentions, and that engaging in them will be enough to destroy the penumbra of awe which ought to attach to at least some of the things he mentions.

While I — like Lord Quinton — would like to see education as a transmitter of culture and an inculcator of value, there is currently a somewhat different conception of education, that by which individuals are led to question received opinion and values and to take it on themselves to decide what they will regard as valuable or not.

The view I am referring to has obvious roots in seventeenth century and Enlightenment philosophy. Its most influential British exponent is the J.S.Mill of *On Liberty*, in Chapter Two of which we are told that all beliefs and values, including and especially true beliefs and correct values, prove their mettle only by being submitted to rigorous and systematic criticism. A consistently Millian approach suggests that all purported values, all proposed goods are always up for critical examination, that, for example, sadism or genocide are things we have to find *reasons* to reject on pain of not understanding the meaning of the prohibitions, and that those values which do not accord with what seems to us to be rational are to be rejected.

The Millian approach did not, of course, originate with Mill. We can remember the words of Francis Bacon, the prophet of much that even now characterises the scientific method (with which the view of education I am now discussing is often closely linked):

> What happiness it would be to throw myself into the River Lethe, to erase completely from my soul the memory of all knowledge, all art, all poetry;

what happiness it would be to reach the opposite shore, naked like the
first man (as quoted in Oakeshott, 1989, p. 73).

— the same Bacon who, as Oakeshott tells us, tried to prevent
Charterhouse being founded, on the grounds that its curriculum
was centred on the ancient classics. Diderot, similarly, was insistent
that a true philosopher would 'trample underfoot prejudice, tradition, venerability, universal assent, authority — in a word, everything that overawes the crowd' and dare 'to think for himself' and 'to
admit nothing save on the testimony of his own reason and experience' (Taylor, 1989, p. 323). And what if the philosopher's 'reason
and experience', as in the case of Diderot himself and even more in
the case of Holbach, told him that it is natural for men to be moved
only by pleasure and pain? Does this not in the end lead — as Taylor
argues — to a blurring of the distinction between moral and
non-moral evaluation: we just do what we are programmed by
nature to do — i.e. seek pleasure and avoid pain — and that is also
what we ought to do. But this 'ought' is no longer the clearly autonomous ought of morality. In this perspective there seems little room
for any 'ought' of a moral as opposed to a causal sort, any ought
which will furnish us with a sense of goods other than those of pleasure and pain, which are hardly moral goods at all, and which do not
require any sense of awe to sustain. Moral thinking thus reduces
either to a Californian plea to 'be natural' or, for those who realise
that such a plea may lead to logistical difficulties at least, to a device
for permitting the simultaneous satisfaction of as many human preferences as possible. (This, I take it, is the essence of the utilitarian
position from Bentham to Hare.) But, once the sense of the moral
ought has been naturalised by utilitarianism, why should any individual feel bound to obey the dictates of the device? Why should each
man not just do what seems to him most pleasant and least painful in
the light of his reason and experience? Why should I as an autonomous individual obey the rules which lead to the smooth running of
society, and not just seek my own pleasure? My argument is that this
is the point at which the individual needs allegiance to constitutive
moral goods and virtues beyond his 'natural' search for pleasure.

It will be said that the elevation of individual reason and experience to be the arbiter of moral judgment does not necessarily lead to
a collapse of autonomous moral authority or value in this way.
Might not one conclude even for oneself that, say, the traditional
moral values of Christianity are the right ones? This is precisely the
situation envisaged by Kant in the *Grundlegung*, where the man con-

fronted with the Holy One of God (Christ) turns away to consider the dictates of his own conscience and reason. But, as Iris Murdoch has urged, the man envisaged by Kant — 'free, independent, lonely, powerful, rational, responsible, brave', the 'ideal citizen of the liberal state' and 'offspring of the age of science', confidently rational and yet increasingly alienated from the world his discoveries reveal — this man actually embodies the notion of the will, of my will, albeit universalised, as the creator of value.

> Values which were previously in some sense inscribed in the heavens and guaranteed by God collapse into the human will. There is no transcendent reality. The idea of the good remains indefinable and empty so that human choice may fill it. The sovereign moral concept is freedom (Murdoch, 1970, p. 80).

I do not want to deny the Kantian insight that morality has to do with the finding of reasons for actions of an interpersonal sort. Morality *is* to do with de-centring one's world and one's motivation. But the de-centring involved in morality requires more than the purely formal demand for the universalisation of one's principles. It requires also, in the jargon, some 'thick' conception of the good and the virtuous, some notion of what true virtue and true goodness consist in beyond rationality in a formal sense, and this is a conception which each one of us inherits first in our culture and tradition, and which we then learn the meaning of in experience.

Particularly in philosophy, the area in which reason is held to be central, we need to remind ourselves at this point of one very basic fact. Despite the claims of Mill in *On Liberty* there is no guarantee that the sort of systematic critical examination of principles which he envisages will lead to an improvement of the principles, behaviour, or of a culture more generally. As Maurice Cowling has pointed out:

> aesthetic and intellectual achievement depend on persistent development of requisite sensibilities, on traditions of professional competence and on patrons and audiences who are willing to be interested, not on the pervading commitment to make men scrutinise their consciences (Cowling, 1990, p. 157).

And, this is where what I have to say bears on education. Mill wanted just such a systematic scrutiny of even the best-founded beliefs and values to be conducted by the young. On pain of our and their losing 'living apprehension' of a truth, he urged the 'teachers of mankind' to find

> some contrivance for making the difficulties of the question as present to the learner's consciousness, as if they were pressed upon him by a dissentient champion, eager for his conversion (Mill, 1859, 1991, Ch 2, part 2).

particularly where there is general agreement on a truth. Yet this kind of rationalistic and dialectical approach to value, encouraging as it will the setting of uneducated preference on the same level as mature wisdom, is likely actually to undermine the sense of value as autonomous, on which both morality and culture depend. Such indeed was the view of Nietzsche, who was more aware than most philosophers of the subtle inter-relationships that exist between value, culture, reason *and* education. In his essay 'On the future of our educational institutions', he wrote

> It is a crime to have incited someone to 'autonomy' at an age when sub-jection to a great guide is to be cultivated.
> Correct and strong education is above all obedience and custom.
> Indulgence of the so-called free personality (by teachers) is nothing but a sign of barbarism.[2]

I will leave it to you to decide the extent to which contemporary educational practice is, in Nietzsche's terms, indulgent and barbaric, and to what extent it is permeated by notions of greatness and of obedience and custom, though I will just say that part of the motiva-tion and attraction of phenomena such as political correctness and the contemporary clamour for what is called equal opportunities in education is that they promise to indulge those who, rightly or wrongly, feel themselves excluded from the customs and culture which prevail (feelings which are often simply a consequence of an educational philosophy which, not stressing obedience and custom, might almost have been designed to induce a sense of exclusion).[3]

Nietzsche's remarks are partly psychological, but not exclusively so. They are of a piece with the ethical criticisms he made of Socrates in *The Birth of Tragedy* and elsewhere. The objection to Socrates is that by his quibbling, his cleverness and his relentless and ultimately fruitless search for definition, he destroyed the confidence of the best

---

[2]   Quoted and translated by Cooper, (1983), p. 38.

[3]   I should also point out that the highly influential system of moral education known as values clarification is predicated on the twin assumptions that 1) the teacher must not impose his or her values on pupils and 2) pupils must be encouraged to explore and express what they think about moral matters. In our own country these assumptions have been embodied in the well-known Schools Council projects on the Humanities Curriculum and Moral Education, and permeate much that goes under the name of Personal and Social Education. It is the combination of assumed relativism on the part of teachers and rationalisation on the part of pupils which I am objecting to, as it is likely to undermine in pupils any robust sense of the objectivity of value. (I am indebted to Fred Naylor for this information.)

in what was best. In this, of course, Nietzsche is following Aristophanes:

> They sit at the feet of Socrates
> Till they can't distinguish the wood from the trees
> And tragedy goes to pot;
> They don't care whether their plays are art
> But only whether their words are smart
> They waste our time with quibbles and quarrels
> Destroying our patience as well as our morals
> And teaching us all to talk rot (*The Frogs*, lines 1491–9).

Why might Socratic questioning and Socratic education destroy morals?

1) Not everything in morals, or anything else, can be given an explicit verbal formulation or, even less, a verbal justification. But the presumption of Socratic questioning as demonstrated in the *Euthyphro* is that what can't be so expounded and justified should be rejected. It is significant that Mill holds up for our admiration the Socratic principle that those who had merely adopted the commonplaces of received opinion did not understand the subject. My feeling, to the contrary, is that morality is better served by people who are content to grow into holding certain commonplaces, and in whom the development of this experience is not held up by the premature exercise of what Mill himself calls 'a negative discussion' (Mill, 1859, 1991, Ch. 2).

2) Even more important, we have to recognise that, particularly in the realm of value, abstracted from a grounding in experience and tradition, 'reasoning' is likely to mislead in the way Nietzsche and Orwell feared. In other words, contrary to the Millian spirit, self-critical examination of principles ungrounded in moral experience can threaten morality, rather than preserve or strengthen it.

Practical reasoning is not just intellectual cleverness. It requires on the part of the reasoner a disposition towards the good and the virtuous and, as I argued earlier, that requires on the part of the agent a sense that in being so moved he — or even more, those whose principles he is examining — are not merely projecting sentiments of their own on the world, or at least, are not necessarily doing that.

Aristotle is very clear about the need for the right dispositions on the part of the man who is to discuss morality successfully. As far as practical reasoning goes, he says:

> it makes no small difference, then, whether we form habits of one kind or of another from our very youth: it makes a very great difference, or rather *all* the difference. (*Nicomachean Ethics*, 1103b 24–5).

The point is that we can reason well about value if we have been brought up so as to acquire habits of respect for the good and the virtuous, a respect which assumes both that certain values are not in any serious sense open to question and that the right values have gradually emerged in the experience and discourse of the many and the wise.[4] It is in its tendency to discount the way in which the experience and knowledge of the many and the wise has helped to delineate the forms of goods we discover as much as we create, that I find the Bacon–Diderot stress on individual instant reason unfortunate. This is especially so in education, where the reasoners are likely to lack the experience and wisdom necessary to judge which things are good and virtuous.

The contrary Aristotelian expectation — or hope — is that once young people have been encouraged to do what is good and virtuous, they will feel attracted to it. In their subsequent reasoning they will both see the reasons for it and have such a respect for it that they will not find basic moral virtues and principles seriously open to question. That they will (and should) subsequently reason about values is taken for granted by Aristotle (and by me) for two reasons. The first is because in life, situations never repeat themselves exactly; so intelligence and flexibility of mind will be required to know just what the good thing to do is in a given situation. And secondly, as rational beings, it is incumbent on us to understand the reason for things, including the reasons for our conduct. Nothing I am saying is intended to suggest that morality is either inflexible or not to be reasoned about; what I am concerned to establish is the motivational and dispositional basis on which good reasoning about morality can proceed.

What I have been suggesting in this lecture is that although we, as human beings, are in a general sense part of nature, we do have orientations towards the good and the true which take us out of the purely natural, and invite us to think of our beliefs and values as subject to demands of truth and goodness in some absolute sense. Reflection on our moral life shows that we do indeed find ourselves obliged and moved by values which we cannot regard purely as mere projections of human feeling. Education has a key role in transmitting such values to the young, but this role is likely to be subverted if the educational process is conceived in narrowly

---

[4]   On Aristotle's account of our need to listen to the views of the many and the wise, cf *Nicomachean Ethics*, 1143b 6-14, and Crisp (1991), p. 522-4.

rationalistic terms, encouraging young people to rationalise or criticise values whose proper understanding depends on the precritical acquisition of certain moral dispositions. Educators ought then to be more concerned with inculcating in the young a sense of awe and respect for the virtues of civilised life than with encouraging their pupils to regard these virtues as open to choice or simply a reification of preferences. A rationalistic approach to values and to education is likely to foster the latter attitude, whereas an education stressing custom and respect is likely to encourage the former.

I have been speaking of education as a process in which children ought to be inspired by the notion of an autonomous and existing order of value. This is an order, not of their making and not of ours as teachers either; but it is one to which some human deeds aspire and which some human works reflect. In formal education, the existence of an autonomous objective realm of value is best initially pointed to by immersion on the part of pupils in those works which — in the Wittgensteinian distinction — show its existence; that is, not in works of philosophy or the social sciences, which talk about it and on occasion talk it out of existence, but in works of literature and the arts more generally, in which its fabric is articulated and illustrated.

In emphasizing the objectivity of value and the centrality of literature to its understanding, I would, though, not want to underestimate the importance of the study of the natural sciences here. Indeed, the pursuit of science itself does give us direct experience of truths independent of us, direct experience of objectivity. In recognizing the independent existence of the natural world, and in studying this world, we learn what it means to submit ourselves to a reality outside of us, and that itself does involve a certain type of virtue and submission to something authoritative over us. Where science is conceived in more than technological or instrumentalist terms, its pursuit actually makes sense only against the background of a concern for truth and knowledge for its own sake, a concern which is hard to justify or explain so long as we conceive human life in utilitarian terms. Science then is part of our existence in a world of interest-free value and certainly has its place alongside literature in an education which recognises the objectivity of value.

The realm of value of which I have been speaking in this lecture has largely been that of moral value. Morality, as I conceive it, is part of the fabric of everyday life, and much of what I have said about it derives from its central place in our everyday lives. So, in dealing with morality, although they will be taking their pupils beyond self-interest, teachers will not be taking them beyond the everyday, even if they may intimate that the everyday has implications beyond the everyday.

But, in human life there are realms with their own objectivity and autonomy other than the moral. The realms I particularly have in mind are those of developed cultural forms, the sciences, the arts and the humanities, and I see their study as having much to contribute to the awakening in children of a sense of higher value and therefore as reinforcing that decentring of desire and impulse which is implicit in morality.

In my second lecture, I will speak about education as a process of initiation into worthwhile forms of knowledge and experience beyond those of daily life. On education seen in these terms, Nietzsche had this to say in *Human, all too Human*:

> The value of the grammar school is seldom sought in the things that are actually learned . . . The reading of the classics — every educated person admits this — is . . . a monstrous procedure: before young people who are in no way whatever ripe for it, by teachers whose every word, often whose mere appearance, lays a blight on a good writer. But herein lies the value that usually goes unrecognised — that these teachers speak *the abstract language of higher culture*, ponderous and hard to understand but nonetheless a higher gymnastics for the head: that concepts, technical terms, methods, allusions continually occur in their language such as young people almost never hear in the conversation of their relations or in the street. If the pupils merely *listen*, their intellect will be involuntarily prepared for a scientific mode of thinking. It is not possible for them to emerge from this discipline as a pure child of nature quite untouched by the power of abstraction (Neitzsche, 1878, 1996, Vol. 1, sec. 266).

Unfashionable it may be, but I like the 'hidden curriculum' of children listening, of their being captivated by the forms and meanings of words they cannot criticise and which, at first anyway, they barely apprehend. Such a hidden curriculum is far more apt to make children receptive to the objectivity of value and to the existence of higher values than is the classroom filled with pupil reaction and the scepticism of the not-yet-educated, the classroom the enlightenment has bequeathed us via Dewey. I realise, though, that Nietzsche's words, along which much of what I have been saying, especially in the closing sections of my lecture, raise the question of *which* or *whose* culture we are to use to inspire our children with notions of value beyond the everyday. They also raise the question of what we should do educationally *if* it turns out that some or many of our children are unable to get very far with the abstract language of higher culture. In my second lecture I will deal with both these questions.

6

Anthony O'Hear

The Pursuit of Excellence – An Educational Value

To my mind, one of the failings of philosophy of education – a Cinderella of a subject if ever there was one – is that it has been far too obsessed with abstruse discussions of concepts and policies and far too little concerned with experience. Like much writing in the educational field, it has been unconfident of itself, unwilling to draw on the knowledge we all have from our experience of educational practice. Even when the conclusions are correct, one sometimes feels in reading educational literature that fifteen thousand pages are being spent to 'establish' something which we always knew in the first place (e.g. that well-organised schools and classrooms are better than ill-organised ones, and likely to achieve better results). So I will begin with a passage, not from an educationalist, or indeed from a philosopher:

> . . . the lecturer was talking about matters and things in the world of art, situations which had never come within our horizon and only appeared now on its margin in shadowy-wise through the always compromised medium of his stammering speech. We were unable to check on it except through his own explanatory performances on the cottage piano . . . and we listened to it all with the dimly excited fantasy of children hearing a fairy story they do not understand, while their tender minds are none-theless in a strange, dreamy, intuitive way enriched and advantaged. Fugue, counterpoint, 'Eroica', 'confusion in consequence of too strongly coloured modulations', 'strict style' – all that was just magic spells to us, but we heard it as greedily, as large-eyed as children always hear what they do not understand or even what is entirely unsuitable – indeed with far more pleasure than the familiar, fitting and adequate can give them. Is it believable that this is the most intensive, splendid, perhaps the very most productive way of learning: the anticipatory way, learning

that spans wide stretches of ignorance. As a pedagogue, I suppose I should not speak in its behalf . . . (Mann, 1947, 1968).

As I am rather in favour of children's minds being enriched and advantaged, and am not even always or in principle against their hearing 'unsuitable' things with pleasure and as I am often told I am no pedagogue, I shall not feel inhibited in this lecture from speaking up for what Thomas Mann through his narrator here calls the anticipatory way of learning.

In my previous lecture, I argued that human life in its civilised form depended on the recognition by us of certain moral values not of our choosing. Although the values and our being attracted by them have their roots in our basic needs and desires, our form of life presents certain virtues and goods to us as good in themselves and, as such, as constitutive of the desires we ought to have, rather than as dependent on the desires which we as individuals or even groups actually have. I also argued that a form of education which stressed first the inculcation of culture and tradition and only secondly the self-critical examination of beliefs and values by the young was more likely to inspire in them the respect for value on which our moral form of life depends. Such as education is also more likely to promote good reasoning about morality than a narrowly rationalistic one, given that practical reasoning depends in part on the reasoner being in possession of the requisite dispositions and experience, the dispositions and experience having to inform and hence precede the reasoning.

In the previous lecture I took morality as the most fundamental of our autonomous value systems, and tried to show how, once established, morality presents us with goals and goods which we regard as good in themselves, and which cannot be reduced to other goods or be regarded simply as means to other, non-moral ends. I also suggested ways in which the study of literature and the arts and, in its own way, the study of science can be regarded both as throwing light on our nature as moral agents and as themselves in a broad sense moral enterprises. In this lecture, I want to look more directly at education as a process not simply concerned with inculcating moral and other values in a general sense, but as a process by which specific forms of knowledge and experience regarded as valuable in themselves are transmitted.

In the previous lecture I spoke of our existence as self-conscious agents. As such we will seek to improve and correct our beliefs and attitudes in the light of what is true and desirable. As part of our self-consciousness, we are also users of symbol systems, systems which stand between us and the world, and which allow us to represent the world in both more and less abstract ways and to express our feelings and experiences in various ways. As self-conscious we have a drive to understand ourselves, to make our roots and our history and our values and institutions transparent to ourselves (which is not the same as submitting them to premature rationalistic criticism). As self-conscious we have a drive to consider our final end and purpose, a drive extinguished neither by materialism nor by the banalities of popular science. As self-conscious and at the same time embodied, we are also capable of aesthetic experience: of contemplating and delighting in what we perceive in various modes — sound, sight, touch, and so on — and also of aesthetic creation and reflection on that creation.

Emerging into our self-conscious existence, then, we begin to produce the various sciences, the arts, the humanities and religions. Each of the disciplines in question has developed its own distinctive style and approach, determined by a complex interaction between its subject matter, its history and its own mode of expression. Disciplines such as physics, mathematics, biology, history, literature, music, painting and philosophy have achieved a degree of autonomy, in that people who work and study in them have to learn their forms and modes of thought and expression as they have come to be in their history. Although they are human activities and dependent on the ingenuity and creativity of the people who work within them, they also provide the culture, the goals and the techniques of those who work in them. Arguably some of the disciplines I have mentioned also aspire to standards of truth or beauty which transcend human activity altogether, and to which practitioners aspire in their work. Whether this is so or not, from the perspective of the newcomer a mature form of knowledge or experience will have all the air of a foreign land whose delights and attractions have yet to be discovered and investigated and whose customs and language have to be learned.

To know about the world one inhabits, to know about one's history and roots, to know about the best attempts men have made to express their feelings, experiences and attitudes, to learn to engage in aesthetic contemplation both of the works of man and of the natural world — all these things come to be part of the good life for agents such as ourselves, both embodied and self-conscious. Engaging in these activities is part of what human fulfilment consists in, quite irrespective of any further benefits doing science, say, or reading good literature might bring. In a developed, literate and articulate culture such as our own, all the fields I have mentioned have traditions, forms, concepts and procedures of their own, which are not innate to human beings. Nor can they be acquired without formal instruction. A major role of formal education in a civilised society must be the preservation, transmission and development of the traditions of learning and expression of the culture in question.

My title speaks of education as the pursuit of excellence as an educational value. Perhaps it would be more accurate and closer to my meaning here to speak of education as the study of the excellent. For each of the realms of meaning I have mentioned is constituted by the existence in it of acknowledged masterpieces, masterpieces which serve to set the standards, to raise the questions, to delineate the possibilities. Here I would extend what T.S. Kuhn (1962) says about mature science and say that without the existence, within a field, of acknowledged masterpieces and standards, we do not have a form of knowledge or experience which could or should form an essential part of anyone's formal education, as opposed to some new field of enquiry which they approach from a background of strength in existing disciplines. Part of the reason for what I say here about formal education is that in being initiated into an established discipline of study, you begin to learn intellectual rigour.

I have spoken of an intellectual discipline being marked in part by the existence within it of acknowledged masterpieces but, it will be asked, acknowledged by whom? Well, in the first place, acknowledged by experts in the field in question, by people who have made it their life's business to study and delineate the field. There might seem to be something circular about this, but this is not really so, or at least not so in a vicious way. For in most traditions of thought and expression in the West at least, there is a high premium, perhaps sometimes too high a premium, placed on creativity and innovation. Nor, unlike the Christian Bible, are literary, artistic or scientific canons fixed. They are subject to constant shifts and revisions with changes in taste and knowledge. And even Christianity, the religion of the Bible, has, as Newman pointed out, a tradition of doctrine developing, a tradition which has served Christianity very well through the centuries in its encounters with new and initially unsuspected challenges. But, along with the shifts, changes and revisions in taste, knowledge and doctrine — shifts, changes and revisions often produced in answer to the quest internal to a discipline for truth or goodness or beauty — alongside the changes, there are certain constants, as Hume pointed out in *On the Standard of Taste*:

> The same Homer, who pleased at Athens and Rome two thousand years ago, is still admired at Paris and at London. All the changes of climate, government, religion and language have not been able to obscure his glory. Authority or prejudice may give a temporary vogue to a bad poet or orator; but his reputation will never be durable or general. When his compositions are examined by posterity or foreigners, the enchantment is dissipated and his faults appear in their true colours. On the contrary a real genius, the longer his works endure, and the more wide they are spread, the more sincere is the admiration which they meet with (Hume, 1757, 1965).

There is also the fact, pointed out by C.S. Peirce, that a historically developed form of knowledge or experience accumulates and grows through the ages, rather like a Gothic cathedral, and that the individuality of each new worker is necessarily dwarfed by 'the gradually increasing sense of immensity which impresses the mind . . . as he learns to appreciate the real dimensions and cost' of the whole (Pierce, 1958, para. 11).

Hume, as was Quinton, is absolutely right to stress the test of time and of cross-social class and cross-cultural corroboration in the recognition of masterpieces, something completely overlooked in the sneer about dead white European males. Against that, incidentally, we might juxtapose Chesterton's adage (in *Orthodoxy*) that tradition is the democracy of the dead and reflect on the arbitrariness of disenfranchising their experience, as arbitrary as disenfranchising any of our contemporaries and far less wise, given that we do not yet know just what mistakes our contemporaries are making. It is because of what Hume rightly says about the difficulty of judging works of the present that in the arts and the humanities education should *concentrate* on works from the past. Such works will often be difficult to read at first, but this is precisely the reason they should be studied and an oblique endorsement of Oakeshott's dictum that no one ever learned to read by concentrating on contemporary writing. In the sciences, where theories are tested against a timeless and a-historical nature, objectivity may not require that we wait for the test of time, although in science, too, we will be assuming implicitly that the best theories will still be recognised as such across time and across cultures.

As a matter of historical fact, in the humanities and in many of the arts, our present day canons can be seen — as Quinton pointed out in his first lecture — as 'continuous with what was picked out as the best by Greeks and Romans, as revived at the Renaissance and ... added to and otherwise varied in composition ever since'. The strength of these canons, their correctness and durability (up to now) are due in no small part to their having been fashioned by many hands of many types, in many places and circumstances and over many centuries (and with luck and goodwill will outlive contemporary claims to the effect that the likes of *The Colour Purple*, Gilbert and George, Andy Warhol, and Sir Andrew Lloyd Webber are the major creative forces of our or any other time). The centrality to a discipline of its masterpieces, amounting almost to being constitutive of its identity, is the reason why people are outraged when they hear of secondary school courses in English which do not include Shakespeare or of music curricula in which there is no room for mention of Beethoven.

Even though, like morality and like aesthetics, it may appeal to transcendent values and will certainly have standards which once set up are autonomous and self-generating, a discipline of study is not given to us a priori, independently of experience and invention, nor can its concepts or procedures be deduced by a beginner a priori. This is true even of mathematics, the discipline which par excellence deals in the a priori and the deductive. Even here, its current shape and form depends on the often chance-ridden discoveries and insights of mathematicians — which, as the story of Fermat's Last Theorem persuasively suggests, sometimes cannot be retrieved even by their discoverer, once lost or forgotten. Even religions depend crucially and centrally on the revelations vouchsafed to their founding spirits — and this is as much true of a tradition such as Vedanta which does not explicitly stress the historical as it is of Judaism, Christianity or Islam, which do.

The fact that a discipline of study or a religion has survived and developed tells us something about its own strength and conformability in some sense to the world and to human nature. But the fact that its survival and development are historically conditioned processes means that the newcomer to a discipline has to be inducted into it, as it happens to stand at the time of his or her induction. Such an induction presupposes on the part of the learner a readiness to submit to a historically given and determinate mode of thinking and experiencing, and a readiness on the part of the teacher to initiate the learner into the relevant modes more or less systematically.

Thus, as Oakeshott put it in his article 'Education: the Engagement and its Frustration', learning (in which all human beings engage much of the time) becomes 'schooling' when

> learning becomes learning by study, and not by chance, in conditions of direction and restraint. It begins with the appearance of a teacher with something to impart which is not immediately connected with the current wants or 'interests' of the learner (Oakeshott, 1989, p. 68).

Oakeshott goes on to speak of five marks of schooling, and as each of these marks goes against the grain of current fashion, I will describe each, indicating how it departs from orthodoxy. The first mark is that what we have in what Oakeshott refers to as School is

> .. a serious and orderly initiation into an intellectual, imaginative, moral and emotional inheritance; an initiation designed for children who are ready to embark upon it.

This initiation will involve a 'considered curriculum' which will direct and focus the learner's attention, and make him aware that learning is not a seamless robe nor its possibilities limitless. Such an initiation clearly cannot be in any serious sense child- or student-led, for this would be a case of the uninitiated attempting to initiate the uninitiated, rather worse than a Daphnis fumbling with a Chloe, as the Chloe is in this case Daphnis himself, and the subject matter no natural act, but one constituted by canonical works which have to be approached on their own terms.

Oakeshott's second mark of schooling is that it is 'an engagement, to learn by study', a 'difficult undertaking' calling for effort. The effort is that of learning to read or to listen, 'allowing another's thoughts to re-enact themselves in one's mind', so that in submitting to the expressions of the rational consciousness of another, our response becomes 'a part of our understanding of ourselves'. The effort of which Oakeshott speaks is very far from the project undertaken by the student on his own initiative. It is also a long way from the thought that in the study of the arts and the humanities at least the main thing is to publish one's own thoughts. But it is not too far from the Platonic complaint about the invention of writing in the *Phaedrus* (275a-b), the complaint being that writing will encourage men to rely on external marks rather than to make the effort to take wisdom into their own souls. In this case, we are being asked to make the effort to etch something of the masterpieces of our discipline on to our souls, and not simply to file away knowledge of where we can find the masterpieces or something about them.

'The third component of the idea "School" is that of detachment from the immediate, local world of the learner . . . "School" is a place apart in which the heir may encounter his moral and intellectual inheritance' not in its contemporary terms and resonances but as an 'estate, entire, unqualified and unencumbered'. As such it is 'an emancipation', achieved by a redirection of attention from the 'loaded' questions of his life towards 'intimations of excellence' as yet undreamed of, offering new interests and pursuits 'uncorrupted by the need for immediate results'. This vision of education is under attack from both ends of the political spectrum; education as an initiation into something unconnected with practical results, and valid precisely because of this disengagement from the temporal, is one which finds favour neither with Royal Society of Arts' 'Education for Capability', nor with the Socialist Education Association, and which in the public arena perhaps has only Enoch Powell and the Prince of Wales to speak up for it in terms which carry any conviction. But education as relevant only to the market place or to some collectivist notion of democratic politics is decidedly education for the last man in Nietzsche's terms, the man in whom aspirations towards the distinctions implicit in culture and civilization are foregone for acquiescence in a new state of barbarism. This is the barbarism of reducing all distinction and all nobility to the values of the market or of the collectivity, values which almost by definition preclude differentiation by quality: for the market place judges everything in terms of one interchangeable and per se valueless value, while the first rule of collectivist egalitarianism is that what all can't have none shall have, a rule which was certainly followed by Dewey in his writings on education.

Oakeshott's fourth mark of School is that education, properly speaking, is a personal transaction between a 'teacher' and a 'learner'. A teacher is one in whom 'some part or aspect or passage of the inheritance' is alive and who renews some part of the inheritance in imparting it to newcomers. Such teachers are the only indispensable equipment of Schools. Apparatuses of other sorts are 'almost wholly destructive' of School. I have known a number of teachers of the sort Oakeshott commends, and have been taught by quite a few. None of them were machines, none of them used machines, and none of them saw their role as the construction of learning packages or modules. They were all different and all priceless, and although some had notable and noticeable personalities, even the most egocentric just about kept their personalities subservient to the demands of their disciplines, as Peirce believed was the case in the makers of the Gothic cathedrals. We should remember Oakeshott's remark about teachers and equipment next time we hear that schools are under-resourced. I am all in favour of transferring funds in education from 'resources' to teachers. In considering Oakeshott's structures against educational technology, we should also remember that in any well-developed form of knowledge or experience, much of what is known will be known tacitly. It is for this reason that contact with someone in whom this tacit knowledge is vested is so vital for a learner, and why contact with a teacher is indispensable for any learning which goes beyond the repetition of formulae, which are in the end but the abridgement of practices which resist explicit formulation.

In his final mark of 'School' Oakeshott takes up a theme redolent of Newman: that a school is a historic community of teachers and learners, one dedicated to the value of initiating newcomers to the human scene 'into the grandeurs and servitudes of being human'. A school in Oakeshott's sense will recognise that the education it is offering will not 'equip the newcomer to do anything specific', it will give him 'no particular skill', it will promise 'no material advantage over other men', it will point to 'no finally perfect human character'. What it will do or try to do is to demonstrate 'how to be at once an autonomous and civilized subscriber to a human life'. Oakeshott sees such a vision of schooling as exemplified in the *paideia* given to children in ancient Athens, in the schools of the Roman empire, in the collegiate, guild and grammar schools of medieval Christendom, in the schools of renaissance Europe and in their successors, our own grammar and public schools and their equivalents in continental Europe.

When Oakeshott says that education in his terms has no extrinsic end or purpose, and that for both teacher and learner it is part of the engagement of being human, I agree; I would, though, emphasize the point I have already made about the connexion between our nature as self-conscious, reflective agents, and the various forms of knowledge central to the educational engagement: mathematics, natural science, history (including social studies), the humanities, the arts and religion. All these forms of knowledge throw essential light on what we are, how we relate to the world and each other and how we express ourselves and conceive our final end. They are, indeed, constitutive of our self-knowledge and self-expression, constitutive of our humanity. Not to be initiated into each of these forms of knowledge and not to have experienced something of what they have to offer in the form of an acquaintance of some sort of what has been best thought and best expressed in each of these areas is to be a stranger to some significant part of the human condition. For a child to enter an educational establishment and not be offered some form of initiation into each of these forms of knowledge is for that establishment to conspire to keep him or her to that extent a stranger to the human condition.

I do not, therefore, accept the apparent implication of Oakeshott's characterization of school, that it is only in grammar or public schools that an initiation of the sort he describes can or should be attempted. Some at least of what has been best thought and best expressed is widely communicable, and can appeal on many different levels. If I may be anecdotal, I once took a party of very average six-year-old boys to see a film of *Henry V*, fully fearing a highly fraught afternoon; in fact they were captivated as much by the language as by the action. The idea of a high culture continuous with popular culture, or perhaps better that of a popular high culture is not a completely empty dream, as examples as variegated as Shakespeare, Mozart, ancient Greek theatre, Russian ballet, the English Bible, the operas of Verdi, and the writing of Tolstoy and of Ruskin all testify. The reasons for the break between high and popular culture are many and various, the development of education itself and the resulting increasing sophistication of intellectuals being perhaps two.

Nevertheless, educators, it seems, have a congenital tendency to underestimate their charges. Sometimes this is because of an arrogant attempt on their part to direct a certain part of the population to menial tasks. Sometimes it is out of an often politically-guided form of slumming on the part of teachers, a pretence that all forms of thought and language are equally valuable. Either way the upshot will be to turn what should be a form of liberation into an intellectual and cultural prison; it will deprive those who most need it of the only magic strong enough to counteract and see beyond the symptoms of real deprivation. In his book *The Disuniting of America*, and not, I think, entirely hyperbolically, Arthur Schlesinger wrote of the sort of slumming I am objecting to:

> If some Kleagle of the Ku Klux Klan wanted to devise an educational curriculum for the specific purpose of handicapping and disabling black

Americans, he would not be likely to come up with anything more diabolically effective than Afrocentrism (Schlesinger, 1992).[1]

By contrast in *The Dean's December*, Saul Bellow has this to say of a teacher who brings *Macbeth* into the ghetto:

About *Macbeth* Corde ... had noted that in a class of black schoolchildren taught by a teacher 'brave enough to ignore instructions from downtown' Shakespeare caused great excitement. The lines
'And pity, like a naked newborn babe
Striding the blast'
had pierced those pupils. You could see the power of the babe, how restlessness stopped. And Corde had written that perhaps only poetry had the strength 'to rival the attractions of narcotics, the magnetism of TV, the excitements of sex, or the ecstasies of destruction' (Bellow, 1982, p. 187).

I agree with the spirit of this, and so commend the efforts of the National Curriculum Council in England to put Shakespeare, Mozart and Raphael before every child in my country. I also, for what it is worth, thoroughly endorse what Thomas Nagel has to say on education in *Equality and Partiality*:

It is essential to maximise access, but that will not promote equality, only mobility. In particular the tendency towards equality and distrust of the exceptional found in the public educational systems of some modern liberal societies is a great mistake. Equality of opportunity is fine, but if a school system also tries to iron out distinctions, the waste from failure to exploit talent to the fullest is inexcusable. It also undermines equality of opportunity ... (if) the lower classes are mired in mediocrity whatever their talent (Nagel, 1991, p. 135)

Nagel's words are significant not just because they are true, but because they come from one committed to some form of egalitarianism in the economic sphere; but he fully recognises that there exist cultural goods which are worth pursuing and which cannot be distributed equally:

A society should try to foster the creation and preservation of what is best ... and this is just as important as the widespread dissemination of what is merely good enough. Such an aim can be pursued only by recognizing and exploiting the natural inequalities between persons, encouraging specialisation and distinction of levels in education, and accepting the variation in accomplishment which results.

It cannot be pretended, and I do not pretend, that every child in my country has either the capacity or the motivation to pursue aca-

---

[1] The sentence quoted is referred to by Frank Kermode in his review in the *New York Times*, 23.2.1992.

demic study very far; in this I agree both with Nagel's stress on variation of accomplishment and with what Oakeshott says about the
difficulty of academic study. Indeed, Oakeshott's continual use of
the notion of inheritance can itself mislead. A cultural as opposed to
a monetary inheritance is, as T.S. Eliot stressed, one which is gained
only by work and effort on the part of the legatee. In recognition of
this fact, there should be a clear differentiation of courses and possibly even of schools at secondary level, and certainly at post-16 level.
The pretence that there is one curriculum and one examination
which all children of 14 or above can do, a pretence which is
enshrined in comprehensivisation and at least in the rhetoric of the
GCSE, helps neither the academically-inclined nor the non-academic. It does not help the academic because it prevents them making the strides they are capable of making in what really interests
and excites them. It does not help the non-academic because it forces
them to do studies for which they have neither ability nor inclination. It also brings home to them daily what will inevitably be
regarded as their failure, without producing any other field of interest in compensation.

To come down to practical policies here, we are often told that we
in Britain, or in England and Wales at least, are very bad at education
and training at the levels of further and higher education. According
to Sir Claus Moser, in his pamphlet entitled 'Our Need for an
Informed Society', we have 40% of 16–18 year olds in full-time education or training, and this is the lowest in any advanced country
(Moser, 1990, p. 15). This figure, though, should be set against
another statistic, one provided by the DES last year (using mainly
1986 data): the DES statisticians discovered that with 15% of the relevant age group graduating from universities and polytechnics with
first degrees, we had a higher proportion of graduates per hundred
of the age group of any country in Western Europe with the excep-
tion of France, which also had 15%.[2] If we are failing in education
post–16, the failure is not at the top level and not in universities. Nor

---

[2]   *International Statistical Comparisons in Higher Education: Working Report,*
1991, table 5. Lest this fact be regarded as some sort of vindication of our
comprehensive system of secondary education, it is worth pointing out the
quite disproportionate contribution made to the gaining of A-levels by the
independent schools. With around 7% of school leavers in the 1980s, the
independent schools produced 32% of those gaining three or more A-levels,
and around 50% of the A grades attained. (These figures were derived from
DES statistics by John Marks (1991), p. 22).

is it at A–level, as Moser and many others argue. If A–levels are the route to first-degree courses, they are doing their job, because our first degrees, though among the shortest in the world, are generally well-regarded and our drop-out rate in higher education has been (at least until quite recently) one of the lowest in the world.

A rational response to the combination of the Moser figure and the DES statistics I have just referred to, given that we are apparently committed to a huge expansion of higher education, would be to introduce sub-A-level and sub-degree level courses. I would have strong objections to reducing standards at either A-level or first-degree level, because this would involve adults or near-adults being forced to suffer the fate inflicted on so many of our more able children at the primary and secondary levels of schooling — i.e. boredom or worse due to lack of intellectual stimulation. Enforced boredom of this sort would be particularly regrettable if it came at a time when students are both able and willing to manifest and exploit a strong commitment to some clearly-defined field of interest. Conversely, forcing post-16 students to do subjects they do not find attractive is likely to produce, not unreasonably, resentment on their part.

Usually at this point in discussions of this sort, mention is made of the narrowness of A-level programmes and the need for something wider, along the lines of the French *Baccalauréat*.[3] One common misconception must be dispelled straightaway. In France, there is no single *Baccalauréat*. There is, in fact, a broad distinction between the academic *Baccalauréat* and the *Baccalauréat Professionel*, a completely separate thing, and which is fast becoming the main goal of technical and vocational study in France. Within the academic *Baccalauréat*, there are no less than 24 possible groupings, and naturally some are esteemed higher than others. The difference between England and France, then, is not that France has one single unitary qualification for all post-16 education and England several. The difference is that France, while maintaining a clear distinction between academic and vocational education, and many other distinctions within the various *Baccalauréats*, has managed to construct a well-regarded vocational qualification, in some sense on a par with academic qualifications.

---

[3]   In my analysis of the French and German systems I have benefitted from Peter Pilkington (see Pilkington, 1991).

The picture is very similar in Germany, where there are actually three main types of distinct school at secondary level, *Hauptschulen, Realschulen* and *Gymnasia*. *Hauptschulen* are roughly equivalent to secondary moderns, *Gymnasia* are in effect grammar schools and *Realschulen* somewhat akin to the technical schools we were supposed to get after 1944, but never did get in sufficient numbers. If, as seems to be true, in Germany there is the much-sought 'parity of esteem' between academic and technical/vocational qualifications, it has not been achieved by comprehensivization, by 'one examination for all' at the age of 16 (as the GCSE is supposed to be), by a unified post-16 qualification (as Sir Claus Moser proposes) or by watering down the academic *Abitur* (as the Royal Society would do to A-levels). It has been achieved by distinguishing clearly between academic and technical qualifications, and by having separate institutions for each type of qualification.

Many commentators have deplored what they regard as the narrowness of typical A-level courses. While it is worth remembering that narrowness here is simply the correlate of depth, and that it might be wrong, or at least bloody-minded, to force a 16 year old to be 'broad' just for the sake of it, I am prepared to concede that critics may have had a point. The subsequently introduced combination for each pupil of A–levels together with a number of intermediate A/S levels, may combine both rigour and depth in his or her chosen subject or subjects, together with worthwhile and serious study from other areas of the curriculum. This may have been a reasonable compromise, provided that university entry continues to be tied to A-level and that there is no pretence that A/S levels are of the same standard as A-levels. Indeed, one might also favour the taking of A/S levels in some of the humanities for pupils opting for vocational training after the age of 16. While I can see no good either for the academic or the non-academic in not differentiating between them at least in the later reaches of secondary school, and while what evidence there is suggests that pupils all through the ability range do better in a grammar/secondary modern secondary school system than do their counterparts in comprehensive systems (Marks, 1991, pp. 7–15). I would not want those on vocational routes to be deprived altogether of education or of 'School' in Oakeshott's sense.

My recent remarks are not a pure digression from my main theme. They are intended as a sketchy, though nonetheless serious attempt to deal with one consequence of a conception of education as the transmission of what has been best thought and best said. Clearly in a developed and articulate culture such as ours, doing this at even the moderately high level presupposed by A-levels or the upper reaches of the GCSE is beyond the ability of many or even most of our pupils. The reaction of many educationalists to this fact is to say, in effect, that what all cannot do, none will do, and to attempt to suppress or mask differences between individuals. This, of course, is what has tended to happen in our primary and comprehensive schools. Too often the upshot helps no one, as we see by comparing standards in British (English) schools with those elsewhere in the developed world. Moreover, Germany, which is far better at technical and vocational education than us post-16, has a differentiated school system at the higher levels, yet many would have us *decrease* differentiation here even more than we have done already, in the name of 'access' or 'flexibility', and expect us to end up with results similar to theirs. This expectation strikes me as obtuse, as does the aim we now have of increasing to 50% of the population the rate of participation in higher education, without any thought of providing new types of course for them. It is no use simply assuming that they will cope with established degree-style courses, or that they can be admitted to such courses without an inevitable drift to reduce standards so as to accommodate them. Yet reducing standards for what are socio-political reasons is to frustrate the engagement education should be, an engagement dictated in the first instance by the nature and demands of the subject and its excellences. The engagement will certainly be frustrated if its processes and standards are determined by extrinsic considerations such as increasing access, the 'need for an informed society' or a 'skilled workforce'. In the last case the frustration of education for its own sake will be particularly ironic, for the differentiation I am suggesting — between academic and vocational education — is one which, if the lesson of France or Germany are anything to go by, will actually promote the acquisition of workforce skills through the development of courses specifically dedicated to producing them.

To conclude: in these two lectures, I have been considering education against the background of a particular conception of human nature and human life. In this conception, I envisage human beings as products of nature, but also as having powers of reflective self-conscious thought and expression. By means of our symbol systems, especially language, we come to possess systems of moral value and other forms of knowledge and experience which possess a degree of autonomy and objectivity. In education, we should seek to make pupils aware of the fabric of these systems. We should be cautious of undermining their objectivity in the eyes of the young by advocating premature and potentially destructive criticism on their part; rationality, indeed, in the full sense is not served by forms of reasoning and criticism which are not founded in the relevant knowledge and experience.

When we come to the developed forms of knowledge and expression in which our existence as self-conscious agents is embodied and expressed, teachers should have as an aim the need to introduce all their pupils to some of the best that has been done in each form as didactically and subject-centredly as is necessary for the integrity of the form. Teachers should understand the role of canons in constituting a discipline of study and contribute to their development rather than to their destruction. While I believe that the aim of introducing all pupils to what has been best thought and best expressed can be achieved to some degree — and to a degree higher than is often attempted — talk of the best implies differentiation and stratification. Not all can achieve as much as the best in any field, and certainly not in the pursuit of articulated knowledge and expression. Lest we cramp the efforts and aspirations of the best — and eventually undermine the foundation on which a tradition of knowledge or expression develops — we should seek to develop a system of education which recognises and responds to the facts of human diversity. That we in higher education should respond in this way is particularly pressing when talk of classlessness and expansion is all the rage.

Part 3:

**EDUCATION, VALUES,
AND THE STATE**

7

Richard Pring

The Aim of Education: Liberal or Vocational?

Introduction

Edward Copleston, Provost of Oriel College, wrote in 1810 a reply to the calumnies of the *Edinburgh Review* which had been directed against the University of Oxford. The *Review* had argued that the Universities of Oxford and Cambridge should reform an outdated system and prepare their students more effectively for the pressures and problems of the nineteenth century. In his reply, the Provost of Oriel argued that:

> the purpose of the University is to counter the effects upon the individual of gross materialism . . . not to train directly for any specific profession but rather to develop 'an elevated tone and flexible habit of mind which would enable them to carry out with zeal and efficiency all the offices, both private and public, of peace and war. (Slee, 1986, p.11)

It is comforting to discover that there is some stability in a world of rapid change, if only in the sense that the controversies which divided people in the nineteenth century continue to do so today. And the theme of these two lectures is the same as that which was raised by the *Edinburgh Review*, namely, the conflict or the balance between a liberal education, on the one hand, and vocational preparation on the other. This debate was by no means unknown to the nineteenth century as Copleston's words would indicate. In his inaugural address in 1867, when installed as Rector of St Andrews University, John Stuart Mill argued that universities should not be places of professional education or vocational preparation as

> their object is not to make skilful lawyers, or physicians, or engineers, but capable and cultivated human beings. (Mill, 1867, 1931, p. 133)

Universities, instead, were places where knowledge was pursued, where the intelligence was perfected, where that culture was acquired which

> each generation purposely gives to those who are to be its successors, in order to qualify them for at least keeping up, and if possible for raising, the level of improvement which has been attained. (*ibid.*, p. 133)

Education was about 'improvement' not about being useful. But it was also assumed that the educated and the cultivated person would *thereby* be useful. Mill argued that

> men are men before they are lawyers and if you make them capable and sensible men, they will make themselves capable and sensible lawyers. . .what professional men should carry away with them from an University is not professional knowledge, but that which should direct the use of their professional knowledge, and bring the light of general culture to illuminate the technicalities of a special pursuit. (*ibid.*, p.134)

Mill, in this respect, reflected a tradition of liberal education which had been enunciated in 1810 by Copleston in his defence of the 'status quo' at the University of Oxford and, in 1851, in the writings of another Oriel man, John Henry Newman, in *The Idea of the University*. Furthermore, it is a tradition which is reflected in the first series of Victor Cook Lectures. Both Lord Quinton and Professor O'Hear would subscribe to the view that the values to be nurtured at university, and indeed through school, are primarily concerned with the intellectual excellence and with acquaintance with 'the best that has been thought and said' — or, in the adaptation of Lord Quinton, with that which 'has been best thought and said'. Neither quite argued that the purpose of education was to 'counter the effects of gross materialism' or 'to develop an elevated tone'. But the aim of education was certainly that which was objectively good in the cultivation of the mind and in the development of virtue. Both would share with Mill the suspicion of Universities as places for professional preparation; and one, Professor O'Hear would clearly like to see university-based teacher training disappear altogether. The positive messages of those lectures (namely, that education is primarily concerned with the pursuit of excellence, particularly intellectual excellence as that is found within a selective tradition) is reinforced by the critical and negative comments on those developments which run counter to liberal sentiments so defined — the rejection of the 'Education for Capability Manifesto' and the dismissal of John Dewey. It was Dewey (1916) who challenged the dualisms between theory and practice, between thinking and doing, between intellectual and useful upon which a particular liberal tradition is founded, and who challenged also the crude identification of 'liberal education' with the academic.

The importance of these first Victor Cook Lectures is that they were a response to what they saw as a fresh challenge to that liberal tradition and to the values which it embodied. Certainly we live in a time of change and those changes affect (rightly or wrongly) the aims that educational institutions subscribe to, the values that they cherish and bequeath to the next generation, the content of the curriculum, the control of what is taught and the nature of the institutions themselves. It is a theme that I want to continue, but, in doing so, I argue that both Quinton and O'Hear have ignored the nature of the changes taking place and thus have been tilting at the wrong enemies — the cockshies of the education correspondent of the *Daily Mail* rather than the real philistines waiting at the gates.

Furthermore, in failing to identify and understand those changes, they too fall victim to the criticisms levelled against the University of Oxford nearly 200 years ago. There are two enemies that I have in mind in giving these lectures. The first are those who, in face of certain changes, retreat to a narrow concept of liberal education which leaves so many dispossessed of education. The other is those who, in trying to make education more relevant, betray the best that is preserved within the liberal tradition. The divide is, and no doubt always will be, between liberal education and vocational preparation. But it need not be, and I shall do my best to see how two quite different traditions might be reconciled.

In this lecture, therefore, I shall do the following.

First, I shall say something about the nature of those changes taking place to which educational institutions are obliged to respond; it will be brief and superficial, but it provides the context in which a debate about the aims of education might be conducted. Second, I shall identify what are the key features of the liberal tradition which, I think, both Quinton and O'Hear subscribe to, and which has shaped the aims of education for both schools and universities. Third, I shall outline the vocational alternative which is increasingly affecting how the changes referred to are met. Fourth, I shall examine how the two traditions might be reconciled. But that will require a fresh look at the aim of education — in particular, what it means to be a person and to become one more abundantly.

Change

It is hardly necessary to rehearse the well-known accounts of the changes that are affecting our society, and thus indirectly the schools. But I shall remind you of some of them because they provide a necessary backcloth to the debate on liberal education.

We are warned by many, particularly those in industry, that the economic changes affecting our standard of living and the pattern of employment are unprecedented. This is obviously related to the massive developments in electronics and in technology. But it goes beyond that to the changing pattern of trade as other countries develop more sophisticated economies. People talk with bated breath about 'the Pacific Rim'. The employment consequences are that just as more than a million unskilled jobs were taken out of the economy in the 1980s and 1990s, a further reduction on a similar scale has been predicted. Furthermore, there is a disproportionate increase of employment in the service industries, requiring different kinds of personal qualities and skills. The bank no longer replies to my pompous letters about errors in their favour with an equally pompous reply starting 'Dear Sir'. Rather does one receive a personal phone call from the friendly bank clerk, Marilyn, asking if she can be of any service.

The impact of all this on the educational system is manifold. First, so we are told, many more need to be educated. Second, such education should provide skills and knowledge which previously have been neglected — in information technology, economic awareness, communication skills, practical numeracy, for example. Thirdly, schools and universities need to form a different, more favourable set of attitudes towards the industrial and commercial worlds; too often, and for too long, argue such as Wiener(1981), a liberal tradition of education has regarded with contempt the useful and the practical, the doing and the making.

It is impossible to make sense of so much that is happening in schools and universities without reference to the impact of these economic changes upon how those, who are in positions of power and influence, conceive the aims of education. This was reflected in the then Prime Minister Mr Callaghan's Ruskin Speech in 1977. There, in initiating the Great Debate in Education, he not only spoke of the importance of raising standards, but referred particularly to standards which related to economic performance. Subsequently, there was a shift of emphasis in the political and administrative sense of educational aims. Looking back on this period, one high-ranking Treasury official felt able to say:

> We took a strong view that education could play a much better role in improving industrial performance. The service is inefficient, rather

unproductive and does not concentrate scarce resources in the areas that matter most. The economic climate and imperatives are clear; the task is to adjust education to them (quoted in Ranson, 1984, p. 223).

Subsequently, efforts have been made to inject vocational skills and knowledge and the newly-discovered virtues of enterprise and entrepreneurship into the curriculum of schools and universities — the Technical and Vocational Education Initiative and the Enterprise in Higher Education initiatives being two examples.

The changes, however, go more deeply than purely economic ones. The number of young people continuing with their education beyond the compulsory school leaving age has risen quite dramatically. In the first half of the 1990s the percentage of seventeen year-olds in full-time education and training rose in England and Wales from under 40% to around 70%; in Scotland the percentage has always been higher than in England. This has forced teachers to reassess the aims of general education for those who traditionally would not have continued in education beyond the age of sixteen and entered university. The word 'relevance', much despised by philosophers of liberal education but essential to those who teach rather than just talk about teaching, enters into the vocabulary of educational aims. Hence, the development of new qualifications and new routes into higher education. And universities look different, with polytechnics having been transformed and professorships now created in subjects unheard of by a Newman, Copleston or Mill..

Furthermore, under the banner of 'relevance', especially vocational relevance, new styles of learning have been explored, embodying different assumptions about the purpose of learning and about the value of that which is learnt. There is an emphasis upon co-operative learning, upon problem solving, upon relevant learning. Old standards, whereby performance is assessed, give way to new ones, as a new generation is taught within a different social and economic context and with different ends in view. All these changes, too often announced through a list of clichés, need to be questioned philosophically. That is, questions need to be asked about the kind of knowledge, about the nature of problem solving, about the meaning of relevance, which underlie the advocacy of these changes. But changes they are and they undermine the erstwhile settled way in which schools and universities saw their aims and in which they served each other.

These changes reflect also deeper social worries. Society is different from what it was ten or twenty years ago. There are less certainties about what is right and wrong; less consensus over the values to be taught and learnt; greater stress upon autonomy (for example, freedom to make up one's own mind on controversial issues); a belief, ill-defined, that the schools should respond educationally to the increasing personal and social dislocations that pupils bring with them into the school; scepticism of the selective culture which once was unquestioned; perspectives introduced by people of different ethnic backgrounds — a minority in the country as a whole but often a majority in particular schools and localities.

At the same time, despite these differences and doubts, despite the scepticism over values and the rejection by many of liberal values, there is paradoxically a growing chorus of people who want schools, through their educational programmes, to counter anti-social forces, to help 'improve' society, indeed to make people good. Even responsibility for the 1993 football riots in Rotterdam was attributed by one newspaper to state schooling. Whereas liberal educators are primarily concerned with understanding behaviour, the teachers of 'relevance' want to change it.

The teachers in schools, colleges and universities have the job of reconciling the different forces — those, on the one hand, of traditional learning with its emphasis upon a readily understood map of learning, established texts and an agreed literary canon, consensus on what is worthwhile and a belief in traditional standards, and those, on the other hand, of meeting the urgent needs of often disillusioned and alienated young people, of answering the call of society to produce the worthy and productive citizen and of doing all this against a background of uncertainty within society over the quality of life worth pursuing. The problem was identified by Derek Morrell, the architect of the Schools Council established in 1964, in his 1966 Joseph Payne Memorial Lectures. He asks

> why educators, in all parts of the world, are finding it necessary to organise a response to change on a scale, and in a manner, which has no precedent . . . Why can't curriculum modification follow the simpler, and in many ways more comfortable pattern of partial and piecemeal change which we and other countries followed for so long? (Morrell, 1966).

His answer is developed through the lectures but it might be summarised in the following words

> The many reasons . . . stem from the pace of change in modern society. Its rapidity, and the extraordinary difficulty which we face in defining its characteristics, and in communicating the implications of change throughout complex systems of human relationships, have destroyed or

at least weakened the broad consensus on aims and methods which was taken for granted when our educational system took its present form.

For Morrell, and for the Schools Council of which he was the main creator, teachers had to address the question of the aim of education anew, in conjunction certainly with those within universities whose voices from within their respective disciplines of philosophy and sociology, of psychology and history, had such an important contribution to make, but in partnership also with those in the wider community who were in tune with the economic and social context within which young people had to live — and make sense of living. The critique of the liberal ideal was that it prescribed the quality of the life worth living without reference to the social reality of those who had to live it. And it must be the teachers, rooted in a liberal tradition of worthwhile learning but seeking also to educate all children irrespective of background and motivation, who had to bridge the gap — explore both the moral base of the curriculum and its content. And that in turn raised the very questions which, in the *Edinburgh Review*, had angered the Provost of Oriel. Perhaps we should examine more precisely the liberal ideal of which I speak.

The Concept of Liberal Education

There are many versions of the liberal ideal. And indeed it is dangerous to assume that all versions were averse to some form of utility.

The arguments were rehearsed, and the different versions clearly exposed, in a nineteenth-century debate which tried to accommodate a liberal tradition to the different conditions of an industrial society. Not all the Victorian exponents of liberal education saw eye-to-eye with Copleston. As Ralph White (1986) points out in his paper 'The Anatomy of a Victorian Debate', there were variations in the degree to which the liberal ideal both could and needed to be justified by reference to some extrinsic goal. How far did the knowledge and understanding which characterised the educated person have to be useful knowledge? For Newman social benefit and virtue might be beneficial by-products of education; that would be a bonus, but not a defining characteristic or a reason for pursuing it (see Newman, 1852, 1919, p. 120). Mill, on the other hand, as we might deduce from his inaugural lecture, was much more aware of the social consequences and of the personal power that a liberal education bestowed — lawyers made more sensible lawyers through exposure to general culture. But he went further than that for, in examining the content of the university curriculum, he constantly referred to its relevance, indirect maybe, to social improvement. This reference to social improvement, not simply to intellectual excellence, and to those subjects which were relevant to that social improvement, was a constant theme in that nineteenth-century debate. For this reason, Huxley complained that

> modern geography, modern history, modern literature, the English language as a language; the whole circle of the sciences, physical, moral and social, are even more completely ignored in the higher than in the lower schools (quoted in White, (1986, p. 57).

The variations in the argument about liberal education — between Newman, Mill, Huxley, Sidgwick and Arnold, all of whom endeavoured to define it — were essentially about the degree of social usefulness which should temper the pursuit of intellectual excellence. Consequently, the argument concerned the degree to which the ideal of liberal education needs constantly to be renewed, as new knowledge, and new organisations of knowledge, transform our ideas of 'social usefulness'. But, whatever the variations, there remained the central significance given to the development of reason and to those studies which enhanced the capacity to know, to understand, to pursue the truth. Such a liberal ideal might be characterised in the following way.

First, its chief aim is to develop the intellect — to improve the capacity to think and to understand and, indeed (in the area of the arts), to appreciate what is worthy of appreciation. 'Improvement' is the word, but the improvement concerns not the character or the behaviour, but the appreciation of what is true — or, indeed, 'the best that has been thought and said'.

Second, that intellectual development was based upon an organisation of knowledge which was not merely practical or convenient but was philosophically sound. It was argued (for example, by Hirst, 1965) that there are different forms of knowledge and understanding. These are not arbitrary and not open to personal choice or arbitrary social reconstruction, whatever the sociologists of knowledge might say. Such forms of knowledge are characterised in various ways by their own distinctive ideas and concepts, by their own central axioms, by their key texts which are the touchstones of debate and argument. Thus, to think mathematically or historically one has to *learn* a way of thinking and to understand what are regarded as concepts and modes of enquiry which are central to these forms of understanding. Liberal education is an initiation into these forms, which underpin our different understandings of experience. Such initiation is normally undertaken in an organised fashion — systematically, through subjects, under the tutelage of a teacher.

Third, the value of acquiring these different forms of understanding requires, philosophically at least, no extrinsic justification (see, for example, Peters, 1965, chapter 5). Education in this sense should not be seen as a means to an end. It would be like asking: 'why be educated?' or 'why should we cultivate the mind?' where the answer requires a statement of value, not of economic usefulness. Of course, the pupils, prevented from enjoying themselves by having to learn, might ask those questions, not seeing the intrinsic value of reading Virgil or understanding theoretical physics. But that is because they are not yet 'on the inside' of those forms of understanding or because they are not yet sophisticated enough to see the philosophical or ethical arguments for the value of understanding for its own sake. A very real problem for liberal education lies in the failure of its proponents to communicate the values felt by the educators. But, then, the argument is not easily accessible, as is apparent from the first Victor Cook Lectures — dependent more on the intuition of the privileged few who already have been initiated.

Fourth, the formation of the intellect is demanding. It cannot, in the main, happen incidentally. 'Learning from experience', or 'learning from interest', attractive though these pupil-centred phrases sound, will not provide the insights that intellectual excellence requires. Such excellence requires there to be teachers, people already acquainted with the best that has been thought and said. And they need to be free from the distractions of the immediate and the relevant. They need, in other words, schools and universities separated from the world of business and usefulness. Indeed, schools ideally should be like monasteries, rather than market places.

Fifth, the responsibility for learning — for its content, its assessment, its emphasis, its direction — must be in the hands of the experts, the authorities within the different intellectual disciplines. They will have proved themselves in scholarship and in critical discussion. Such people work mainly in universities. But if schools are to address the problems of change within that liberal tradition — to relate intellectual excellence to social improvement — the school teachers too must be regarded as authorities within the development of liberal learning. That, surely, was the main rationale behind the Schools Council — teachers supported in their deliberation about ends, not simply about the means to ends decided by politicians and business people.

Liberal education so conceived has been likened by the philosopher Michael Oakeshott (1972), to a transaction between teacher and learner, in which the learner is introduced to the conversation which takes place between the generations of mankind in which the learner listens to the voices of poetry, of history, of philosophy, of science. We live in a world of ideas. And education is the initiation into that world. It has no purpose other than to let people into that conversation and to enjoy it.

There have been, however, critics of this ideal of liberal education. It is under attack in a number of ways. And, since these attacks have political muscle and money behind them, they are undermining a liberal tradition and the values which it embodies. The vocational imperative goes beyond social improvement as that was understood by Mill or Arnold. It questions the very rationale and content of the liberal tradition — but not in the way that Quinton and O'Hear have appreciated. Before, however, we turn to the vocational alternative, it is important to attend to the criticism of the liberal education of those who are seeking to change it.

First, the liberal tradition, in focusing upon the world of ideas, has ignored the world of practice — the world of industry, of commerce, of earning a living. It is claimed that there has been a disdain for the practical intelligence — indeed, for the technological and the useful. The great nineteenth-century engineer, Brunel, had his own sons educated at Harrow School so that, in concentrating upon the classics, they would not be corrupted by technology. In 1980, the Royal Society of Arts, an ancient and much respected society which for 250 years has striven to bring together theory and practice, thinking and making, intellect and skill, produced its Manifesto for Capability, signed by distinguished scientists and philosophers:

> There exists in its own right a culture which is concerned with doing and making and organising and the creative arts. This culture emphasises the day to day management of affairs, the formulation and solution of problems, and the design, manufacture and marketing of goods and services (RSA, 1980).

The notion of 'capability', though hard to define, is an important one, but is neglected by those who, in pursuit of liberal learning, ignore its significance for intelligent living. This, surely, is part of the divide between those who inhabit academe and those who dwell in the world of business.

The second criticism is that the tradition of liberal education which we have inherited writes off too many young people. They fail the initiation test. Their voices are not allowed into the conversation, and the voices they listen to are not considered to be among the 'best that has been thought and said'. It is as though the liberal education is but for the few — those in the English system who, until recently, were selected for the grammar school or who were able to afford an independent education. That cultivation of the majority as a basis of social integration, which is what Arnold aspired to, has not occurred, and the injunction 'try harder' seems misplaced. Perhaps the tradition itself needs to be re-examined. In the absence of such a re-examination, a more practical, useful and vocational training is recommended for the majority — one which, despite political protestations to the contrary and whatever the Howie Report (1992) might have argued, has lower status and which is perceived as such by those who are selected for it. There were indications within the Dearing Report (1994) that that might be the solution to the criticisms of educational achievement from fourteen to eighteen. Certainly they were contained in the Howie proposals for the two-track system leading to the SCOTBAC (Scottish Baccaluareate) for the more able and to the SCOTCERT (Scottish Certificate) for the others. Many young people are thus 'written off' as *educational* failures, though able to benefit from vocational training, as if they did not have minds to be developed and human qualities to be nurtured.

Vocationalising the Liberal Ideal

There are two curriculum responses to these criticisms. The first is that of having two curriculums — preserving the liberal ideal for the few, and offering a vocational alternative for the many. The second is to dilute the liberal education with a vocational emphasis. Before, however, I get to the detail, I need to spell out the contrast between the liberal ideal as I have portrayed it and the idea of vocational preparation.

The following seem to be the characteristics of vocational training, which, in varying degrees, affect the liberal ideal as it responds to the criticisms outlined above. First, the aim is, not intellectual excellence for its own sake, but competence at work — or in the tasks which adults have to perform at work, at home and in the community. Preparation for citizenship, or for parenting, are but extensions of vocational preparation. The dominant idea is 'competence'.

Second, the content of the education and training programme is not derived from the intellectual disciplines, or from the best that has been thought and said, but from an analysis of the work to be done.

People in industry say what skills are needed to run a business or to be an electrical engineer or to supervise staff, and the training programme is geared to produce those skills. There is an emphasis upon the 'can do' statements, on practical competence, as an object to be achieved through learning. Thus, the National Vocational Qualifications are based upon the basic elements of skill which the Industry Lead Bodies say are required for jobs to be done efficiently.

Third, the value of what is learnt is justified by reference not to intrinsic worth or, indeed, to social improvement, but to the usefulness of it. This usefulness might apply to the economy as a whole or to the economic well-being of the learner or of the community at large. Consequently, a different set of virtues characterises vocational preparation — enterprise rather than disinterested pursuit of the truth, entrepreneurship rather than love of ideas, efficiency rather than the display of imagination.

Fourth, the best place for this useful learning is not away from the busy world of commerce and industry, nor away from the practical problems that the young person will face after school and university. Preparation for adult life is best done through a kind of apprenticeship in which the young learner is engaged practically in the adult world, though of course under supervision and with a systematic introduction to the skills and competences required. No one doubts the need for systematic learning and thus for periods set apart. But those are dictated by the learning needs, not by some liberal ideal of separation from the distractions of the practical world of economic and industrial reality. Implicit in vocational learning, therefore, is a view about how learning best takes place — practically, relevantly, with useful and specific goals in mind.

Fifth, such a view of learning — its aims, its content, its value and its location — cannot be left in the hands of the academics. After all, it is argued, they and their ideal of liberal education have been responsible for economic neglect and for the impoverished idea of education in which the majority is excluded and in which important areas of experience play no part. Therefore, education and training must be under wider control. 'Authorities' over what should be learnt, and over what counts as successful learning, must include those from industry who know best what learning is useful and what research should receive public support. They must include, also, those teachers who, whether or not they be academics, know the students, their motivation and their personal needs — and who, therefore, can provide the kind of learning experiences which will make the students competent citizens, parents and employees. They must include, finally, the government which has broader interests and purposes to serve and which ultimately pays the bill.

Vocational preparation, therefore, uses the language of usefulness, fitness for purpose, effective means to an end. It cherishes different values. It respects different personal and social qualities. It requires a different process of control and accountability.

The effect of the vocational intent shows itself in many ways. Universities were promised a lot of money if they incorporated the skills and virtue of enterprise in all their undergraduate courses, including Ancient Greek and Old Norse. 'Core skills', that are vocationally relevant, are incorporated into otherwise academic courses such as A-Level. 'Economic awareness' becomes a cross-curriculum theme, supposedly giving a different dimension to the teaching of history or geography. Young enterprise schemes find their way onto the curriculum so that students can have first-hand experience of running a business. The Technical and Vocational Education Initiative was introduced into schools in 1983 so that students would acquire the work-related skills and attitudes neglected in the liberal education which otherwise prevailed. Concern in schools over the alienation and underachievement of so many children encouraged the schools to provide vocational alternatives — the City and Guilds courses and Business and Technical Education Council courses in particular. The Government insisted that all pupils have work experience and that 10% of teachers each year have placements in industry. The Howie Report was concerned about the many who left school without a marketable qualification and pointed to the need for ladders of progression into employment as well as into higher education.

The options in SCOTBAC offer more vocationally-oriented studies. Compacts with industry have been established in which jobs and training are guaranteed if agreed learning objectives are met. There has even a Burger King school in Tower Hamlets, based on a form of sponsorship in the USA where good behaviour is rewarded with vouchers which can be cashed in at the local fast-food store. Such modifications of the liberal ideal — justification of educational activities in terms of extrinsic utility rather than intrinsic worth, educational content reflecting economic relevance rather than intellectual excellence, assessment and control in the hands of employers rather than academics, education in the workplace rather than in places set apart — are sometimes confined to the less able for whom training rather than continued education is deemed more appropriate. But increasingly it affects the idea of liberal education itself, challenging the values for which it stands. And this is best illustrated, first, by the changing language of education and, second, by the emphasis upon preconceived and measurable objectives, often expressed in terms of competences.

First, then, the changing language: education is increasingly seen as a commodity to be bought or sold; the transaction takes place between provider and customer, rather than between professional and client; value is defined by popularity in the market rather than within a selective educational tradition; success is measured by external auditors against performance indicators rather than by the peer review of fellow academics; judgment of intellectual development is reduced to measurement against a few criteria. This changing language through which the education of young people is described and understood — the shift in metaphor from that of conversation to that of business audit — has received little philosophical attention, and yet it does more to undermine the liberal ideal than any innovation in content or emphasis upon relevance.

Second, and connected with this change in language, is the emphasis upon skills and competences. By competences is meant the 'can do's', the list of skills which a well-trained person can employ in specific contexts. Such skills should ideally be related to an analysis of what is necessary to do the job effectively. To express, for example, the professionalism of teaching in terms of competences is to assume that the task of teaching can be reduced to a limited (i.e. what can be put on two sides of A4) range of context-specific skills. It ignores the wider cognitive capacities. The outcomes in terms of 'can do's' are logically separated from the processes by which they might be achieved. Syllabuses and periods of study and contact with a teacher are not essential for, having clarified the specific outcomes and the limited list of competences, one starts with the assessment points not with the learning experiences. Courses or teaching are arranged as a sort of remedial response to the failure to measure up to these assessments. There is nothing wrong with untrained teachers — with a Mums' army — so long as their performance measures up to a finite list of behavioural indicators. Furthermore the assessments should be in the real situation of the workplace, not the unreal environment of the university.

The language of 'competence' is used rather elastically, likened to specific, measurable and context-bound skills for planning purposes, but then stretched to cover knowledge, judgment and understanding where that is convenient. The result is an impoverished concept of knowledge and understanding — one which results in the measurable behaviours specified by those who teach. Indeed, the distinction between education and training disappears as teaching is defined in terms of imparting specific content and behaviours. No longer is it a conversation, a meeting of minds, a seeking after goals the nature of which is transformed in the very search. Indeed, the teaching is a means to an end logically disconnected from the process of teaching itself; it is no longer that transaction in which the ends themselves are subject to examination and scrutiny. In the language of the former Youth Training Scheme, personal development becomes personal effectiveness.

Again, I repeat, this may be only for the less able, even though they might be the majority, leaving a wider chasm still between the education of some and the training of others. But this vocationalising of education, as is reflected in the audits of universities (my department has been audited six times in one year) and in the assessment of schools, now permeates the idea of liberal learning itself.

Re-Examination of the Liberal Ideal

Following the last Victor Cook lectures, it may seem unwise of me to refer to John Dewey. In the eyes of many who defend the liberal ideal, Dewey is seen as the source of all our ills — the advocate of child-centred education, the promoter of 'collectivist egalitarianism' (whatever that means), the supporter of 'the classroom filled with pupil reaction and the scepticism of the not-yet-educated'. But Dewey it was who questioned the dualisms which seem to bedevil our thinking about education — the divide between the academic and the vocational, between the theoretical and the practical, between the intrinsically worthwhile and the useful, and indeed (a point lost on his detractors) between subject-centred and child-centred education (see Pring, 1989).

I want in this final section, and in anticipation of my second lecture, to make two major points about how this dichotomy between the liberal ideal and the vocational preparation might be challenged, and with it the mistaken solution to our educational problems of establishing two- or three-track systems.

First, there is a mistaken tendency to define education by contrasting it with what is seen to be opposite and incompatible. 'Liberal' is contrasted with vocational as if the vocational, *properly taught*, cannot itself be liberating — a way into those forms of knowledge through which a person is freed from ignorance, and opened to new imaginings, new possibilities: the craftsman who finds aesthetic delight in the object of his craft, the technician who sees the science behind the artefact, the reflective teacher making theoretical sense of practice. Indeed, behind the liberal/vocational divide is another false dichotomy, namely, that between theory and practice. Theory is portrayed as the world of abstractions, of deep understanding, of the accumulated wisdom set down in books, of liberation from the 'here and now'. Practice, on the other hand, is identified with 'doing' *rather* than 'thinking', with the acquisition of skills rather than knowledge, with low-level knowledge rather than with understanding. Intelligent 'knowing how' is ignored, the practical way to theoretical understanding dismissed, the wisdom behind intelligent doing unrecognised. I cannot understand why the practical science in BTEC Intermediate and Advanced courses is called vocational, unless it is because it is practical, which presumably much good science is. Because of the dichotomy of theory from practice, of thinking from doing, science teaching, rather than be contaminated with the label 'vocational', enters into a mode of symbolic representation which loses the vast majority of young people — cuts them off, at an early age, from an understanding of the physical world in which they live. Real science is for the able; craft is for the rest; the science within the craft goes unrecognised, and for that both the able and the less able suffer.

There is another false dichotomy which has permeated our educational system at every level. Certainly, the concepts of 'education' and 'training' do not mean the same thing — education indicates a relatively broad and critical understanding of things, whereas training suggests the preparation for a relatively specific task or job. But, despite the different meanings, one and the same activity could be both educational and training. Thus, one can be trained as a doctor, as an electrician, as a bus driver, or as a pharmacist, but that training can be such that the experience is educational. For example, the student teacher can be trained to plan the lessons, to manage the class, and to display the children's work. But the training can be so conducted that the student is educated *through* it — in becoming critical of what is happening, in understanding the activity, and in coming to see it in a wider educational context. Competence as a goal might be limiting. But it need not be. Indeed, without a certain degree of competence in playing the piano, one might be denied the chance of appreciating the finer points of a musical score, or, without some competence as a politician, one's political theorising might miss the mark. Furthermore, a critical stance requires very often the practical competence — as, for example, in the understanding of the use of technology. Skills training is not the opposite to understanding, but very often a precondition of it.

The first way of challenging the liberal/vocational divide lies in questioning the way in which certain distinctions are employed as though the same activity cannot be both educationally liberating and vocationally useful, or both theoretically insightful and skilfully engaged in, or requiring both intelligence and practical training.

Secondly, however, this acknowledgement of false dichotomies goes only part way to bridging the liberal/vocational divide. Once more we must return to the aim of education — aim in the sense not of something extrinsic to the process of education itself, but of the values which are picked out by evaluating any activity as educational. The liberal ideal picked out intellectual excellence, although we noted at the beginning of this lecture the link that Mill and Arnold tried to make between individual excellence and social improvement. But much more needs to be said than that.

I am reminded of the letter sent to the new teachers in an American High School by the Principal:

> Dear Teacher,
> I am the victim of a concentration camp. My eyes saw what no man should witness: gas chambers built by learned engineers; children poisoned by educated physicians; infants killed by trained nurses; women and babies shot and burned by high school and college graduates. So I am suspicious of education.
>
> My request is: help your students become human. Your efforts must never produce learned monsters, skilled psychopaths, educated Eichmans. Reading, writing, arithmetic are important only if they serve to make our children more human.

That effort to make everyone more human must, of course, include the perfection of the intellect. After all, what is more distinctively human than the capacity to think and to act intelligently? And what is best that has been thought and said other than what cultivates the intellect in its many different manifestations, practical as well as theoretical? But being human, and becoming more so, is the privilege of everyone. Each person, whatever his or her individual capacities and talents, is engaged in thinking and doing, in feeling and appreciating, in forming relationships and in shaping the future. All this can be engaged in more or less intelligently, more or less sensitively, more or less imaginatively. So long as there are thoughts to be developed, relationships to be formed, activities to be engaged in, feelings to be refined, then there is room for education. But that is possible only if those thoughts, feelings, relationships and aspirations are taken seriously — not contemptuously rejected as of no concern to the tradition of liberal education. And that requires bringing the educational ideal to the vocational interests of the young people, educating them through their perception of relevance, helping them to make sense of their social and economic context, enabling them to be intelligent and questioning in their preparation for the world of work.

For any young person, assistance with how to live one's life, in which the sort of job one does plays such a significant part, is the most important of all educational experiences — clarifying the style of life judged worth living, identifying the training and work that will enable one to live that life, questioning the ends or values embodied within it, acquiring the necessary skills and competences.

Philosophy of education needs a more generous notion of what it is to be human than what has too often prevailed or been captured in the liberal ideal. Consequently, many young people have been dismissed as ineducable. A focus upon intellectual excellence has ignored the wider personal qualities, informed by thought, feeling and various forms of awareness, which need nurturing, even if this must be for many in the context of the practical and the useful.

The vocational alternative has, however, missed the point entirely, substituting a narrow form of training for a generous concept of education, transforming learning into an acquisition of measurable behaviours, reducing understanding and knowledge to a list of competences, turning educators into technicians.

The result has been two- or three-track systems — the SCOTBAC and SCOTCERT in Scotland, the A-Level, the GNVQ (General National Vocational Qualification) and NVQ (National Vocational Qualification) in England and Wales. Such systems have ignored the intuitive sense of so many teachers that education, helping young people to become human, is not like that. Certainly that education must be rooted in an educational tradition as that is captured in literature, in history, in the human and physical sciences, in philosophy, in poetry — in the voices that make up the conversation between the generations of mankind. But that education must also establish a continuity of experience with the young people themselves as they sort out their future employment or establish the quality of life which *for them* is worth living.

8

Richard Pring

The Context of Education: Monastery or Market Place?[1]

Introduction

'Education is big business'. Those at least are the opening words of the fifth chapter of the National Commission on Education's Report (1994), 'Learning to Succeed'. And well they might say that. The total annual bill to the taxpayer for education in the year prior to the Report's publication was, we are told, £27 billion. At a time when the country had to do something about the £50 billion national debt, there was no escaping the importation of business metaphors and practices. Corporate providers of taxes ask about the ROI of education — the Return On Investment. The Government questions its cost-effectiveness. It is the Institute for Economic Affairs which advises the Government on educational policy. It is the Audit Commission which proposes how schools should be re-organised.

Furthermore, the main drive to expand education and to improve standards arises from a concern about economic competition from abroad. The National Commission sets the tone for its recommendations on 'learning to succeed' by pointing to the *economic* necessity of doing so — and in relating that success to what is referred to as 'the knowledge industry' and in particular to the importance of training in information technology. Therefore, twenty-seven pages are devoted to information technology, whereas the expressive arts (which include drama, music, art and physical education — clear distinctions are not made) get a mention on two pages only, and then

---

[1]   In my analysis of the French and German systems I have benefitted from
        Peter Pilkington (1991).

only as a subject area to be included in the non-core part of the curriculum. What is lacking in a Report which incorporates a section called the Commission's Vision and which has a chapter called 'The Vision of the Future' is any *educational* vision — that is, following my previous lecture, any picture of the quality of life, the life worth living, which is logically associated with the notion of a community of educated persons and embodied in the liberal ideal. The Report is an excellent example of how, even with liberally-minded people, vocational preparation, necessary though it is as I have argued, can pervert the idea of a liberal education. It, therefore, demonstrates (which is the purpose of these two lectures) the need to reconcile the two traditions — that of liberal education and that of vocational training — within the context of the system of education which it is the Commission's aim to reform.

In my previous lecture I pointed out the essentially evaluative nature of any judgments about education. 'Education' picks out those activities which form the educated person, and our concept of the educated person, contestable though it is, refers to those qualities and accomplishments which we value highly in people. 'Educated' is a commendation, granted by virtue of certain achievements. But those achievements have a cognitive core; they entail some sort of learning and the development of understanding. However, the nature of that understanding and the selection of the achievements thought worthwhile, depend on wider ethical questions concerning the kind of life worth living and the kind of society which we think is desirable to live in. Moreover, just as the economic base of society changes, so will change the list of accomplishments which we see the educated person to need if he or she is to live intelligently within that society and to make a significant contribution to it. The liberal ideal of education needs constantly to be reexamined as our moral ideas develop concerning what it is to be a person and indeed how that person might adapt intelligently to changing economic and social conditions. And the question that I have been addressing concerns the extent to which such an ideal needs to incorporate the idea of vocational preparation. One danger of its failing to do so is that the vocational tradition — its language, its dominant concern for utility, its indifference to moral deliberation and to philosophical speculation, its reduction of successful learning to the efficient achievement of someone else's goals, its equation of personal development with personal effectiveness — nudges out the liberal ideal, impoverishing the aims of education.

In this lecture, I approach the issue from a different angle. It is a common mistake — and one encouraged by certain interpretations of the liberal ideal — to perceive the educated person on the basis of purely personal accomplishments without reference to the greater social good to which that person contributes (or from which he or she takes away). The intellectual excellence, to which Newman refers, needs, as Mill and Arnold argued to be related also to social improvement. But that requires reference to the context of education within which the aims of education are to be achieved. It requires, too, reference to the kind of society which one believes to be appropriate for fulfilling those moral goals. Questions about the aims of education may be a matter of ethics, but they shade quickly into the area of social philosophy. One cannot disassociate the quality of life from broader questions about the institutional framework through which that quality is to be achieved.

In this lecture, therefore, I want to examine more closely the social context of the separation of the liberal and the vocational — the way in which this dualism (and its values) are maintained and how possibly the reconciliation might be achieved. In so doing, I shall ask the following questions:

1. Where should education take place?

2. How should education be described?

3. Who should control education?

4. Who should own education?

The Place of Learning: Monastery or Market Place?

The monastery was a place where people could get away from the world of business and commerce and, through concentration upon salvation, ensure the safety of their own soul and, through prayer rather than social interaction, help too with the salvation of others. Therefore, schools and universities have sometimes been likened to monasteries — places, like our major and prestigious private schools and like the old 'new' universities, set apart in a rural idyll, undistracted by the affairs of commerce and industry. There intellectual excellence might be pursued, and individual salvation found. And the people so educated would also be of value to others, since they would constitute the guardian class, the clerisy, as Coleridge argued, who would be the leaders of society. For the philosopher T.H. Green, this social benefit of liberal education was the best way of preparing his students in Oxford for the professions and public service. Indeed, the impact of Green and the idealist philosophers of Oxford on the development of a tradition of public service in Britain is a story still to be told.

The most famous of English civil servants concerned with Education, Michael Sadler, and his successor as Permanent Secretary at the Board of Education, Robert Morant, architect of the 1902 Education Act, owed their initiation into a liberal ideal of education to T.H. Green's educational idealism. This was, and was seen to be, a preparation for public life — vocational preparation, if you like, but not explicitly so, much more the preparation arising from a well-trained mind and a moral formation.

Such an achievement, however, took place in a place set apart. As Oakeshott describes it in his essay 'Education: the Engagement and its Frustration',

> In short, 'School' is 'monastic' in respect of being a place apart where excellences may be heard because the din of worldly laxities and partialities is silenced or abated. (Oakeshott, 1972, p. 69)

And why does it have to be a world apart? Because, as he explains in another essay,

> Liberal education is a difficult engagement . . . It is a somewhat unexpected invitation to disentangle oneself from the here and now of current happenings and engagements, to detach oneself from the urgencies of the local and the contemporary, to explore and enjoy a release from having to consider *things* in terms of their contingent features, *beliefs* in terms of their applications to contingent situations and *persons* in terms of their contingent usefulness . . . (Oakeshott, 1975, p.32, my italics).

For that reason, Oakeshott's school must be a place set apart, to be contrasted with the world of vocational preparation, that is, the world of the contingencies and the 'here and now' which are a distraction from the difficult engagement of learning. In a school, there is a need for order and silence, for recognition of the world of ideas which the learner is seeking to enter, for periods of undistracted attention. There is time to reflect and to imagine and to enter into realms which are forbidden in the practical world. There is opportunity for moral formation, for the personal development necessary prior to vocational choices and training.

The vocational tradition on the other hand is scathing of this aloofness. The real world of practical living, into which the products of our school and university system must enter, is, it is argued, the more appropriate arena for preparing young people. That world defines the problems which need to be tackled and disciplines the thinking through the demands of relevance to the task in hand. Certainly there will be periods when there needs to be time and space set apart for undistracted learning, but these are largely determined by the nature of the problem. On the whole, people learn by 'doing', although preferably under critical supervision. Thus, the BTEC (Business and Technology Education Council) and the new GNVQ are practical though demanding, assignment-led rather than based on intellectual disciplines, drawing upon the resources of the community rather than remaining aloof.

The market, therefore, provides a different metaphor from that of the monastery. It points to a shift from the centrality of contemplation and reflection to the importance of intelligent practice and of getting things done. It conjures up the image of a busy world in which, less dependent on authority, people make choices, purchase what they need or want and determine by their choice what is worthwhile selling.

It suggests, too, a different set of dispositions or virtues as desirable characteristics of the educated person. 'Enterprise' is the key word. Training and Enterprise Councils have assumed much of the funding for further education; an initiative called 'Enterprise in Higher Education' put millions of pounds into universities so long as they incorporated enterprise-generating activities into all their undergraduate programmes, including those of Ancient Greek and Medieval History; thousands of schools now have young enterprise schemes whereby pupils form companies and engage in business; the Training, Education and Enterprise Department of the Department of Employment provided millions of pounds for educational research and development projects so long as enterprise was firmly embodied in the proposal. Enterprise is the most distinctive virtue of the market-based educational system — the disposition most needed by the entrepreneur whom schools and colleges are now seeking to produce. Such a person, and such dispositions, had no place in that liberal tradition I have spoken about — for which reason that liberal tradition is criticised as too remote from the practical and economic world that young people must be prepared for.

And yet one of the ironies of the new dispensation is that it is so difficult to pin down what is meant by enterprise. Presumably it refers to a certain readiness to take risks; a propensity to think laterally in problematic situations; an ability to think imaginatively where solutions are not readily available. It indicates, too, a certain practical energy, an unwillingness to give in to barriers where they

are erected against one. And all this is said within the context of business and economic initiative. One rarely refers to the painstaking
and scholarly ancient historian as enterprising — or, if one does,
then it might be interpreted as a term of abuse. The *enterprising* historian would be the one who imaginatively thought of putting his or
her historical knowledge to financial gain — tours of medieval Britain for the foreign tourist, for example.

Despite its vagueness (indeed, despite the very elasticity of the
concept as it was stretched to cover an enormous range of activities,
as the Department of Employment sought to disburden itself of
money intended to promote it), 'enterprise' reflects the market-
oriented understanding of both schools and universities and of the
curriculum which they try to develop. A new and different sort of
value system. Education in a different sort of place. The enterprising
headteacher will be the one who finds alternative sources of money
and who creates thereby an atmosphere, much loathed by those
within the liberal tradition, in which the competitive ethics of the
market enter into the educational values of the school.

A place of learning set apart? Or a place immersed in the practical
and busy world for which the young apprentice is being prepared?
Certainly vocational training favours the latter. And, as liberal education becomes vocationalised, so too will that apprenticeship be
linked with the world of work, be made relevant, be assessed in the
practical world and incorporate the core skills that adult life
demands. Universities now credit assessment in the work place; and
the three or four year course — a period of reflective learning in a
place set apart — is under threat. Part-time study is seen not as a
necessity for impoverished students, but as a virtuous opportunity
for all students. The integration of the world of learning and the
world of work is on the agenda.

The Description of Education

The market enters into, and indeed controls, our thinking about education in several important respects. First, it has changed our language — the moral language — through which we describe that
transaction which takes place between teacher and learner. That, in
turn, transforms the values we attribute to these activities; it negates
the value of some activities (those concerned with doubt and deliberation, with reflection and speculation), central to the liberal tradition, and it attaches importance to others which otherwise would be
neglected (those concerned with practical business, with practical

problem-solving, with enterprising and money-making activities). It also provides, as I shall demonstrate in my next section, a language of control, affecting that transaction in a deeper sense — indeed, affecting what we *mean* by learning as that is understood within the liberal tradition. In my final section, I shall show how the market, once a metaphor, becomes a reality in the organisation of institutions — bringing them in line with the new language of learning and bestowing on them a different set of relationships.

The language of education, therefore, is changing dramatically, as new metaphors dominate the political scene. One can see how this happens. For example, my department at the University of Oxford was audited (not my word, but one I am now forced to use) six times in the course of one year (1994). Such audits require the appraisal of what we do in a language which only a few years ago was quite foreign. Not to employ that language, requiring different criteria for evaluating success or achievement, would be financially fatal. The changes in language, and their significance, are illustrated in a report in 1991 of Her Majesty's Inspectorate, a body, you must remember, first led by Matthew Arnold, author of *Culture and Anarchy*.

> As public interest in *managerial efficiency* and *institutional effectiveness* has increased, there has been a general acknowledgement of the need to use *performance indicators* to monitor the higher education system . . . some concrete information on the extent to which the *benefits expected from educational expenditure* are actually secured . . . [an] approach finding most favour in 1989 and 1990 is the classification of performance indicator within an *input, output, process model* . . . (HMI, 1991) [my emphasis].

In searching for indicators 'which allow institutions to assess their own *fitness for purpose*', the report suggests a range of reference points which enable an 'assessment of *achievement against a defined objective* — cost effective indicators', 'academic operations indicators' such as 'inputs' (e.g. application in relation to numbers or ratios per place), 'process' (e.g. value added) and 'output' (e.g. employer satisfaction). There will be *enterprise audits* which evaluate teacher and learning styles and *annual school audits* where senior staff spend one day reviewing all aspects of a school's work. Many institutions are working to sharpen their quality assurance procedures by systematising the use of performance indicators and peer review.

Hence, my department (and increasingly all university departments subject to the audits of AAU, of the QAC, of the HEI) adopts the 'performance indicators' provided for us, however alien to a more defensible tradition of education. Measurements are made which are irrelevant to the richness of the relationship, to the quality of the conversation, which takes place between teacher and learner. The slow dawning of understanding, depth of insight, imaginative grasp of a problem, critical probing of a text — all of which emerge at different paces and in different ways for different learners — have little place in outcome measures that are imposed on all and that are administered at a preconceived time. The richness of that personal encounter with the ideas of a previous generation escapes the language of competence, of the observable 'can dos', and of the outputs measured against inputs, against which success can be assessed, value-addedness assigned and the purchaser of a service assured that investment is worthwhile. In the audits we have undergone, check lists have been produced against which the myriad activities which take place have been judged; a course solidly based on research into trainee teachers' and mentors' learning is made to fit an impoverished framework created by civil servants, who do not know that research but who are trapped in a language of audit.

Hence, teaching becomes the delivery of a curriculum, no longer an engagement with other minds; that curriculum becomes a commodity to be bought and sold, not a range of activities that are differently engaged in by pupils with their distinctive agendas; the value of that commodity lies in its popularity amongst independent purchasers, not in its access to ideas and imaginings; the controllers of the commodity are those who establish the outcomes or competences, not the teachers, the authorities within a selective culture — although (as a Secretary of State for Education explained) education is also a business in which employers are *shareholders*; the achievements are audited against *performance indicators* from without, not judged by the authorities from within. There are, then, frameworks of *quality assurance* and *quality control* for ensuring the achievement of prespecified outcomes, all within a framework of TQM or Total Quality Management.

That has the language of Her Majesty's Inspectorate, of OFSTED, of Vice-Chancellors, of Headteachers, as they conformed to the managerialism of business and competitive commerce. Headteachers are redesignated *Chief Executives*, and their deputies *Directors of Human Resources*.

This changed language affects profoundly the nature of the activity as it is perceived and the nature of the relationships between those who engage in the activity. Education shifts from being an evaluative word, picking out as valuable that formation of the mind through an encounter with the best that has been thought and said — the value of which can be judged only against broad and often barely articulated criteria. It becomes instead a description of a set of activities which lead to certain outcomes, those outcomes being worthwhile or not simply in so far as either the controller (the Government, says) or the customer finds them so. The *judgment* of the teacher — the one already initiated into an educational tradition — is relegated to insignificance in a world of mechanical rationalism, captured within this superficial language. It is little wonder that ethics, and indeed philosophy generally, are no longer considered to be a worthy component in the professional preparation of teachers, or that Dewey has been placed on the index of forbidden books, for no longer are the teachers expected to engage in ethical considerations about the aims of education any more than a Kellogg's worker is expected to raise questions about the nutritional value of cornflakes, or the car worker the environmental consequences of car exhaust. Furthermore, the personal needs of the learner give way to the imperatives of ensuring certain outcomes — stuck on, perhaps, as with chewing gum or sellotape, but outcomes nonetheless. Indeed, as the prevocational courses leading to General National Vocational Qualifications become standardised, so external tests are imposed upon the mandatory modules — tests that are increasingly conducted through massive item banks of multi-choice questions that can be machine marked and that relieve teachers of any judgment of quality. An 80% pass mark, essential in each of the eight units, guarantees teaching to the test. But where then can there be that *significant learning*, that learning whereby the learner is changed in some important way, rather than the acquisition of a few facts for examination purposes?

The market, therefore, imports a language through which the relation of teacher and learner is perceived differently and through which questions of value are eliminated from serious professional consideration.

The Control of Learning: Politicians or Teachers?

Connected with the way in which business metaphors affect our description of education is the new scope for social control which these metaphors provide. The very comprehensive list of objectives or attainment targets through which the National Curriculum of England and Wales is defined are of course the peg on which to hang an assessment system. Through such an assessment system every pupil, and thereby every school, can be labeled in a standardised way. This is necessary within a system of education wherein the schools are seen as providing a commodity to be purchased, or chosen, by autonomous consumers. To make rational choices, consumers need to have the product, which they wish to purchase, labelled with all the ingredients explicitly stated. The future parent is able to see what has been achieved subject by subject within a school, and also to see where that school is placed in relation to others in a league table. The present parents are able, on the same measures, to see where their children are placed in relation to other children. These measures, therefore, become exceedingly important and would be justified in the need for a market system of schools wherein the marketable product is displayed for all to see and can be rationally chosen or not in the light of the knowledge provided.

The importance of such measures gives unprecedented powers to those who establish the targets and the measures. They — the non-accountable bodies, such as the Schools Curriculum and Assessment Authority, and the Secretary of State who endorses the recommendations or not — are able to define what exactly should be learnt, what literature should be read, what music should be appreciated, indeed when history ends. Under the guise of the market in which there is a need for precise labelling of that which is to be chosen, there is an unprecedented political control of what is learnt. The language of competences and precise objectives, consequent upon the reconceptualisation of education as a system of providers and purchasers within a market framework, is the language of control. It is not the language of a conversation within the liberal tradition, for the very essence of a good conversation lies in the unpredictability of the outcomes. The significant result of a serious engagement with a text lies in the effect upon the person, the contribution it makes to that growing enlightenment and involvement within a tradition of learning.

There are two aspects of this new language as a basis of social control which I wish to expand upon further. The first lies in the underlying concept of learning whereby the relationship between teacher and learner is defined. The second lies in the role of the teacher in interpreting and defining the values which shape the task of teaching.

There is a distinction between 'education' and 'training'. 'Education' is an evaluative word. Education lays down broad criteria which any activity which one claims to be educational must conform to. Such activities must bring about learning; that learning must be significant — it transforms the understanding of the learner in a valuable way and is not simply stuck on superficially; the value of that learning lies in the deepening and broadening of understanding. To that extent any specific activity *might* be educational — might bring about the inner reflection, the stimulus to further thought, the insight into something significant. In fact, we know that certain activities are more likely to do this than others — obviously, because that broadening and deepening of the understanding is logically related to the different forms of knowledge or experience through which our thinking is logically structured. Many learning activities are, by their very nature, unlikely to do this. They close or limit or deaden the mind; they lead up culs-de-sac which terminate the search for understanding; they result in boredom which for Dewey was the mortal sin of education. To educate, therefore, one needs to get the learner on the inside of these different forms of understanding whereby yet further questions can be asked and new enquiries embarked upon. It is to ensure the grasp of basic concepts and principles (in science, say, or in literature) through which experience is organised in a distinctive and fruitful way and through which new perceptions and imaginings are made possible. An understanding (which can be pitched at many different levels — we talk of the depth of understanding) of 'elasticity of supply and demand' in economics or of the nature of tragedy in Othello or of the principles of leverage in classical mechanics provides more than the predictable output that can be machine marked on a multi-choice examination paper. Rather does it provide the power to talk intelligently about a range of issues, which talk cannot be confined to behavioural outcomes but can be recognised as intelligent, valid, defensible by those who are authorities within that forum of understanding. The role of judgment cannot be replaced by assessment according to pre-ordained and observable outputs. To do so is to confuse the process of thinking with the specific behavioural outcomes of thinking, a position we are increasingly led to by the insistence upon performance indicators.

Training, on the other hand, may or may not be educational. One is trained to *do* something. Circuses train dogs and horses to perform certain tricks, but we do not claim that these animals have been educated. People are trained to be plumbers and electricians. There are training courses for teachers. The implication is that there are specific skills — 'can dos' — which, following a course of training, these people can demonstrate in the place where these skills are applied. There is certainly learning, and there may be much understanding. To be trained as a plumber requires understanding — not only how to diagnose problems but also how to think imaginatively about solutions. A well-trained teacher is useful, but an educated one is better — one whose skills are informed and applied through a broader intellectual grasp of the issues of the nature of learning, of the social context of the child, and of the values worth pursuing. Hence, one can be educated *through* training — that is, training conducted in a particular way, through the acquisition of critical reflection on what one is doing and through the wider perspective which places one's specific job within a wider context of values. The efficient joiner may have no aesthetic sense; he turns out furniture to order; on the other hand, he might be so trained as to see his work within an aesthetic dimension, appreciating the beauty of what is created and striving for standards beyond those of efficiently doing the job.

Behind this distinction lies different understandings of learning. On the one hand, it is an achievement, a change of consciousness which meets certain standards, those standards being defined by the nature of knowledge or of that which is to be learnt. That is why learning theory should not be (as it often is) divorced from the philosophical analysis of what it means to have understood a particular concept or a particular principle or a way of doing things. There is a logical structure to learning which defines the standards whereby success is assessed. On the other hand, learning is associated with changed behaviour, with whatever measurable outcomes that the trainer wishes to see. There is no claim to *understanding* in the successfully changed behaviour of the circus animals. And there is no need to refer to the processes of learning or to the depth of understanding or to the mode of seeing in the input/output model through which educational institutions are now to be audited.

The significance of this shift of language and of the conception of learning is yet to be acknowledged or indeed properly analysed. This lecture can only point to what is happening, hoping that others more able than me will see the issues worth exploring in greater depth. One consequence, however, is the severance of assessment from course or curriculum, for what now becomes centre stage is not the quality of transaction between teacher and learner, reflected inadequately in a final examination system, but the quality of the assessment — the measurement of the 'can dos' within the context of the practical world — for which a course may or may not be thought necessary. The growth of item banking, of TAPs (Training Assessment Points), of accreditation of prior learning are instances of a shift of curriculum to assessment, as though the quality and significance of learning acquired through the curriculum are captured entirely in the outcome measures of the assessment. The liberal ideal of a place set apart where, *for a time*, the young learner can enjoy poetry and philosophy and science and where each, at his or her own pace, can become acquainted with a world of ideas, succumbs to the metaphor of the market in which the product is distinguished from the process and in which the product is what alone counts, a product assessed not in a place apart but in the context of the practical world into which the learner is entering.

The second aspect of the new language as a basis of social control lies in the changing understanding of teaching as a profession. Teachers are part of a social tradition of learning in which they are the mediators of what is thought, within that tradition, to be worth passing on to the next generation. Their position is held not by virtue of personal qualities (although certain personal qualities might be seen as a condition for successful teaching) but by virtue of their expertise within an area of learning. That expertise is of two kinds. There is the proven understanding of that area of knowledge and understanding into which the learner is to be initiated. Second, there is the expertise concerned with the nature of learning — how to represent that which is to be learnt in a mode which is intelligible to those who do not yet understand. The teacher teaches by virtue of being 'an authority' within an area of understanding and within the art of communicating that understanding.

That, at least, is a necessary condition of the claim to professional status. Of course, in practice this claim may often be difficult to sustain. Teachers may have a weak mastery of their subject and little opportunity is given for that mastery to be enhanced, improved, kept abreast with developments in the subject. Furthermore, their expertise in pedagogy might itself be practical and unreflective, rarely challenged, not responsive to critical enquiry. It was for that reason that in Scotland, but not in England, there has for 80 years been a close relationship between the Educational Institute of Scotland representing the teachers and the Scottish Council for Research in Education. The Research Committee of the EIS, when that connection was established in 1928, exhorted its members to justify their claim to professional status by showing a greater keenness in all that concerns the science and art of their profession (Wake, 1988, p. 8).

Research, practical research, into the aim, context and methods of education was seen as essential to teaching as a profession — communicating that selective culture in a mode that would be intelligible and perceptibly relevant to the uninitiated learner.

But more needs to be said about that professional relationship between teacher and learner other than the distinctive expertise through which a service of a particular kind might be offered. Another feature of being a professional is the distinctive set of values which shapes the relationship with the client. These values — the ethical code under which the provider of the service works and under which the client can expect a certain level of service — are reflected in the rules which govern and define the relationship. They set boundaries. They give grounds, too, for complaint and for disciplinary action where they are breached. In this respect, teaching is like medicine, or law, or social work — each having a set of values which shapes the relationship between professional and client and which, internalised, affects how the professional sees his or her task. The doctor aims to cure, the lawyer to defend, the social worker to counsel. Moreover, the practice of teaching, curing, defending or counselling is first and foremost in the interests of the receiver. The doctor, acting professionally, will recommend the medicine which is most beneficial to the patient, not the one which is most profitable to the doctor. The lawyer will defend the accused however personally obnoxious the accused may be and undeserving of acquittal. The social work counsellor sees his or her professional duty to listen to and to help the client to find an acceptable solution — not to be judgmental.

In teasing out the underlying rules and values which shape the relationship between *teacher* and learner within a tradition which we have inherited (but which is so easily vulnerable to an enterprise seen increasingly as a business, subject to market forces), can one go much beyond the rather general statement that it is the interest of the learner which is uppermost? Such an acknowledgement, though in itself not taking us very far, would not itself be empty. After all, it is conceivable (and there is the danger) that the system might serve solely or principally the interests of the economy, irrespective of the interests of the learner. For example, the Government under the 1993 Trade Union Reform and Employment Rights Act, opened up the Careers Service to competitive tendering, giving it a market discipline which previously it lacked. The tenders will be judged on cheapness and on performance indicators which relate to employment targets. The danger is that, as a result, personal guidance, the responsibility to the client, will be neglected. People become potential fillers of job vacancies, not persons who need, as Dewey so well argued, to find personal fulfilment in a life worth living, of which an appropriate occupation is part.

Such professional values of the teacher must include a defence of the learners' interests against pressures to the contrary from Government, parents or employers (and the rejection of Key Stage 3 testing in English was an example of such professional judgment), a defence, too, of a cultural heritage which it is their duty to communicate, a commitment to enquiry and to questioning, a respect for the confidentiality which is entrusted to one by the learner.

One could go on. But suffice to note the significance of professionalism namely a body of people who, by reason of distinctive expertise and values, are to be regarded with respect in what should be learnt, how it should be learnt, and what purposes that learning should serve. The importance for my purposes of such a concept of professional is that it denies the right of the market place to regulate what is worth learning or what is the appropriate relation between teacher and learner. These are set within an educational tradition of cultural transmission and of moral relationships, which cannot be reduced to the exchange and the values of the market.

And there is the rub. The inherited language of business and the market, providing an impoverished notion of learning and introducing thereby the mechanism for social control, undermines the independent authority and autonomous role of the teacher as an expert, as an interpreter of an educational tradition, as a defender of the learner against the encroachment of government or business, as the protector of values which may be economically irrelevant or indeed subversive. In that way, the liberal ideal is challenged and undermined.

The Ownership of Education: Public or Private?

The final way in which the market enters into our thinking about education lies in the changed relationship between institutions. The White Paper *Choice and Diversity*, known popularly as Chaos and Perversity, extols the virtues of schools being different and, in being different, offering different kinds of services to the consumer. Thus, for example, in the interests of variety and choice, the Secretary of

State has proposed to transform selected secondary schools into Technology Colleges — an educational culture which 'is scientific, technological and vocational', and as a further extension of consumer choice. The reason given why such colleges can be created only within the grant maintained or voluntary sectors (that is, outside the control of local education authorities) is that only these are empowered by the 1993 Act to appoint governors from firms which have agreed to sponsor them. Employers will be rewarded for their sponsorship by places on the governing bodies so that they can influence staffing, curriculum policy and admissions. Thereby will be secured (to quote) 'a better trained and more motivated *local* pool of workers, all with some understanding of the sponsors' business'.

The competitive and diverse framework of schooling, therefore, reflects a shift in ownership, undermining the role of teachers as both public servants and as professional guardians of an educational tradition. Certainly there is, both in the example I have given, but so too in many other developments, a transfer of responsibility both for the content of the curriculum and for the purposes that the curriculum must serve, to people external to the educational tradition itself, namely, in this case, to business people whose interests lie in very different directions.

This is, however, but one aspect of that diversity, for choice must be between self sustaining, autonomous institutions which are empowered, in response to the market, to offer and advertise different kinds of service. And they will sink or swim depending on the desirability of services offered and of the efficiency of their delivery. To make the market work the schools and the parents have to be treated autonomously. That is, the schools need to be in full control of their affairs (having , for example, almost all money devolved to them) and the parents need to have the right, in the light of the information provided, to select the school — or to transfer allegiance to another school if the one of their choice does not come up to scratch. As the then Conservative Secretary of State said a decade ago:

> Parents know best the needs of their children — certainly better than educational theorists or administrators, better even than our mostly excellent teachers (DfE, 1993, p. 2).

Therefore, the system of education requires no buffer such as Local Authority between the central market regulator, namely, the Government, and the 25,000 providers, namely, the schools. Such providers are maintained, or not, by the choices of well informed 'purchasers', and their standards are improved in the normal commercial way, namely, through competing for allegiance within a framework of choice.

The appropriateness of such a framework is a matter of argument. Certainly there are those who like John Gray (1992) argue for a moral foundation of market institutions, albeit without explicit reference to educational establishments. One such argument is the epistemic one, namely, that there is a logical limit to the amount of knowledge that central planning institutions can know about the intentions and wants and values of the consumer. And those logical limits are due to the vast amount of intelligent but unarticulated or tacit knowledge which people have and which, by definition, cannot be in the hands of central bureaucrats. That tacit knowledge may be about local institutions or it may be about the kinds of things they want and the values they have which they cannot convey to others explicitly. But it is manifested in the choices they make and in the values which they recognise in the institutions they visit. The millions of decisions that people make based on such tacit knowledge must necessarily escape the planner. And, therefore, a system that values the wishes of the consumer, that believes that parents know best, is obliged to devolve that control to the parents.

And yet it is too often forgotten that markets themselves are artefacts. They are created by people and can be so created that they serve the interests of the creator. The rules on which the competition is legitimised are the rules created not within an educational tradition pursuing a liberal ideal but within a training tradition concerned with economic advancement and social differentiation. On this let me make the following points.

In establishing the rules of the new market in education, the views of those who, by profession, guard an educational tradition, are ignored. The 1944 Education Act established a partnership between government, local authorities, the teachers and the churches. In that partnership, the government played a back seat minimalist role, seeing its main duty to be that of ensuring the proper resourcing of the system. Central advisory councils were established with representatives of all interested bodies, particularly the teachers, with the statutory right to be consulted on educational policy. One member, appointed to the Central advisory council in 1947, when she asked what the main duty was of a member of that council, was told by the then Permanent Secretary Sir John Maude 'to die at the first ditch as soon as politicians try to get their hands on education'. There was nothing controversial in such a view. The job of government and politicians was to ensure the framework through which the transaction between teacher and learner might be achieved — not to influence the transaction itself. The government had no privileged position in determining what constituted an educated person.

The political philosophy which determined this limited role of the state reflected a tradition of liberal education which was the inheritance of those who framed the legislation and implemented it. Indeed, these people (especially the civil servants) were themselves the products of a liberal tradition of public service whose essential task was to facilitate, to make possible, rather than to provide. Schools, therefore, were not (and, strictly speaking, still are not) *state* schools; they are church schools or local authority schools, though maintained by the state. However, in abolishing the Central advisory councils, in decimating Her Majesty's Inspectorate as an independent protector of educational standards established over 130 years ago, in getting rid of civil servants who offered impartial advice, in enfeebling the local authorities, and in placing education and curriculum decision-making in the hands of government-appointed quangos, so the ownership of education has changed — away from the guardians of a liberal tradition, and into the control of the government in terms of its substance and mode of delivery, and into the control of parents, the consumers, in terms of the places where it shall be delivered.

Conclusion

In these two lectures, I have outlined two competing traditions of education and training — the liberal and the vocational. In the past, they have not competed for our allegiance because they have related to different sorts of people — a liberal education for a privileged minority and vocational training for the rest. The first Victor Cook lectures — those of Lord Quinton and Professor O'Hear — represented that liberal tradition.

But now those different traditions are in competition, as the development of education and training is increasingly driven by economic need. Above all, we see that liberal ideal being vocationalised as the language of the market transforms our understanding of education — the values that shape the relation between teacher and pupil, the concept of learning, the professionalism of the teacher, and the control and ownership of education. Paradoxically, the appeal to the market has increased the power of the state, as the regulator of that market.

On the other hand, the disdain of that liberal ideal for practical relevance and vocational concern has made it vulnerable to such an encroachment. The question that I asked in my first lecture was not a practical or a political one, namely, 'What might the protectors of that liberal ideal do to stave off the vocational predators?' Rather was it an ethical one concerning the aims of education, namely, 'Ought not education, liberally conceived, also include vocational relevance and preparation?'

Such a question, if pursued, raises further questions about what is worth learning and about the quality of life that learning prepares young people for. Such quality of life cannot ignore the kind of occupation or vocation to be pursued, the practical talents and intelligence acquired, the capability of engaging creatively and imaginatively in the practical world, an awareness of the social and economic context in which one acts and lives, the moral framework of the relationships which one enters into. Vocational preparation in that broader sense must surely be part of a re-examined idea of liberal education. Furthermore, such an idea must have appeal to everyone, not just the privileged possession of the few. Everyone, in his or her different way, and no doubt at different levels, is capable of thinking intelligently and sensitively, of having hopes and aspirations, of entering into relationships, and of having a sense of achievement and of personal worth. Teaching is first and foremost an attempt to achieve that in young people, and to do so through the mediation of a diverse and rich culture that we have inherited. But such a mediation must address those practical questions, concerning the preparation for the future, which are uppermost in the minds of the young, and which are not unrelated to the economic context into which they are entering. In that sense, there is a need to vocationalise the liberal ideal — to question the dualisms between thinking and doing, between theory and practice, between the world of education and the world of work, between education and training, which for too long have impoverished the educational experience of many.

On the other hand, I have, in the lecture, pointed to the dangers of an impoverished tradition of vocational training transforming education into something which is educationally indefensible, importing inappropriate metaphors through which that transaction between teacher and learner is described, is valued, is controlled and is owned.

9

Mary Warnock

The Educational Obligations of the State

Meeting Educational Needs

Most people have come to take it as a matter of course that education should be compulsory for all children, by law. It is also generally agreed that the state must, at least to some extent, finance education not only for those who are bound by law to attend school, but also for those who choose to be educated beyond the age when they are compelled, and that not only post-16, but higher education is inevitably dependent on state funding. These assumptions can be taken to show either that education is a good of which no one ought to be deprived by poverty or the fecklessness of their parents, or that the state itself needs educated members and will finance education in its own interests, rather in the way that it finances defence. In 1859 John Stuart Mill argued that it was a 'moral crime' to allow a child to be uneducated, a crime both against the child itself and against society. He used this, incidentally, as an argument for making education, up to a certain stage, compulsory, but not for the provision of education by the state, which he held to be a 'mere contrivance for moulding people to be exactly like one another'. Whatever we may think of this argument, Mill's view that education is good both for the individual and for the state seems to be now generally accepted. Moreover, those who believe this do not usually feel much need to explain in what this goodness consists. Just as it is manifestly better for an indi-

vidual to be healthy rather than unhealthy, and better also for the
state that its members should enjoy good health, so with education.

It is against the background of such assumptions that the idea of
an educational need arises. The concept of a need is hypothetical. We
need something if something else is to be achieved. Thus it is proper
to talk of needs when there are things that are required either for the
sake of life itself, or for the sake of a decent or satisfactory life. No one
would dispute that people need food, water, clothing and a roof over
their heads; for a need exists wherever, without its satisfaction, a valued end would be unattainable. Since these basic needs are required
for life itself, and we all suppose that life is to be valued, there is no
disputing about such needs. But education does not fall into this category: no one will die for lack of it. It is only that their lives will be
less than satisfactory. And here at once we enter the realm of values
that can be the subject of debate. If the state regards education at
least partly as a good of which no one should be deprived, something which constitutes a need, the state must have a view about
what makes a satisfactory life which could not be attained without
education. Thus a child will need to be taught to read if it is the case
that a life of illiteracy is thought to be unsatisfactory. To say that this
is so is to say that literacy is highly valued. Now to hold that literacy
is highly valued as a component of a satisfactory life for individuals
is not incompatible with holding that the state itself is better off if
most of its members can read. But it is the individualist rather than
the corporate view of the matter which generates the concept of an
educational need, a need, that is, which must be satisfied for the sake
of the individual himself.

The satisfaction by the state of individual needs is the aim of the
so-called welfare state. Although any democratic state might be supposed to be concerned with the welfare or well-being of its members,
the term 'welfare state' has traditionally been used for one in which
some, fairly limited, measures are supposed to ensure that certain
needs are met. These measures include financial hand-outs in the
form of pensions, children's allowances, unemployment benefit and
other benefits directed towards the meeting of specific needs. The
measures also include the provision of services, such as the health
service and education, designed to meet other manifest needs. In
such a state, government, or the civil service, determine what the
needs are which must be satisfied if 'welfare' is to be ensured. It is
not necessary that the beneficiary himself should see the point of
what he is given. Someone else has decided that he has a need and

goes about to meet it. The welfare state is thus intrinsically and necessarily paternalistic, and this is the charge most often brought
against it. The other charge is that it is inevitable that the welfare
state, any welfare state, should sooner or later run out of money. As
the standard of living increases in the population at large, so what
counts as a need will change. Moreover the meeting of needs literally
creates its own demands. The health service ensures that people live
longer, and thus, each individually, have ever greater needs; similarly the education service creates its own demand for more, better
and longer-lasting education for the individuals who benefit from it.
That all this was to a certain extent foreseen in the 1940s makes it no
easier to keep up with the demands. Historically, the result was that
by the 1980s, at the height of the conservative domination of politics
in this country, the welfare state, (the nanny state as it was often
called) fell increasingly into disrepute. I shall argue that, for all its
hazards, we must not forget the concepts that lay at the heart of
welfarism, and in particular we must try to retain the idea of meeting
educational needs as a positive obligation on the state.

The first step in this argument must be to examine the notion of
paternalism, the first of the accusations brought against welfarism.
There is an important sense in which all education is paternalistic.
Certainly in the sense in which Lord Quinton, in the first of the Victor
Cook lectures, spoke of education as having the task of handing
down 'High Culture', the element of paternalism is ineradicable. For
the concept of high culture entails the thought that someone other
than the person to whom it is to be handed down shall determine, or
have a part in determining, what is to count as worthy of that
description; and not just any other person, but some person himself
brought up to love and respect the culture. I shall return to this
theme in my second lecture. And I entirely agree with Lord Quinton
that if this traditionalist element in the notion of education were to
be lost then a large part of the value that we attach to education
would be lost with it. The canon, in some form or other, is crucial to
the idea of education; and so one among educational needs is the
need that individual children have to be introduced to this canon,
the encapsulation of the culture within which they live.

The objection to paternalism is that it is an illegitimate denial of
human freedom, the imposition from outside of rules or standards
which ought to come from within. The traditionalist argument,
indeed I would say the educationalist argument, is that, on the contrary, such standards cannot come from within unless they have, in

the first place, been introduced extrinsically, from without; and this has always been the role of parents, or of those temporarily *in loco parentis*. Of course children rebel against their parents; and young persons being educated rebel against those whom they regard as unduly authoritarian with regard to what must be learned. This is why J.S. Mill's essay, *On Liberty*, to which I have already referred, is such an immediately and properly popular text among students. The doctrine that no one should have the right to tell another what he ought to do, even for his own good, is a doctrine with instant appeal to those still under subjection to their parents and teachers. It has to be remembered, however, that Mill was speaking of adults, not children or students. Moreover it is more than likely that, at the forefront of his mind at the particular time when he wrote the essay, was the condition of women, adult persons, yet still, at that time, denied their freedom, and above all denied the right to make up their own minds, form their own tastes, control their own property and, if necessary, go to hell their own way. With this special case in mind, it is not surprising that his voice became unusually shrill and his argument a bit exaggerated.

Educational issues apart, paternalism is to some extent a necessary correlate of government. It is the duty of government to make decisions of public policy, such as, in the nature of the case, cannot be made by individuals one by one, and each for himself. The law itself is paternalistic; and so is government when it decides how much is to be spent on health, housing, transport, environmental protection or any other public service. There is a good deal of dishonesty, therefore, in the Thatcherite gibe that the welfare state had become 'Nanny'. What is supposed to be objectionable about nannies is both that they claim to know best, and that they stunt the aspirations of their charges to freedom and maturity, keeping them wrongly attached to everlasting apron-strings. But the state, in making decisions of public policy or public expenditure, is fulfilling a function which individuals cannot fulfil: it is not inhibiting their freedom, nor treating them as less than competent to do things they are perfectly capable of doing for themselves.

But of course it makes all the difference how the decisions of the state are arrived at; and this is so obvious that it should not be necessary to say it. Yet one of the most notable features of recent government thinking has been its forgetfulness of democracy, especially democracy at the local level, where most people notice it. If nanny makes her decisions quite arbitrarily, if there is no way that she can know what her charges think of her plans, above all if she doesn't care what they think, then nanny is a tyrant, due to be sacked. In a democratic state, public policy goals are not set arbitrarily. They are set not only with a view to the common good, but also in the awareness that without some kind of underlying consensus about what is an acceptable goal, government cannot continue. It is this reliance on consensus, however inarticulate, which mitigates the inevitable paternalism of government. This consensus, which can be referred to loosely as a moral consensus, is instrumental in determining what, in any specific area, is to count as a need.

The necessity of determining what is to count as a need to be met has obvious relevance to the second charge usually brought against the welfare state, that it will never be able to fulfil the obligations it has taken on, because of the inevitable growth in demand. There is no absolute once-and-for-all rebuttal of this charge; nor could there ever be a theoretical answer, which would enable a government to say that so much and no more was the correct amount to spend on services, so much and no more the amount to raise by taxation or by individual contributions to welfare hand-outs. The whole business of meeting needs will always, and necessarily, be subject to financial restraint, and doubtless also to periods of especial retrenchment and, on the other hand, of relative liberality. But no government department will ever be able to persuade the Treasury to allow it all the money it could usefully spend. The business of ministers is to argue for money where they see genuine need, to try to keep a balance and to exercise judgment, Alas, there is no way out; and that there will always be competing claims on the exchequer to be pressed, more or less successfully, by individual ministers does not provide an argument against adopting as an ideal the meeting of people's needs.

It is easy, in any discussion of welfarism, to be over-impressed or indeed overwhelmed by the difficulties of establishing what is to count as a need which must be met. I have already said that it is essential to the notion of a need that it is relative to a hypothetical goal; and those who argue that it is an inherently shifting, ever-expanding, subjectively determined concept make much of this fact. I would undoubtedly need a very large number of piano lessons if I were to hope to become a respectable pianist. If my son were to aim to become a country gentleman, he would need an enormous income. But such goals as these, though they can be seen certainly to generate related needs, are essentially egocentric and personal.

There are, on the other hand, goals that are general, common to everyone and pretty readily agreed. It is needs related to such goals as these that it should be the purpose of the state to satisfy. A need in this sense is very different from a mere wish or aspiration. For a need, unlike a wish, may not be immediately recognized by the person whose need it is. As I have argued, what counts as a need may be settled externally, without reference to any individual's actual desires. All humans have some needs in common, and can be brought to recognize them, both for themselves and others. Of course things are not as simple as I suggest. There will be some cases where it will be difficult to decide whether there is an actual need or not. In the educational climate of the 1960s, for example, when the prevalent metaphors of education were to do with flourishing and growth, and the cliché concept that of fulfilment of potential, an educational need was flexibly interpreted. If a child showed marked musical talent, then he needed instrumental lessons, and these would be provided. At other times needs would mean something more basic. But again, that there may be difficult decisions to be made should not blind us to the fact that in some cases the need will be manifest and agreed. That I cannot draw a line with certainty does not entail that there is no line to be drawn; nor does the continued existence of dubious cases entail that there are no clear cases. When we think of educational needs, it will be as well to concentrate on these clear cases.

It must be the purpose of any democratic government to aim for the common good, the well-being or welfare of the country as a whole. But this might not necessarily entail any strong commitment to equality of provision. What has come to be designated the welfare state had such a commitment built into the ideal of meeting people's needs. The National Health Service, for example, aimed to give equally good health care to everyone. Paying for private medicine could doubtless give one greater choice; but the actual quality of the service was to be no better for those who paid than for those who did not. This was the particular glory of the ideal. In education, the ideal was certainly to meet the needs of everyone who could benefit from education. But, in the 1940s, it was held both that children would benefit from different kinds of education, provided in different kinds of schools, and that there were some children so intellectually disabled that they could not benefit from education at all. These children fell outside the scope of the various education Acts, and were the responsibility of medical and social services only. It was not until the early 1970s that all children came to be entitled by law to *education*, in addition to other kinds of services. It was at this stage, then, that the state took on the responsibility of educating everyone. This duty was taken on because it had become clear that, even for the most severely disabled, education was not only possible, but it was the greatest possible good that they could have; that is to say, it made more difference to a severely disabled child whether he was educated or not even than to other children. And since this was so there was a moral obligation to provide the education the child needed. I emphasize the perceived moral nature of this obligation because unless there had been such a moral commitment the law would not have been changed so as to include all children within the scope of educational provision. Moral philosophers sometimes argue that 'ought implies can', that is, that you can have no moral obligation to do something that is impossible. I believe this to be a dubious axiom. But however that may be, there often exists a hidden argument that 'can implies ought', and this argument is especially powerful if conjoined with an argument based on justice or fairness. If the severely disabled *can* be educated, then education *ought* to become their right as much as anyone else's, at whatever cost. This was the moral principle that lay behind the inclusion of all children under the responsibility of the then DES. It was also the principle on which the 1981 Education Act on the education of the handicapped rested. Unsurprisingly, it was in this Act that the concept of meeting educational needs first became explicit, as the policy of Government.

It is perhaps worth looking back to consider how this policy was explained and justified at the time. In the report of the government committee of inquiry that led up to the legislation of 1981, it was plainly stated at the beginning that education was a benefit to which all children were now entitled by law; and it was a benefit that the State could therefore not withhold from any child. It was presumed, indeed positively asserted, that education was an instrumental good, beneficial in so far as it led to a life after education was over which was better, in various specifiable ways, than it would have been if education had not been provided. Thus an educated child, as he grew to be an adult, would become competent, and possess a reasonable understanding of the world, able both to look back on the past and forward into the future with imagination. His competence would show itself in his freedom, that is his ability to make choices for himself and ultimately to lead an independent life, usefully employed. Now it is plain that these are high ideals, and that education alone cannot secure them for anyone. Nevertheless, no one can progress far along the road towards their realization without good education. It was crucial to the thinking of the committee of inquiry that the goals of education should be shown to be the same, whatever the abilities or disabilities of the pupil. In the first half of the century, if children with disabilities were educated at all, they tended to be educated in special schools, with aims and curricular goals entirely different from those in ordinary schools.

On the whole the targets set for such children were modest and, after the age of sixteen, if not before, the word 'training' tended to be used, not education. As I have already said, the concept of the 'ineducable' was used to embrace children with the most severe disabilities. The conceptual change or rather revolution embodied in the report of the committee of inquiry, though not necessarily making a great immediate difference to the kind of education provided, was nevertheless extremely significant. For once it was recognized that it was possible to set common aims for all education, then it was according to the criteria implied in those aims that educational needs could be determined, for all children. Thus if a child was to become competent and self-reliant, he must be taught the skills, linguistic, mathematical and technical, demanded by life in the modern world; if he was to aim to understand the world he lived in with imaginative grasp, he must have some knowledge of history and of the concepts and methods of science. The needs children had would dictate the school curriculum; and one would envisage this common curriculum as a path along which all children were supposed to progress. But it is obvious that children's abilities differ dramatically: for some the school curriculum is never going to present many problems, and their passage through it, along the common path, will be easy. For others the obstacles on the way are extreme and, if they are to make any progress, they need help gradually to overcome the obstacles. These children then have special needs, over and above the needs that all children have if they are to come near the attainment of the educational goals. This was the idea of Special Educational Needs that found its way into the 1981 Education Act and reappeared in the 1993 Act. A child with a special need is defined as a child who has a need which a school could not be expected to meet without extra resources, or which could not be met at all in an ordinary school without undue expense, or damage to other pupils.

I have gone into this example at some length, because it shows how ready the Government was in 1981 apparently to embrace the view that its duty, as far as education was concerned, was to satisfy needs, identified against the assumption of the benefit that education would be to the child himself. In seeming to accept this duty, Government, through legislation, also accepted that the scope of what had hitherto been known as 'special education' was much broadened. Instead of being that which was provided, usually in 'special schools', for about 2% of the school population, it was to be that which was provided to meet an extra need, temporary or permanent, and experienced by any child at whatever kind of school he might be. The number of children having such a need at any one time was thought to be about 20% of the school population. Most of these children were of course in ordinary classrooms in ordinary schools; and the bulk of special provision to meet special needs was to be in ordinary schools.

However, in spite of the apparent acceptance, perhaps even the first clear enunciation of the doctrine of educational needs in the 1981 Act, there was no money set aside to meet these needs, and the Act itself contained cautions. Individual children's needs would be met if this was deemed economically feasible. By itself this caution might have been a matter of mere prudence: no one who preached the gospel of meeting needs thought that money was limitless. But meanwhile the Government had already embarked on a quite different policy, strictly incompatible with the policy of meeting needs. The early eighties were the years of the first genuine and severely felt cuts in the education service and, four years before, in 1977, a Labour Government had initiated a different way of looking at education which was destined to be taken over by the Conservatives, and played for all it was worth. It is still, fundamentally, the policy that is followed today, and was embodied in the 1993 Education Act, in which, although the 1981 Act is invoked, and the definition of an educational need repeated from that Act, in fact the very concept of an educational need is out of place.

1977 was the year of the Great Debate, set up by the then Prime Minister, James Callaghan, as a result of a speech he made at Ruskin College, Oxford, in October 1976. The debate was on the educational curriculum and it reflected a general and growing belief, shared by industry and the public at large, that the whole educational system was failing. Children were leaving school in large numbers knowing few, if any, of the things they needed to know, and society, equally, was being deprived of people competent to carry out the work that needed to be done. The regional debates on the curriculum in schools were open to parents and indeed to anyone who wanted to attend. The idea of the Debate was bitterly opposed by the teachers' unions, who foresaw an unprecedented intervention by government in the preserve of the curriculum and how it should be taught. Max Morris of the TUC executive described the debate as a 'shoddy public relations gimmick' intended to divert attention from the cuts in educational spending that were already foreshadowed. For ever since the end of the 1960s, when Britain's affluence began to decline, governments had been obliged to go back on their commitment to expand educational services and to meet all educational needs, regardless of cost. And so, from 1977, the focus of education began to shift from the pupil and the classroom to the outside world. What did society, and especially the wealth-generating parts of society, want schools to teach? What would it benefit society that pupils should learn? It was assumed that parents would, in answering these questions, side with 'society', and especially with industry; for it was assumed that parents would want for their children, above everything else, that they should be employed after school, and should be capable of working, if they were ambitious, to rise to the top.

Such supposedly vocational demands on the education service caused a great deal of distress and outrage to liberal educationalists and probably to some, though not many, teachers. The arguments of this time tended to dichotomies: vocational education was opposed to 'true' education, and pupils' needs were opposed to the needs of society. Of course, in fact, such polarities are unrealistic and damaging. I have already suggested that the goals of education at school must lie outside school, and that education must be directed towards what is to come afterwards. If the aim of the system is to make children as far as possible independent when they leave school, or finish higher and further education, then this entails that they must be competent to work, including to work in industry. Independence demands no less. So it is essential to regard the educational needs of children and the needs of society as interlocking concepts; most of what people need to learn at school is dependent on what other people require that they should know. But at the time, and in the heat of a battle that had not been foreseen, it was difficult to remember these simple truths.

The battle was violent because the Great Debate itself had arisen out of a negative and critical attitude towards what was going on at school. It was not to be wondered at that teachers and Local Education Authorities should become defensive. The next ten or eleven years were characterized by an ever increasing hostility between government and both the teaching profession itself, and those who employed teachers at a local level (and we should not forget this bit of history, when we may be inclined to lay all the blame on Conservative governments: it all started when Shirley Williams was Secretary of State, though it must be said that she herself had little enthusiasm for the Great Debate). At last, in 1988, there was legislation: what was grandly named the Great Educational Reform Bill, commonly known as Gerbil. This Bill was enacted late in the year, and was followed, in 1992 and 1993 by two more Education Acts, one relating to Higher Education, the other to education at school, and especially to the method of funding it (further Acts were passed in 1996, 1998, 2002 and 2004).

Since the 1988 Act was specifically supposed to reform the system, it ought to be easy to discover in it the principles on which educational policy was now to be founded, and the values which were, from now on, to be incorporated into the educational system. However, it is in this respect that the essentially negative attitude towards teachers and schools, inherited, as I have suggested, from the days of the Great Debate, turns out to be most damaging. The inspiration of the Act is a determination to stop the rot, and to inhibit those supposed to have caused it from doing further damage. In direct line from the thinking of the Great Debate, the crucial first step in rot-stopping was to introduce a National Curriculum, adherence to which would, it was hoped, ensure that pupils would know, when they left school, that which society, and especially industrial society, wished them to know. In itself, the introduction of a national curriculum, to be followed by all children at school, is an excellent move, (however much J.S. Mill would have deplored its uniformity). The existence of such a curriculum could well be interpreted as part of a policy to meet the educational needs of all children. For, as I have already argued, there is no incompatibility between the needs of society and the needs of pupils who are, or will be, members of that society. Moreover the existence of a national curriculum, to be accessible to all, might well be thought to be the outcome of a moral commitment to genuine equality. There should be no child, whatever his circumstances, and whatever school he attended, who should be deprived of the possibility of progressing along the common educational path of which I have already spoken. I believe that this was at least part of the thought lying behind the introduction of the national curriculum, or at least its introduction was so interpreted by numbers of teachers and other educationalists. However, because of the deep hostility and mistrust of schools, teachers and Local Education Authorities to which I have already referred, along with the new curriculum there was introduced a system of compulsory testing, with the publication of results, so that there should be a quick method of distinguishing teachers and schools that succeeded from those that failed. Obviously almost no one who has ever taught would object to tests, or examinations from time to time, to find out how well pupils were getting on along their educational path. It was the nature of the particular tests proposed, their publicity and the fact that they were to be used to compare one school with another (or one teacher with another) that revealed a quite different principle underlying the Act from that of equalizing provision. The principle was that society, and in this case especially parents, must be allowed to judge among schools, which were good and which were bad and choose between them.

This was the second, and less direct, outcome of the Great Debate. That debate had been open. It was suddenly proclaimed as a matter of principle that people other than educationalists, that is to say politicians, industrialists and the man in the street, had the right to determine what education ought to be like. And so increasingly, from the late 1970s, parents became the people supposed to wield power in the school world. Parents had duties as governors of schools; and when schools began to become financially independent of their local authorities, to the extent of being given a budget and funds which they had to handle themselves, it was increasingly parents who made financial and therefore even educational decisions that affected the schools their children attended. The publication of test results was the next step: parents were to be enabled to decide between good schools and bad, to seek out the good and avoid the bad. The principle of parental choice was added to that of parental knowledge and responsibility.

The final step was to allow parents, by a ballot, to decide to take schools out of local authority control altogether, so as to transform the schools into free-standing self-governing institutions, funded by a centrally appointed council, set up specifically to distribute resources direct from government to this new kind of schools. What might happen in such schools, provided only that the National Curriculum is followed, becomes a matter for the governing body of the school. The details of the scheme, so far as they were worked out, were set out in the 1993 Conservative legislation. So what had happened to the educational policy that seemed to be discernible behind the Education Reform Act? The intention of the National Curriculum, to raise educational standards, and raise them for everyone, was still there. But it had slipped from the first to, perhaps, the third place in the list of priorities. Joint first came the principle of parental choice, and that of the removal of control from local authority hands. The introduction of the National Curriculum, in the Education Reform Act, could have had the effect of strengthening what had long been the guiding principle of British education, that it should be a national system, locally administered. It could, by itself, have made the policy of meeting children's educational needs both more uniform and more efficient. For the national curriculum could have defined more clearly than ever before the common goals of education and made the assessment of pupils' needs more accurate and more useful, with the help of nationally-accepted criteria. The Local Education Authority, which has always been in a position to know its own schools, could have distributed funds for schools to administer, bearing in mind the special needs which children in particular schools might have, if they were to have proper access to the common curriculum. For local authorities, in collaboration with their schools, and also their health and social services departments, were uniquely well-placed to understand where educational needs arose, not only out of specific disabilities, but out of different kinds of deprivation. They could at any rate partially target funds to, for example, nursery classes in geographical areas where early education could prevent much greater educational obstacles arising later in a child's career, obstacles that might then be expensive or even impossible to overcome. Whatever the origin of a child's special educational need, it has been found that local management is by far the most effective way of ensuring that the need is, as far as possible met. It is local management and local policy that has now been sacrificed to the ideal of parental choice, and the right to schools, one by one, to choose freedom.

The concept of freedom from the yoke of local management was a recurring theme in the government's defence of the 1993 Bill, in its passage through Parliament. And of course it is true that local authorities, having become increasingly short of money, not always through their own mismanagement, have often seemed mean and tyrannical to the institutions that fell under their rule. As there is often extra capital for building or refurbishing to be given out by government when a school votes to become grant maintained, the temptation to try out the new system was great, and in some areas, such as Kent, half the secondary schools left the local authority, while in the London borough of Hillingdon nearly all the secondary schools became grant-maintained. What happened, then, was a fragmentation of the education system. Each individual school is on its own, (though schools are permitted to form themselves into consortia for certain purposes). It is parents, in theory at least, who have chosen to be free; it must therefore be parents who go on to determine the policy each school shall adopt. As far as government policy was concerned, educational values are safeguarded by the National Curriculum. Other values are for schools to adopt, each for itself, subject only to the monitoring of performance by teams of (non-government) inspectors. (Reviewing the situation ten years after the enactment of the 1993 Bill , and under a different administration, the relation between schools and English local education authorities is no nearer to being settled.)

The central principle of educational policy, then, seems to be the principle of freedom, within a framework of measurable educational standards. This emerges as the way to achieve what society requires of education. It is the least paternalistic principle that can be imagined, except that the National Curriculum itself was laid down, and enforced, by the Nanny who knows best. Yet, paradoxically, in Part III of the 1993 Act, the 1981 Education Act raises its head, that which was devoted primarily to the duty of government to meet children's educational needs and, in particular, those extraordinary needs known as Special Needs. The 1981 Act was, as I have suggested, ideologically out of date before it became law. It looked to what individuals gained from education, rather than what society required. It inevitably had the stamp of Welfarism upon it; for in the case of the most severely disabled, society would never get what *it* wanted out of the money spent on education. There will always be people, who, though benefiting vastly from education, will never live an independent life, and will never work in industry. It cannot even be plausibly argued that the further along the educational path such severely disabled people travel, the less expensive they will be for society to support. For, at worst, in the old days, such people, as was often said, were treated as 'vegetables', who could be looked after relatively cheaply in hospitals. The more we recognize the rights of this group to a proper life; the more we discover that they can learn and enjoy through education, the less we can relegate them to sub-human conditions. But our recognition of their rights cannot come cheap. There can be no motive for the meeting of the educational needs of this group except the compassionate motive of doing for them, through the state, what a parent would do for his child.

Paternalism is a necessary concomitant of the right of everyone to education, not just the children of the pushy and the ambitious, nor even only of those children likely to succeed in the terms recognized by an industrial society. It is not enough to speak, as has been the habit since Thatcherism was born, of a safety net, to catch those who cannot help themselves. For the metaphor of the safety net strongly suggests that those who fall so far are rescued out of charity, but will not thereafter get the best treatment. In the Health Service, the safety net used to be the panel, for patients too poor to afford private medicine; and no one even pretended that panel patients got the best of contemporary medical treatment. Now it cannot be supposed that individual schools, or individual parents, could possibly embrace such paternalistic values as are implied in the meeting of needs. Nor, if they did, would they be able to finance their being put into practice. Unless government is to shoulder the burden of a paternalistic education system, we shall be back as we were in the 1940s, when the only source from which funds would be forthcoming for the education of the handicapped would be funds (and human resources) from charities and from the churches. I cannot think that we want, as a society, to go back to such total reliance on charity, however highly we rate such contributions. It is therefore, in my view, necessary for the government to recognize that, as part of its educational policy, there must be a moral commitment built in. The values embodied in public educational policy must include the value of helping everyone along the educational path they are entitled by law to embark on. To say this does not entail a naive belief in limitless resources: it does however entail a belief that moral obligation should be weighed in the balance, along with other more apparently hard-nosed considerations; and that there should be an attempt to build up once again a trust in local authorities who can most realistically carry out the common moral imperatives.

10

Mary Warnock

Good Teaching

In my first lecture, I argued that in any state within which education is a legal entitlement for all children (and which is compulsory for all children up to the age of sixteen) educational policy must be to a large extent paternalist. It must be directed towards supplying something deemed by the state to be good for all those who are to submit to it, whether they like it or not. I argued that, with a view to providing this good, the state must determine what children need, educationally, if they are to move in the direction of the desired goal. Once these needs have been ascertained, it is the duty of the state to satisfy them, as far as it is possible to do so. The priority, in the distribution of limited funding, should be to meet the needs of all children, leaving none of them out. This, I suggested, was the moral imperative which should lie at the heart of educational policy and which should not be lost sight of.

Now education manifestly does not simply occur; does not even occur inevitably if children attend school. To satisfy their educational needs, children must be taught; and it is to the role of their teachers that I want to turn, in this second lecture.

Individual schools cannot be responsible for overall educational policy (and this is recognised at least insofar as concerns the curriculum to be followed at school, now laid down at national level) and so they should not be asked by themselves to be responsible for the nature of the training which teachers must have if they are to be accredited as fit to carry out that policy. However they have a crucial role in the training of teachers and a role which is increasingly recognised.

One part of the duty of the state must be to ensure that a proper number of well-qualified teachers exists. In the past, the responsibility of government, through civil servants, was more or less confined to the attempt to get the numbers right; and in fact far more often than not they got them wrong. The content of training was left to universities and colleges of higher education. But since the introduction of the National Curriculum and an avowed governmental policy of raising the standard of school education, it is only reasonable that government should recognise some responsibility for the actual content of teacher-training. Often this recognition of responsibility has been largely confined to complaints about the quality of teachers, and especially the supposed ideology of their training. However, beginning under the Conservative administration in the 1990s there have been new and important moves to shift the main burden of training to the schools themselves. Initially two hundred schools were involved, experimentally, in school based training, where all the training was conducted in school, and there was no necessary link between the trainees and any institution of higher education, though the training school was able to seek advice from such institutions if it wished. In 1994, under the Education Bill of that year, it was proposed that such a method of training should be enshrined in law, as one possible option. Schools could form themselves into consortia for training purposes, or could act on their own, and could devise their own training curriculum without reference to any university or college. The funding of all training, school-based or conventional, was handed over to a new body, the Teacher Training Authority, itself quite separate from the Funding Council which distributes resources to Higher and Further education. This Authority would decide whether the courses are adequate, and would validate the qualification of the successful trainees (a situation which, notwithstanding a change of government, obtains today).

It is important to distinguish between so-called school-based training and school-centred training. For a number of years there have been increasing numbers of university education departments, and some colleges of education, that have worked in close partnership with schools, and where trainee teachers have spent far more time in school than at the institution of higher education to which they were attached. In my view this has been an excellent tendency, enabling the trainees to have the opportunity constantly to put the theory and principles they are learning to the test in the classroom. They have had far more contact with practising teachers who in turn have taken more responsibility for helping them as tutors or mentors. There are various versions of this kind of partnership, and its results, as far as I know, have been wholly beneficial. Even though school-centred courses have now become universal it remains to be determined what the best form of that partnership may be. Some schools entered agreements with universities, but were then obliged to pull out, because of the amount of time and extra work that the scheme they had entered was demanding of the teaching staff, or because they were not getting paid enough for the students they took to enable them to give the tutor–teachers the time to attend to these duties, by appointing replacement staff. There is no doubt that these problems could have been settled in time. And the mixture of knowledge (of such subjects as child development, or the psychology of learning) with practical experience has been found to be the best way to train professionals of all kinds, not just teachers, but doctors, nurses and lawyers as well.

The connexion of such professional training with higher education should, in my view be preserved as essential. There are elements of expertise, such as those I mentioned just now, which a student must acquire in general terms, not to be picked up by working in one or two class-rooms. A student–teacher must learn, among other things what a vast range of ability there is among children of the same age, something which it is unlikely he could learn in just one school. In any case, it is not and cannot be the task of teachers in schools to teach students the general principles that lie behind teaching. To bring such principles to bear and apply them in a particular situation is a different thing from abstracting them and subjecting them to analysis and criticism. This aspect of professional training cannot be omitted, and must rest with university departments or the equivalent. A nurse who was trained only in the wards would no longer be regarded as fully professional. So it must be with teachers.

It is difficult to avoid the conclusion that exclusively school-based training will in the long run be damaging to good teaching. It is as if the orthodoxy of government, that university departments of education and training colleges are ideologically dangerous (an orthodoxy based on recollections of the 1960s and 70s) created a desire to cut out such departments altogether. Although in other contexts the schools themselves, and the teachers in them, had been held to be highly suspect, incompetent and left-wing, they were then asked to take on the task of training their own successors, presumably because the university education departments were thought even worse. Those who opposed the 1994 legislation were told that very few schools would choose to become training establishments. But if the principle is wrong, that there might be few instances of its being put into practice is hardly relevant. In any case it was also alleged by government ministers that students would greatly prefer this option; and this might well be so: theory and the grasping of general principles is boring and many students would be glad of the chance to cut all that out and begin real teaching a year earlier than if they took a regular postgraduate certificate. Their views, at this stage of their education, should not be taken as conclusive.

In whatever way the training of teachers is carried out in future, one thing is certain. We need to find a set of criteria by which to distinguish good teachers from bad, competent from incompetent. A government committed to improving educational standards for all children, as I have argued it should be, must have an idea of what good teaching is. The publishing of examination results, the league–tables of truancy, and all the rest of the data by which parents are supposed to be able to decide which school is good, which bad, will give only the roughest notion of whether the teaching in these schools is actually good or not. It is therefore worth considering what actually constitutes good teaching, what the status of teachers should be, and how they are to be enabled to teach well rather than badly. These are the questions I want now to address.

However, I must first say a bit more about the short period in the history of education when teaching, not teachers nor even their training, but the very concept itself, was suspect. This period is, thankfully, now part of history; but it has had its effects on public, and especially governmental attitudes. It formed the ideology so much feared and disliked by government, and which appeared to dominate education departments in universities, and to which I have already referred. In the late 1960s there grew up, as part of the turmoil in American and French universities (and universities in the UK, to a lesser extent), an obsession with equality in the school classroom, as well as in the university lecture hall and seminar room. There was to be no hierarchy and no authority. The teacher was not to impose his version of knowledge on his class. Thus the idea of learning became more important than that of teaching. A kind of democratisation of the classroom, based on the ideas of the American educationalist and philosopher, John Dewey, became the vogue. Teachers were to be redefined as enablers, allowing learning–experience to occur for those in their charge. All knowledge had to be discovered by the students themselves and, if the teacher already had this knowledge, he must conceal the fact, and certainly not pass the knowledge on. The very concept of knowledge changed and became fragmented. There was not common knowledge; there was your knowledge and my knowledge. (Such views are still in fashion in, for example, feminist circles, where there is much talk of 'male knowledge' as opposed to 'women's knowledge', a part of the relativism against which Lord Quinton argued in his first lecture in this series). In schools, these theories were not confined to methods of managing the classroom: since it was thought to be artificial to get students to discover knowledge in fields in which they were not interested, the content of what they were to discover had to be changed so as to seem 'relevant'. The old distinctions between one subject and another were seen to be themselves hierarchical, based on a preference for abstraction and specialisation, arcane secrets of a self–perpetuating priesthood such as teachers had been, it was said, in the past. So both traditional methods of teaching and the traditional content of the curriculum were to be thrown out. (An influential book in this movement was Michael Young's *Knowledge and Control*, published in 1971. But there were many lesser texts, some of them forming parts of Open University education courses.) The Great Debate, about which I spoke in my first lecture, was partly the outcome of growing dissatisfaction with this kind of ideology; and since the Debate, in the late 1970s, its power began to wither away. It must be said that the democratisation, or pupil–centred movement was not all barmy: there were doubtless aspects of old–fashioned education that benefited from so thorough a blast of fresh air. As usual, the issues became unduly polarised. Ideology often prevailed over common sense and experience. At any rate, what was left behind was a strong suspicion that teachers, and still more university education theorists (those who were responsible for the content of teacher–training courses) were anti–authority, hostile to tradition, and uninterested in teaching children the so–called 'basics', those skills that would enable them to be useful members of society. This suspicion, as I shall argue, is perhaps the greatest obstacle that good teaching has to overcome, immediately and in the foreseeable future.

To return to the question how we are to judge good (or bad) teaching: there is no doubt that this question is urgent at the present time, especially given the powers that the Secretary of State has newly acquired to take over schools which are 'failing', or to close them.

For this means that schools, as institutions, are to be judged by the quality of the teaching they provide; and the knowledge that this is so leads institutions to try to set up safeguards against bad teaching, and to put in place formal mechanisms to ensure that teaching is good. How far can such measures be successful?

There is not yet a large body of research concerned with the difference it makes to an institution if teaching is put at the top of the list of its priorities, though I suspect that in future we shall see an increasing number of such studies. However, as far as schools are concerned, Michael Rutter's study of some comprehensive schools in London, though more than thirty years old, is still highly informative (Rutter *et al*, 1970). The schools that came out best from this study, providing satisfaction to both students and parents, showing the highest proportion of leavers in employment and the fewest hours of training, were schools where teaching was thought of as a team activity. This does not necessarily mean 'co-teaching', that is having more than one teacher in any one class, though this may very well be part of the pattern, especially where a number of pupils in the class have been identified as having special educational needs. Essentially it entails that members of the teaching staff feel free to consult each other, to go into each other's lessons in certain circumstances, to discuss problems regularly. Senior teachers have a particular responsibility for new members of staff. Above all there is a consistent and well articulated policy within the school (what is now called a 'whole school policy') with regard to such issues as discipline, special needs, homework, the marking and return of work to students, communication with parents and other matters. The ethos of the good school is positive and hopeful. Pupils are praised whenever possible and there is no violence, physical or verbal, against the pupils.

What is revealing in this study is the crucial importance to an institution of its overall agreed attitude to pupils, an attitude both of hope and charity, based on a desire to do the best possible for them in terms of what will happen to them after school. A commitment to the life–chances of pupils is a mark of a good institution. The other indispensable ingredient is consistency of policy and open discussion among the staff of what this policy should be. Finally there needs to be confidence and mutual respect sufficient to enable members of staff to ask one another for help, advice and support. I believe that this last is crucial, but will involve a major change in attitude in some schools. Only skilful and determined leadership will bring it about.

It is relatively easy to set up 'mechanisms' for consultation between different levels within an educational institution. These mechanisms may take the form of faculty or departmental meetings or regular meetings between heads and heads of department, or between governors and members of staff. But such mechanisms may easily become formalised or ritualised, producing, mechanically, reports that are not acted on, leaving attitudes unchanged. It is only an openness of communications based on a mixture of the formal with the informal that will work. Informal communications within an institution, though often helpful, are dangerous, in that they can degenerate into gossip and can always leave some people outside the circle of talk or memoranda. It is therefore of the utmost importance that the channels of formal communication should be in place and be used as a means of disseminating bright ideas that may have started life in a less formal way, as well as being the forum in which established policy is discussed.

There is another way in which institutions must be prepared to show themselves devoted to the ideal of good teaching as a top priority, and that is by listening to, and talking to those sometimes depressingly designated 'consumers'. These are pupils, former pupils, parents, and those who will receive the students at the next stage of their career, whether employers or those engaged in further and higher education. It is difficult and expensive to set up regular lines of communication with all these groups. But the use of questionnaires and the occasional seminar, discussion group or conference within which what pupils have learned, and how they have learned, or failed to learn it can be responsibly discussed would, I believe, be extremely productive. They might do more than demonstrate a willingness to talk about teaching: they might actually produce some concrete suggestions for improvement which the institution could use. Seeking finance for such consultations would be an important concern for school governors and one where industrial or commercial sponsorship might reasonably be expected.

Yet it remains true that, however much an institution may do to ensure good teaching, it is individual teachers who are educated and trained to teach well. Teaching is, and will always be, in part at least, a transaction between individuals. Though there are institutional values, these are necessarily both derived from and sustained by the imagination, knowledge and professional conscience of individuals. While recognizing that to consider a teacher apart from the institutional environment in which he works is to some degree an abstraction and, while acknowledging that it is easier to teach well in an institution which values and supports good teaching, I want now to consider what a good teacher is as an individual.

Most of us have an image of a good teacher, drawn usually from experience. The most important thing that such remembered teachers have in common is their ability to hold the attention, and a kind of manifest hopefulness that their pupils will be able to understand the new fact or practice to which they are being introduced. In principle it might seem that a good teacher will not necessarily teach what is good. Just as a skilled doctor, as Plato argued, could equally be a skilled poisoner, so it might be thought that a skilled teacher could teach anything, for good or ill. Up to a point this may be true. Yet the content of the curriculum is of fundamental importance to a teacher. He will be unable to perform well unless he believes in the purpose of what he is teaching. He must not only know what the point is supposed to be but he must 'internalise' the aims and work towards them with enthusiasm. The fear that this might no longer be possible when the National Curriculum was imposed on schools from outside was what led to an initial hostility to the idea. But in fact there is a considerable consensus about what the outlines of such a curriculum should be and it is now generally seen to be in the interests of the pupils, and to have an internal coherence of its own. It is the details that remain to be agreed. But in any case whatever the source of the curriculum, the good teacher will believe in it, make what he teaches seem worth learning, and above all never bore his pupils.

This is not a trivial point. Our poor record of staying-on rates at school is to a large extent explained by the boredom children experience there. They sense that what goes on at school is too often artificial, a kind of ritual in which they have no concern. The good teacher is the person who will break down this barrier of apparently pointless ritual, will make the curriculum accessible to the student, by whatever means, and will give him the satisfaction of short–term aims successfully achieved. These aims need not always be what would be called 'relevant', or directly related to the outside world. A good teacher can make a student think a subject interesting and worth pursuing, or a skill fascinating and worth acquiring, whether or not this knowledge or this skill is seen to be directly useful.

In order to teach well, that is to make the contents of the curriculum genuinely available, a teacher must have authority to take charge of his pupils' learning (though necessarily with their active co–operation). Now people are given authority to do this that or the other; and so authority partly comes from outside and I shall return to this. But the exercise of authority must ultimately depend on the person who exercises it. He is the author. He must possess his own '*auctoritas*' or the delegation of authority to him simply will not work. It is often said both here and in the USA that teachers have lost their authority, and so can no longer teach. If we are to find out how to restore this authority and so make good teaching possible, we must explore the nature of the authority, and what its source should be.

One obvious source for teachers in school is that they are older than their pupils and therefore know more and have a better entitlement to speak of what they know. They can also do more and do it better, on the whole. It may be said that children no longer have any sense of this natural hierarchy, and none of them believes that age carries any authority whatsoever. This may be so; but it is a part of the function of school to introduce, if necessary for the first time, just such a sense. This is a large part of the proper function of nursery school; and it is the reason why nursery education is of such importance in a society where school may be the first introduction to the idea that someone has a right to speak in a way that means obedience; and that responsible grown–ups exist, who do not abuse or neglect or use violence, but who command respect, just from their generally benevolent function as teachers.

A good teacher should also derive authority from his ability to speak as 'an authority' on whatever it is that he teaches. He will enjoy his subject, with luck; but more than that he will show himself able to arrange its elements so as to make it intelligible, and to connect it with other subjects that the pupils may be learning, and to answer questions about it in a knowledgeable and interested way. So certain must he be that the subject is worthwhile that he must be able to cajole his pupils into learning the parts of it that they may think tedious or pointless, by showing them how they are necessary to a desirable end. And if he cannot do this, he should be able to show that mastery of a subject, any subject, is fun in itself.

It is, as I have said, increasingly recognised that people must be taught if they are to learn. There is also an increased insistence that at school one learns skills. In the process of becoming able to do something, acquiring a skill, there is need for constant practice; and the good teacher is one who encourages and helps pupils with their practice, whether the skill to be acquired is speaking a foreign language, carrying out numerical calculations, writing intelligible English or playing a musical instrument. The duty of the teacher is to pass on all the tips he can, and inspire confidence that the trick can be learned, with perseverance. The old-fashioned 'discovery' methods do not apply to most skills. It would simply be too time–consuming and inefficient to suppose that a pupil must find out for himself how to multiply, or spell correctly, or get the right *embouchure* for playing the flute.

As part of teaching the good teacher will test his pupils from time to time to see how much they have actually mastered. Testing is crucial to teaching. What has been wrong with the testing proposed as part of the National Curriculum is that it has too rigid and too tied to the particular age of the pupil. Its aims have also been confused. It has been supposed that whole classes of children will display, by their test–results, how much the teacher has succeeded in teaching them. Tests ought to be aimed to demonstrate rather how much children can do; and if they are to some extent competitive, so that it is revealed that some children do better than others then this is no bad thing. We are still too much in the grip of the belief that, though competition between schools is necessary as part of the market within which parents are to make choices, competitiveness in the classroom is deplorable. In fact children enjoy competition, and are not on the whole cast down by there being some who do better than they. They tend to be proud of their class-mate who does outstandingly well, describing him admiringly as 'brilliant', but beneficial competition depends on children being set to compete only with those who are at least potentially capable of holding their own or winning. This tells against totally mixed-ability teaching, in itself a difficult and doubtfully efficient way of managing the classroom. I personally believe that it is better for children's self-confidence to be taught alongside others of roughly the same or comparable ability; and that the teacher's skills are best used in these circumstances, though it is also necessary that, within the classroom, there should be a spirit of generosity to the efforts of others. It is in any case characteristic of the good teacher that he is sensitive to the differences between children, and alive to the possibility that some will have obstacles to overcome that will need extra help. I believe that the spirit of competition must be harnessed by the teacher in such a way that his pupils want to do as well as they possibly can, not necessarily for the sake of the high aims towards which the teacher is working, but for the low aims of beating the examiners, doing better than the parallel form, or proving to home or school that you are not such a fool as they think. Beneficial competition and successful testing of course crucially depend, as well, on the children's recognition of the fairness of the teacher who sets the tests and assesses the children. Without that, nothing can be gained.

To go back, then, to the good teacher as we remember her or him: he will have held our attention; and this is often done, as I have suggested, by successfully teaching a skill. For what I have referred to as boredom may, as often or not, be a kind of frustration; and there is nothing so calculated to make one despair as the feeling that no progress is being made. The good teacher can often bring frustration to an end by causing his pupil to be able to do things he could not do before.

However, in our new-found enthusiasm for the teaching of skills, we must not forget that we also need to be told stories. Here the authority of the teacher will consist in his both knowing the story to tell, and being able to tell it, as a traditional spell-binder; and many of our remembered good teachers were just that, I am using the word 'story' in a wide sense. Story-tellers may tell us how things are now, how they were in the past, and how they might be in the future. The essence of teaching is to help people to see the world as intelligible (and therefore to see themselves not as mere passengers, carried along by mysterious forces, but as able to intervene, to choose and to control). It is for this reason then, to show his pupils that there is some manner in which the world can be rendered intelligible, that the teacher must be a story-teller. He cannot fulfil this role by constant problem-setting and solving, but largely by talking, answering questions, allowing his pupils to explore themselves, their past and their future by the exercise of imagination. The teacher is an actor. He has to present a drama which seems significant to his pupils because it involves them, appealing essentially to their imagination. History is one way of making this presentation; and so is literature. But science, mathematics and languages are just as proper stages for the actor-teacher to use in order to induce in his pupils a feeling of coherence and significance, to catch and then free their imagination. In this sense the authority of the teacher is real and cannot be denied, any more than can the authority of the good actor. We are forced to listen. Like the Ancient Mariner, he stops us in our tracks, even though we thought we had something better to do, and not just one in three of us either.

The good teacher, then, has an authority which derives largely from himself. It comes from his being older and better at doing things than his pupils, from his manifest willingness, as well as ability, to help them to master skills, without making them feel foolish or inadequate, and from his power to present himself and, like an actor, command attention, through the force and uniqueness of his persona. He will, as well, be quite prepared to teach an ethos, a preferred way of being as well as specific skills and understanding. Just as an authentic writer has a 'voice' through which we come to know him (even though we cannot wholly separate the voice from what he tells us), so the good teacher has a way of doing things, a personality as well as a persona which comes over with his specific teaching. Thus teachers have moral, as well as intellectual effects on their pupils; and this is part of their task. I do not mean to imply that teachers should always be 'drawing morals' from their subject–matter. But I suggest that teachers, as well as priests, politicians, solicitors, doctors or directors of companies, have to exercise moral judgement in the course of their professional lives, and that they, more perhaps than members of other professions, often have to make their moral principles explicit. This is because their pupils are, relatively, young and ignorant. They need teachers who will speak up in defence of fairness, generosity, honesty, industriousness and charity. If there are student teachers who are ashamed or afraid to adopt a clear moral position and defend it, then I would strongly advise them not to go in for teaching as a career.

The first priority in moral teaching is to teach by example. This means an instant readiness to intervene when manifest wrong is done by one child to another, or by a teacher to a child. Fairness, as I have already suggested, truthfulness, punctilousness about fulfilling obligations, kindness, unselfishness, these are the classroom virtues which a good teacher must at all times practice, and try to get his pupils to admire, so that they will practise them too.

In the case of such virtues as these I suppose few teachers would fear to seem moralistic, or 'judgmental', a dread insult as a rule. The difficulty begins when children must have their interests engaged in broader matters, issues outside the classroom or games field. It is here that teachers are liable to become suspect, as unduly political, and to be accused of indoctrinating their pupils. But teachers cannot, and should not, try to appear neutral between all points of view. Neutrality is easily interpreted as indifference. It is, after all, impossible wholly to separate morals from politics. Since no-one would advocate a teacher's being neutral on matters of morality, matters of right and wrong, I conclude that, at least on some issues a good teacher must express his own political opinions, since these will also be moral issues. Though there is no sharp line to be drawn here, yet when dealing with something which manifestly divides political parties or religious communities, the good teacher will take care to make it clear that the arguments he gives are those which support one point of view, which is his own, there being people who adopt a different view, and would argue against him. He cannot be expected to talk this open line about matters of agreed common morality (and there are many such, like the wrongness of bullying or intimidation). But the very distinction he draws between those cases where he is and those where he is not required to speak as a moral absolutist will demonstrate the wisdom of the teacher, and his good sense. It is just here that he must be trusted to exercise good judgment.

The matter of trust is fundamental. A good teacher is, as I have argued, one of whom an enormous amount is asked. His authority as a teacher must come, in large part, from his being the kind of person his pupils can trust, both intellectually and morally. He must be completely reliable and consistent. In addition if he is to succeed he must, in my view, be enthusiastic and funny. But he cannot perform well in isolation. There are too many instances of teachers entering the profession full of the optimism without which good teaching cannot exist, and finding this eroded by the feeling of being alone, with no help from colleagues, shut in a classroom without support. There is in fact no guarantee that teachers, whatever their potential qualities, will perform well except that which is afforded by a commitment to teaching on the part of the whole institution. Thus I am arguing that good teaching must be placed at the top of the list of institutional priorities. Children and parents must both have trust in the school itself, must like and accept its ethos, as well as having trust in individual teachers.

But, as I have argued, authority comes not only from within, but from outside. And government in the end is the source of this part of a teacher's authority. It must be government who not only sets up the curriculum but sees to it that it is taught by professionals who are equipped properly to do the job, and who are then trusted to get on with it. It is highly paradoxical that the Conservative Government of the 1990s which was committed to pouring scorn on teachers and the schools in which they work should nevertheless have sought to remove them from local control and set them up as largely independent units. It is still odder that the same Government should have proposed to bring in a system of teacher-training which is almost entirely school-based. The explanation, I suppose, is that little though that government trusted the teaching profession, it was still more hostile both to the university education departments hitherto responsible for teacher–training, and to local authorities. Between them, these two groups combined, in the then Government eyes, a habit of reckless and nonaccountable squandering of public funds ('tax–payers' money as it is called) and an unacceptable ideology, of which I have spoken. It was supposed that teachers themselves are the pawns of these two institutions, those who train them and those who employ them, and that they are capable of change, if they are released from the thralls of both. Teachers were thought to be at least potentially non–political, whereas both teacher–trainer and local authorities were all of them tarred with the brush of extreme political (in)correctness. I do not want to go into the rationality of such beliefs. My purpose is simply to explain how it came about that teacher–training, on which in the end the implementation of government educational policy must depend, was placed in the hands of the teachers themselves, subject only to the restraints of the national curriculum and, presumably, some form of independent inspection and assessment.

Paradoxical though this may be, it is necessary to make the best of it. It is impossible to predict how many schools will want to establish themselves as training institutions. We must wait to see how well they manage their responsibilities. My own view is that if teachers are to be respected as true professionals it will be necessary for any school–based training to retain its links with Higher Education; and I believe most of the teaching profession would agree with this judgment. A close partnership between schools and universities or colleges will have many advantages.

First, because of it, there will, I hope be a gradual change in the public image of school teachers. They will, less and less, be regarded as failures, dependent for their qualifications and their positions always on people higher up the professional ladder than themselves. Other professionals (doctors, for example, or lawyers) are thought worthy of respect because they are, relatively speaking, autonomous — establishing and maintaining their own professional standards, carrying out their own training in collaboration with the universities and bearing the responsibility of admitting people to the privileges of belonging to a respected profession. Teachers may gradually aspire to this position. To complete the process, however, it is absolutely essential that there should be a statutory body, a General Teaching Council, to set up and oversee standards, both of qualification and of continuing practice. It is another extraordinary paradox that a government committed to placing responsibility for training in the hands of teachers should refuse to contemplate the establishment of such a body. They seem to be torn asunder by their various suspicions. On the one hand suspicion of colleges and departments of education has forced them to transfer responsibility for training to schools; on the other hand terror of the teachers' unions makes them refuse the last necessary step. But in the end, it will have to be taken and the public's belief in and respect for teachers will be thereby enhanced. Teachers will ultimately receive their authority from government, from the general public and, as I have argued, from their own competence and confidence. Good teaching will be increased by professional pride.

Finally, I come to the second general advantage that I see in the new system, within which teachers are to be entrusted with the task of training their successors, in collaboration with the universities. Everything I have suggested about the definition of good teaching and about ways to make such teaching possible is to be taken within the context of a specific view of education, what it is and what it is for. There is no such thing as good teaching in a moral or political vacuum. The teacher who exercises that proper authority without which I have argued he will not be able to teach will possess it partly because of his own personality and his own training, partly because he will be seen, by government and parents alike, to be able to help his pupils along an educational path whose goal is more or less agreed. A good teacher, above all else, wants success for his pupils. And this entails a commitment to the belief that all of those pupils who come before him are entitled to education. The virtue of hope is the chief educational virtue, both in individuals and in institutions; and this means a belief that there is no-one who is ineducable, however great the obstacles that confront him. There is an egalitarianism built into the law which lays down that all children must be educated. Good teaching must take place within the context of that law. The commitment to improving the competence and understanding of all pupils has a moral and political dimension which cannot be overlooked: it is identical with the commitment to meeting educational needs. It is teachers themselves, necessarily, who have this aim most firmly in their eye, there in the school, where the needs of the child are most clearly to be seen. Teachers training their successors in school will train them to keep this target in their sights, and will thereby be instrumental in realising the moral ideal which, as I have tried to argue in these two lectures ought to be at the heart of public educational policy.

Part 4:

**EDUCATION, VALUES
AND RELIGION**

11

Jonathan Sacks

Political Society, Civil Society

Whereby it is plainly to be seen, the societies of men among themselves, to have been at first sought out for the leading of their lives in more safety and quiet: and then first of all to have sprung from the love which was betwixt man and wife: from them to have flowed the mutual love betwixt parents and their children: then the love of brothers and sisters one towards another: and after them the friendship between cousins and other kinsmen: and last of all the love and good will which is betwixt men joined in affiance: which had at length grown cold, and been utterly extinguished, had it not been nourished, maintained and kept by societies, communities, corporations and colleges: the union of whom hath for a long time maintained many people, without any commonwealth, or sovereign power over them (Bodin, 1606).

From time to time, in their more reflective moments, people have asked the fundamental question common to both morality and politics: what is it that leads individuals to form associations and sustain them over an extended period? Not every thinker has given the same answer, nor has every society formed the same kinds of institutions. In fact any complex society is a confusing mixture of reasons and associations which emerge, like a great river from its countless streams and tributaries, out of a vast range of histories and traditions. None the less, sometimes it is helpful to simplify, to draw a diagram rather than a map, in order to understand what may be at stake in a social transition. In this talk I want to tell two stories that, between them, provide us with a framework for understanding much of what has happened in our social landscape over the past few centuries and, with increasing speed, for the past thirty years.

Western society was largely formed from two primary influences, ancient Greece and ancient Israel, and it owes their combination and dominance to Christianity, formed in the encounter between these two civilisations. At the height of the Victorian age Matthew Arnold, in *Culture and Anarchy,* made much of the distinction between these two sources: he called them Hellenism and Hebraism. To Hebraism, he said, we owed morality, to Hellenism, culture (I would also add politics). The one emphasised proper conduct, the other, great flights of the imagination. For Arnold, Victorian society had erred on the side of Hebraism and now needed a greater injection of Hellenism. *Culture and Anarchy* was published in 1869. It is this contrast, though in a different and more modest way, that I want to re-explore.

Both Greek and Jewish civilisations have a philosophical tradition. The most distinguished representative of the first is Aristotle, the second, Moses Maimonides. There are profound similarities between them, not surprisingly, since Maimonides was a neo-Aristotelian. But there are differences too, and these are no less telling. Each used a phrase to describe our tendency to form groups. Aristotle described man as a *political* animal, Maimonides described man as a *social* animal. There is a distinction between these two ways of seeing things and it may help us understand certain tensions in contemporary life. My concern here is not to discuss Aristotle and Maimonides, but simply to meditate on those two phrases, taken out of context and used as metaphors of human association.

I want to suggest that behind them lie two different stories of how individuals move beyond their isolation to form communities. Both are true, but they describe different aspects of our collective life and give rise to different kinds of institution. Man as a political animal creates the institutions of *political society:* states, governments and political systems. Man as a social animal creates the institutions of *civil society:* families, friendships, voluntary associations, charities, congregations and moral traditions. There is a significant contrast between the two and the forms of life to which they give rise. Much of the history of our attempts to live together can be written in terms of their relationship, sometimes close, sometimes distant, with now one, now the other, in the ascendancy. But to understand each, we have to begin at the beginning, in this case with the most famous of all starting- points: 'In the beginning God created heaven and earth.'

The opening chapters of Genesis form one of the great metanarratives of Western civilisation, and their literary form is designed to draw attention to certain fundamental features of our sense of location within the world. They open with a repeated construction: 'And God said, "Let there be . . ." And there was . . . And God saw that it was good.' The repetition induces a certain mood.

The universe unfolds according to a plan and it is good. What breaks the mood is the sudden appearance, in the second chapter, of the phrase 'not good'. Nothing has prepared us for this expression. Thus far we have encountered only God, the natural world and its highest life-form, *Homo sapiens,* the one being on whom the Creator has set His own image. Almost by definition there is no resistance or drama, since there is only one personality, the artist — who is not merely fashioning a work of art but also bringing into being the materials out of which it is made. What, in such a universe, can be 'not good'? In a single sentence — five words in the Hebrew — the origin of all love and conflict is set forth. 'It is not good for man to be alone.' In its initial verses, therefore, the Bible sets out two propositions that will frame its entire vision of mankind. The first affirms the sanctity of the human individual as individual. Every person is in 'the image of God'. The second asserts the incompleteness of the individual as individual. 'It is not good for man to be alone.' Hence the human need for relationship, association, and for stable structures within which these can grow and be sustained. In fact much of the rest of the Hebrew Bible is the story of the unfolding of these relationships, from the nuclear family of Adam and Eve, to the extended family of Abraham and Sarah and their children, to the confederation of tribes in the days of Moses and Joshua, to the sovereign state in the age of kings and prophets.

So the Bible begins with the recognition that it is difficult for human beings to live alone. Almost immediately, though, it recognises that it is also signally difficult for human beings to live together. With Adam and Eve comes conflict, with Cain and Abel, fratricide. By the sixth chapter, the generation of the Flood, 'the earth was full of violence' and a social order was nearing its end in disarray. The problem which has haunted humanity from its origins and which is rarely far from the surface has been posed in its full drama and starkness. How do we move from unbearable isolation to some form of tolerable association? By way of answer, I want to tell two stories, both implicit in the Bible, but quite different in their implications.

The first is told in its most influential form by Thomas Hobbes in the *Leviathan.* Hobbes takes as his starting-point the condition of humanity before any structured form of relationship. He calls it the 'state of nature', and it closely resembles the biblical description of the era of the Flood. As does the Bible, Hobbes pictures a situation of unmediated conflict. When human beings converge without rules or institutions there is an inevitable collision of purposes and desires. People find themselves 'in that condition which is called War; and such a war as is of every man, against every man'. The outcome is simple, and no one has described it more bluntly. In such an environment, said Hobbes, life would be 'solitary, poor, nasty, brutish, and short'.

How then do human beings create societies? Hobbes' answer is this. What drives individuals to form associations is fear of violence and death. Some of us are stronger than others, but none of us is so strong that we are invulnerable to attack. Indeed each of us has reason to fear the pre-emptive attacks of others. Therefore it is in the essential interests of each of us, as a minimal precondition of peace and security, to hand over some of our powers as individuals to a supreme authority which will make laws and enforce them.

This, the social contract, brings into being the 'great Leviathan' of the state, and thus is born *political society* – the central repository of power needed to bring about a social order. Hobbes' story is a central narrative in the evolution of Western society over the past three centuries. *Leviathan* was published in 1651, but it has certain features that make it a more contemporary work than, say, Locke's treatises on government, or Rousseau's *The Social Contract* and this will become clear during the course of the presentation. But for the time being, I want to step back from the story and think about the assumptions that lie behind it.

The central character in Hobbes' drama is the individual, the 'I'. Hobbes has a certain amount to say about institutions like the family, but his primary concern is with the individual as such, pursuing his or her own interests, concerned for safety and the protection of life, an individual detached from any binding loyalties to family or friends, community or traditions. This became an extremely important feature of political thought as it has evolved to recent times. In an important modern work, John Rawls' *A Theory of Justice* (1971), a different kind of social contract is envisaged, under different starting conditions, but with this same feature: that it is about an agreement formed by persons for their several interests, regardless of their ties or backgrounds. They are 'abstract' individuals, and their histories, loyalties and loves are regarded as irrelevant to the political contract they make. The hero of Hobbes' story, then, is that peculiarly modern figure, the individual seeking self-preservation.

What motivates the individual? Hobbes' answer is *interests*, not moral commitments. This is not accidental but essential to his way of thinking, because for Hobbes there is no motivation beyond the pursuit of interest. Morality, he claims, is simply a dignified way of talking about desire: 'But whatsoever is the object of any man's Appetite or Desire; that is it which he for his part calleth *Good;* and the object of his Hate, and Aversion, *Evil* . . There being nothing simply and absolutely so; nor any common Rule of Good and Evil.' This too is a strikingly modern way of speaking: there are no moral absolutes. What we call good is no more than what we as individuals choose or seek or desire. Hobbes, of course, is not saying we are incapable of conferring benefits on others. He would understand the argument that we should give up part of our income to be redistributed by government for the sake of peace and social stability. But that is always because we gain more than we lose thereby. Man as a political animal is driven by calculation of rational self-interest.

It follows that the political arena will be one of conflict. My interests are not yours, and there is no objective moral standard by which we are bound. One of the central issues of politics is the distribution of finite goods — wealth, power or honour — whose short-term character is such that if I have more, you have less. The political domain is therefore peopled by contending claimants, historically institutionalised in the form of classes, interest groups and political parties. That conflict is contained by the use of external power, by legislation or taxation backed up, *in extremis,* by the threat of coercive force — an army or police force. Power, for Hobbes, is the essence of the Leviathan. There therefore arise the perennial questions of politics, namely the forms and legitimation of power. To the first, our answer (not Hobbes') is representative democracy; to the latter, it is that, without power, conflicting interests would result in chaos and a return to the state of nature.

Thus is born political society. I have told the story according to Hobbes, but with variations it could have been told according to many other thinkers. Among them I have mentioned John Rawls, and I would add a further great modern thinker, Robert Nozick, whose *Anarchy, State and Utopia* (1974) is another modern political classic. The common theme running through this, the single most influential story about our common life for the past three hundred years, is of humanity as an aggregate of rational self-seeking individuals; of society as an arena of conflicting interests; and of the resolution of conflict by a central power given legitimacy by a social contract. In and through this contract, individuals recognise that it is in their interests to yield up part of their freedom to governments, which then become the sole or dominant source of power through which violence is prevented, order maintained, obligations enforced, and conflicts mediated.

I now want to tell a quite different kind of story, beginning at the same starting-point, but using different concepts and evoking a distinct set of themes. The simplest way of proceeding is to ask what actually happens in the Hebrew Bible after the words: 'It is not good for man to be alone'. God creates woman. Man then responds with the first poem in the Bible:

> This is now bone of my bone, flesh of my flesh; she shall be called woman [*ishah*] because she was taken from man [*ish*]. (*Genesis*, 2:23)

I have included two Hebrew words, because the Hebrew text contains a nuance often missed in translation. Until this point man has been called *adam,* man-as-part-of-nature (the word *adam* signifies 'that which is taken from the earth'). Now for the first time man is called — indeed calls himself — *ish,* which means man-as-person. Significantly, he does this only after he has named woman. The Bible is suggesting, with great subtlety, that the human person must first pronounce the name of the other before he can know his own name. He or she must say 'thou' before he can say 'I'. Relationship precedes identity.

In this narrative the primary social bond is not the state, but marriage ('Therefore a man will leave his father and mother and be united to his wife, and they will become one flesh' (*Genesis*, 2: 24)). What kind of bond is this? Clearly, given the way the Hebrew Bible describes it, it is not a Hobbesian contract between two independent individuals, each seeking their own interests. It is instead — in a key word of Jewish thought — a *covenant (brit* in Hebrew), and this is neither an alliance of interests nor, strictly speaking, an emotional state. Instead it is a bond of identity, as if to say: 'This is part of *who I am.'*

This central concept is taken up in various ways in the Hebrew Bible. There is a covenant handed on by parents and children (the subject of much of *Genesis*) and another and more structured covenant at Mount Sinai, with the Israelites as a people. This affects the way the Bible understands certain obligations. Consider welfare. The book of Leviticus defines the duties of citizens to one another with such phrases as 'If your brother becomes poor'. On this view, I owe help to others, not because it is in my long-term interest to do so, nor because a government has so decreed, but because the other is part of my extended family, and thus in a certain sense part of who I am. The members of a society are linked by a bond of kinship and fraternity.

Kinship, however broadly conceived, is an exclusive concept. In a world in which there are kin, there must also be non-kin. In one where there are neighbours, there must also be strangers. This creates a question (deeply troubling throughout much of human history) of the moral status of outsiders. The Bible therefore explicitly and repeatedly extends the domain of obligation to the 'stranger', the person who is not a member of the extended family. The book of Leviticus contains the famous command: 'You shall love your neighbour as yourself' (19: 18), but the same chapter includes the far more significant and strenuous command: 'You shall not oppress the stranger ... instead, you shall love him as yourself, for you were once strangers in the land of Egypt' (19: 33-4). The historical reference is significant. Theologically, the obligation to love the stranger follows from the first chapter of Genesis. If God is parent, humanity is indeed a single extended family. But simple reflection on creation has not always sufficed to persuade people to love as themselves people who are manifestly unlike themselves. The Bible suggests that the Israelites underwent exile and slavery precisely to know what affliction feels like, and thus to learn the lesson that we must not inflict on others what we ourselves have suffered. Morality is sometimes taught by history.

How then does this narrative differ from that of Hobbes? Its central figure is not 'I' but the 'We' of which I am a part — marriage, the family, the nation understood as an extended family, and ultimately humanity itself, considered as a single family under the parenthood of God himself. On this account, our afffiliations and attachments are not irrelevant, but essential, to the structure of obligations we form. We owe duties to others because they are a part of who we are.

What then of motivation? The driving force of the biblical drama is not self interest but something else, for which the Hebrew word is *hesed,* usually translated as 'compassion' (a key word of politics of a certain kind). More accurately, though, *hesed* should be translated as 'covenantal obligation'. It means the duties and responsibilities that flow from identification and belonging, the kind of relationship that exists between husbands and wives, or parents and children.

What constitutes society, on this view, is not a contract but a *covenant (brit).* One difference between them is that those bound by a covenant are 'obligated to respond to one another beyond the letter of the law rather than to limit their obligations to the narrowest contractual requirements'. Another is that covenants have a moral component that renders them more binding and open-ended than could be accounted for in terms of interest. As Daniel Elazar puts it, covenant 'expresses the idea that people can freely create communities and polities, peoples and publics, and civil society itself through such morally grounded and sustained compacts (whether religious or otherwise in impetus), establishing thereby enduring partnerships'. To put it simply, parties can disengage from a contract when it is no longer to their mutual benefit to continue. A covenant binds them even — perhaps especially — in difficult times. This is because a covenant is not predicated on interest, but instead on loyalty, fidelity, holding together even when things seem to be driving you apart.

This helps us understand the significance of another key word in Judaism, *emunah*, often, and wrongly, translated as 'faith'. Faith is a cognitive or intellectual attribute. *Emunah is* a moral one. It signifies the willingness to enter into and to stand by a long-term, open-ended commitment. It is what is needed to sustain a covenant. It means 'faithfulness'.

One of the key differences between a society based on contract and one built around the idea of covenant, is what holds it together. A social contract is maintained by an *external* force, the monopoly within the state of the justified use of coercive power. A covenant, by contrast, is maintained by an *internalised* sense of identity, kinship, loyalty, obligation, responsibility and reciprocity. These promptings cannot always be taken for granted and have to be carefully nurtured and sustained. Hence the centrality, within covenantal associations, of education, ritual, sacred narratives, and collective ceremony.

A social contract gives rise to the instrumentalities of the state — governments, nations, parties, the use of centralised power and the mediated resolution of conflict. It is the basis of political society. A covenant gives rise to quite different institutions — families, communities, peoples, traditions, and voluntary associations. It is the basis of civil society. This is one way of understanding the difference between man as a *political* animal and man as a *social* animal.

So there are two stories about human associations, one told in our political classics, the other in our great religious texts. Clearly they are not mutually exclusive. Civil society requires the institutions of politics for the resolution of its conflicts and the maintenance of peace and defence. Political society, according to most of its theorists, needs the undergirding of civil virtue. Both stories represent enduring truths about the human situation and both need to be told if people are to live together peaceably for any length of time. To some extent they represent a difference of emphasis within the Greek and Jewish traditions, which is why I mentioned Aristotle and Maimonides. The ancient Greeks emphasised political structures as the context of the good life. Jews, with their long history of dispersion, tended to locate it within the family, the community and the educational system. But Western civilisation is the product of both influences, heir to both stories.

By telling these two deliberately simplified narratives, I have constructed a framework, a template, which will allow us to understand what happens, and what is at stake, when slow, imperceptible changes take place in the ecology of associations. For there is a third story to be told, about the relationship between the two other stories. Though they are both true, their relative force and authority, their salience within a culture, differs from one age to the next. For some time now, the Hobbesian narrative has increasingly displaced its alternative, and much in our current social environment flows from that fact. A fateful drama has been enacted which can be described in two movements: the domination of political society, and the progressive de-institutionalisation of civil society.

12

Jonathan Sacks

Languages of Morals

No home, no tea. Insouciant carelessness. Eternal indifference. Perhaps it is only the great pause between carings. But it is only in this pause that one finds the meaninglessness of meanings — like old husks which speak dust. Only in this pause that one finds the meaninglessness of meanings, and the other dimension. The reality of timelessness and nowhere . . . nothing is so meaningless as meanings (Lawrence, 1923).

In 1357 a certain Eleazar, living in Mainz, sat down to write a letter to his children. It was a will, not a conventional kind of will disposing of this or that item of property. It was what came to be known as an 'ethical will', a custom, indeed a literary genre, through which Jewish parents handed on to their children advice and instruction in how to behave. The existence of the genre recognises that parents bequeath their children more than possessions. They leave them ideals, sometimes large, sometimes quite specific. The letter covers several pages. This is how it began:

These are the things which my sons and daughters shall do at my request. They shall go to the house of prayer morning and evening . . . As soon as the service is over, they shall occupy themselves a little with the Torah, the Psalms, or with works of charity. These are the things which my sons and daughters shall do at my request.

Their business shall be conducted honestly, in their dealing both with Jew and gentile. They must be gentle in their manners, and prompt to accede to every honourable request. They must not talk more than is necessary, and by this will they be saved from slander, falsehood and frivolity.

They shall give an exact tithe of their possessions; they shall never turn away a poor man empty-handed, but must give him what they can, be it much or little. If he beg a lodging overnight, and they know him not, let them provide him with the wherewithal to pay an innkeeper. Thus they shall satisfy the needs of the poor in every possible way.

My daughters must obey scrupulously the rules applying to women; modesty, sanctity, reverence, should mark their married lives. Marital intercourse must be modest and holy, with a spirit of restraint and delicacy, in reverence and silence. They shall be very punctilious and careful with their ritual bathing. They must respect their husbands, and must be invariably amiable to them. Husbands, on their part, must honour their wives more than themselves, and treat them with tender consideration. If they can by any means contrive it, my sons and daughters should live in communities, and not isolated from other Jews, so that their sons and daughters may learn the ways of Judaism. Even if compelled to solicit from others the money to pay a teacher, they must not let the young, of both sexes, go without instruction in the Torah. Marry your children, O my sons and daughters, as soon as their age is ripe, to members of respectable families . . . (Abrahams, 1976).

There is nothing remarkable about this letter. Israel Abrahams, from whose work this translation is taken, calls the author 'an average Jew'. He was doing what parents did. Nevertheless, from this distance of time, the letter, like a medieval woodcut, evokes a world of simplicity and not a little dignity. Eleazar, of whom we know little, was not a rabbi. He simply belongs to a tradition which, having received it from his parents, he now prepares to entrust to his children. Its values are not personal. They are those of rabbinic Judaism from the first to the nineteenth century, and which may still be found in orthodox circles today. He speaks of a life of prayer, study and good deeds, laying special emphasis on honesty, civility and charity. Relations between husband and wife are formalised and charged with religious meaning. Marriages in such a world are arranged. The concept of romantic love, though it has existed since biblical times, has not yet developed the power to override such considerations, though the medieval sages did recognise the right of children to marry the partners of their choice.

Eleazar, like most Jews at most times, is aware of the vulnerability of his way of life. In the Middle Ages, Jews were everywhere a minority, surrounded by a religious culture different from, sometimes hostile to, their own. Hence his concern that his children stay attached to a Jewish community rather than live in isolation. He knows that a family alone is not sufficient to sustain a tradition. It needs the support of fellow believers. And hence his insistence, again utterly characteristic, that his children do all they can to ensure that their children are educated in the texts and ways of Judaism, which they must do even if they have to borrow money to do so.

The conceptual world from which this letter is drawn is what is sometimes described as a 'thick morality'. In it, obligations flow from facts. This is a poor person, *therefore you* must give him charity. This is your wife, *therefore you* must give her honour. This is your child, *therefore you* must give her an education. Between the premise and the conclusion there is no intervening act of choice. This is a morality received, not made. It is embedded in and reinforced by a total way of life, articulated in texts, transmitted across the generations, enacted in rituals, exemplified by the members of the community, and underwritten by revelation and tradition. It has no pretensions to universality. It represents what a Jew must do, in the full knowledge that his Christian neighbours in Mainz are bound by a different code. But it is not voluntaristic. Jews received their identity, and thus their obligations, by birth not personal decision. What separates his world from ours?

One key difference can be traced to a justly famous sentence in David Hume's *Treatise of Human Nature*. Hume notes that:

> In every system of morality, which I have hitherto met with, I have always remark'd, that the author proceeds for some time in the ordinary way of reasoning, and establishes the being of a God, or makes observations concerning human affairs; when of a sudden I am surpriz'd to find, that instead of the usual copulations of propositions, is, and is *not*, I meet with no proposition that is not connected with an *ought*, or an *ought not*. (Hume, 1740, 1964).

This, Hume observes, breaks one of the rules of syllogistic reasoning, namely that there should be nothing in the conclusion that was not already contained in the premisses. 'This small attention,' he writes, 'cou'd subvert all the vulgar systems of morality.' The significance of this discovery was hardly apparent at the time. Hume himself said about his book that 'it fell dead-born from the Press'. What he had done, though, was to open up a fateful gap between 'facts' and 'values', description and prescription. There was no way of reading off values from an external world, from the objective properties of things. The hairline fracture which Hume had noticed would eventually grow into an abyss. Where there had been one world, there were now two. There was the world of *is*, charted and explained by science. And there was the realm of *ought*, whose foundations would become increasingly problematic as the centuries passed.

A second, no less momentous, transformation occurred later in the eighteenth century, in the work of Immanuel Kant. For Kant, goodness is to be found not in acts but motives. The good will, the only thing that is unconditionally good, is that which seeks to do its duty for the sake of duty. All other inclinations yield hypothetical imperatives ('You ought to do this if you want that'). Only the good will yields categorical imperatives, absolute commands. But this means that if I am to act morally, I must issue these commands to myself. I must be self-legislating or 'autonomous'. If I do something because someone else has commanded me to do so, my obedience will be based on some extraneous consideration. I act because I want to win favour or avoid punishment. But that means I am pursuing inclination rather than duty, acting prudentially rather than morally, and this applies even if the person whose commands I am obeying is God. To put it another way, if I act morally by doing what God commands, this can only be because I have independently arrived at the conclusion that what I am doing is right. Any other consideration is inappropriate. With this single argument, authority has been transposed from revelation to personal reflection, from 'the starry heavens above me' to the 'moral law within me'. If Hume had released morality from its moorings in the physical world, Kant had liberated it from the Divine will.

Neither man was a revolutionary. Hume described himself as 'a man of Mild Disposition, of Government of Temper, of an open social and cheerful Humour, capable of Attachment, but little susceptible of Enmity, and of great Moderation in all my Passions'. Bertrand Russell paints a charming picture of Kant as 'a man of such regular habits that people used to set their watches by him as he passed their doors on his constitutional'. Neither envisaged that what he was doing was paving the way for vast changes in our moral life. To the contrary, each took the content of morality as more or less given. The question was: what was its basis? The traditional answer, religion, would no longer do. Since the Reformation, Catholics and Protestants had argued over religious truth and, far from agreeing, their disputes had led to two centuries of conflict throughout Europe. There seemed to be two other alternatives: reason and emotion. Kant chose the first, Hume the second. For Kant emotion was too arbitrary to provide the basis for moral judgment. For Hume reason was too detached to provide a motive for action. It was too early for either to see that their answers cancelled one another out and that the search for a foundation of ethics might ultimately prove fruitless. If Hume or Kant were to be followed, however, one thing was clear. Moral certainty could not be found in the world outside. It was neither written into situations nor readable in sacred texts. Morality had travelled from 'out there' to 'in here'.

Perhaps because he wished to avoid such an outcome, Jeremy Bentham proposed an alternative. Morality could borrow the methods of science, especially the new science of economics. Hobbes had said that 'good' and 'evil' simply represented what people desired or had an aversion to. What was observable was that people desired pleasure and sought to avoid pain. These were the 'two sovereign masters' of human motivation. It should be possible, therefore, to construct a science of optimal behaviour. Its principle was simple. Borrowing a phrase from Adam Ferguson, he stated that an action was right if it promoted 'the greatest happiness of the greatest number', happiness defined in terms of pleasure and the absence of pain. The theory, which developed a number of internal variants, became known as 'utilitarianism'. As time proceeded, it became clear that it was open to a number of serious objections. Not least, as one of its disciples, John Stuart Mill, realised, it threatened individual liberty itself, for it meant that the sufferings of the few could be justified by the satisfactions (not always benevolent) of the many. Long before its fatal flaws were exposed, utilitarianism became a most powerful means of overthrowing every kind of moral tradition. Within the utilitarian frame of mind itself is a transition from 'traditional' to 'modern' consciousness. Hitherto, behaviour had been justified by reference to the past. Now it was to be judged by reference to the future, to outcomes or consequences. The question was no longer: 'Is this sanctified by revelation or custom or age?' but: 'Is it effective, does it yield the best results?' With the confidence of his age, Bentham assumed that these could be counted, aggregated and quantified. They could be known. One of the insights of traditional systems was lost in the translation to modernity, namely that consequences of change can sometimes be very distant indeed and impossible to know in advance. But this was out of tune with the temper of the age, and so the scientific approach to human behaviour, later known as social engineering, was born. Bentham's theory was hardly practicable for individuals. It meant long chains of calculation before even the simplest decision. But it was to become vastly influential in the way governments viewed their purposes and procedures, and the theory had a certain symmetry with democracy, government by the greatest number for the greatest number.

As the nineteenth century progressed, however, more radical voices could be heard. Society was moving rapidly. The idea that morality, the established consensus of reasonable people, could be taken for granted came to seem more and more tenuous. Travellers had long noted that other cultures organised matters differently, but the increased speed of travel and the expanding field of anthropology now made people increasingly aware of the diversity of human cultures. Charles Darwin's theory of evolution opened up the possibility that a particular form of life might not be the result of a conscious process of design. If natural selection held true for human societies there might be a fundamental discrepancy between what happened and what people thought they were doing. As two of his modern commentators, Michael Ruse and Edward O. Wilson, put it, 'In an important sense, ethics as we understand it is an illusion fobbed off on us by our genes to get us to cooperate.' The idea, first mooted by Plato in *The Republic* that a society might be maintained by a 'noble lie' — that our moral convictions might be no more than myths designed to mask quite different underlying realities — now began to seem more plausible. Three immensely influential figures took up the case: Marx, Nietzsche and Freud.

For Marx, the significant human realities were material ones. The superstructures of consciousness — morality, religion and philosophy — were by-products rather than the causes of what people did. They were 'phantoms formed in the human brain'. Moral and religious systems concealed rather than revealed the true nature of society: the division of labour, the exploitation of one class by another, money relationships, and the bourgeois interests of the capitalist system. As Engels put it

> What is good for the ruling class is alleged to be good for the whole of society with which the ruling class identifies itself. The more civilization advances, the more it is found to cover with the cloak of charity the evils necessarily created by it, to excuse them or to deny their existence: The only way to address real problems was to proceed without illusions, to circumvent the 'false consciousness' by which people accept their situation, and directly to change the social and economic structure. (Engels, 1902).

Nietzsche's aims were different, but his method was strikingly similar. Morality, by which he means primarily the Judaeo-Christian ethic, is an invention designed to further the interests of a particular class. Nietzsche's bold thesis is that the class in question was not the rulers but the slaves. The 'slave revolt in morals' taught people to value self-restraint, compassion, charity, the protection of the weak, the defence of the vulnerable. In so doing it inverted the values of life itself, of which the most important is the will to power. 'The slave', he wrote, 'is suspicious of the virtues of the powerful: he is sceptical and mistrustful, keenly mistrustful, of everything "good" that is honoured among them'. Instead he favours 'those qualities which serve to make easier the existence of suffering', namely 'pity, the kind and helping hand, the warm heart, patience, industriousness, humility, friendliness'. It is precisely these virtues, cherished in the

West since the rise of Christianity, which Nietzsche sees as contemptible, false, at odds with nature itself. 'Wherever slave morality comes to predominate, language exhibits a tendency to bring the words "good" and "stupid" closer to each other.' Like Marx, Nietzsche aims at the overthrow of conventional morality, a 'transvaluation of values'. For both, an essential prelude is the 'unmasking' of ordinary moral language to uncover the harsh reality beneath.

Freud's views on morality are difficult to summarize and underwent revision in the course of a long career. In their simplest outline, though, they are that in their primitive state people are driven by a set of aggressive and sexual instincts which have to be repressed for civilisation to be possible. In the individual this takes the form of an internalized restraint, the superego. In the case of cultures it takes the form of myths and rituals. In *Totem and Taboo,* Freud argued that their origin lay in an ancient memory of parricide. The sons of the tribe had risen against their father, envious of his monopoly of the tribe's women, and had killed him, only to be haunted by guilt which was then assuaged by rituals of atonement and reparation. All civilisation, whether of the individual or society, depends on the suppression of instinct, which generates internal conflict and neurosis. Religion was simply this conflict writ large and projected onto the universe; it is 'the universal neurosis of humanity'. Freud himself believed that discontents are an inevitable outcome of civilisation, but this did not prevent a number of his followers from arguing for a new and less repressive form of existence, in which instinctual gratification came to be seen not as a hazard to society but as a route to health. This was the origin of what Philip Rieff calls the 'therapeutic ethic'.

These three thinkers, quite different in their concerns and aspirations, nevertheless share important points of similarity. Unlike Hume and Kant, they no longer merely bypass religion. They take active pains to explain it away in the hope of overcoming it. Each is engaged in a massive revisionary enterprise, whose ultimate outcome will be to change the way we think and speak about ourselves, even the way we structure society. Their aim is not to vindicate morality but to offer a language from which morality, in the Judaeo-Christian sense, has been removed. Most significantly, each expresses (or in the case of Freud, makes possible) a new and adversarial relationship between the individual and society. The external order was, in Marx's key word, 'alienating'. It had come to seem something foreign and oppressive, hostile and falsifying. The very failing of morality was that it postulated a harmony between 'in here' and 'out there', a harmony that did not exist and which, in the striving to create it, divided man against himself. If Hume and Kant sought to justify morality, Marx, Nietzsche and the post- Freudians undertook to free us from it.

By the time the impact of these thinkers had been felt, the radical conclusions already implicit in Hume and Kant could finally be spelled out. In 1936, A.J. Ayer took Hume's argument to its logical conclusion. If there is no legitimate transition from *is* to *ought* then moral judgments can be nothing more than expressions of emotion. Unlike scientific statements, which can be tested and verified against experience, sentences containing 'good' or 'ought' are pseudo-propositions, apparently meaningful but actually not. They do not convey information. They merely express emotion. They are the communication of subjective states. If so, not only can there be no moral knowledge, there can be no meaningful moral discourse.

What Ayer did for Hume, Jean-Paul Sartre did for Kant. Autonomy, the self as sovereign over its own choices, might have meant, in the eighteenth century, no more than free assent to established custom. But after the Second World War, for Sartre, it meant radical, 'existential', choice, freedom without guidance or constraints, the courage to face a world without external meanings. As he puts it,

> Dostoevsky once wrote 'If God did not exist, everything would be permitted'; and that, for existentialism, is the starting-point. Everything is indeed permitted if 'God does not exist, and man is in consequence forlorn, for he cannot find anything to depend upon either within or outside himself (Sartre, 1989).

For Sartre, 'Man makes himself; he is not found ready made; he makes himself by his choice of morality, and he cannot but choose a morality, such is the pressure of circumstances upon him.' Kant believed that we could discover morality through reason. Sartre has no such illusions. All that remains is autonomy itself, in which the individual discovers 'that there is no legislator but himself; that he himself, thus abandoned, must decide for himself.

Let us now return to Eleazar in fourteenth-century Mainz. What is clear is that within our present frame of discourse we cannot make sense of much of his world. What interests us — private emotion, individual choice — does not overly concern him. He speaks not of the self and its dilemmas but of family and community, the relations between husbands and wives, parents and children, the importance of living and handing on a tradition. He does not believe that his is the way of all people. He knows only too well that it is the way of a minority. But it defines who he is, who his children are, where he belongs, and what he is dedicated to continue. He can speak easily to his children of duty because it is a language he and they share. There is a certain coherence to his world which we may have lost.

By contrast, Ayer's and Sartre's individual has many more choices; indeed they are almost open-ended. But he has no particular reason for choosing one thing over another. The language of objective justification of choice is in principle ruled out. He has been taught and has accepted that all choices are equally valid. Nor, if he has absorbed popular versions of Marxism or sociobiology, has he any reason to suppose that his decisions are particularly significant. The world is as it is because of inexorable forces of which we are only dimly and intermittently aware. Choice becomes simultaneously open-ended and inconsequential. The modern individual has no reason to enter into binding commitments such as marriage or membership in a community, for these will restrict his options in a way he has learned to find intolerable and unjustifiable.

He might as a result find it difficult to say who and what he is. It will not be surprising if his life consists in a series of temporary engagements — jobs, relationships, lifestyles — none of which, since they come and go, gives shape and unity to a life. He may even have little relationship with his parents or his children. Perhaps the cruellest realisation will be that for no-one does he hold unconditional worth. A world without moral bonds, of free-floating attachments, is one in which we are essentially replaceable — as employees, sexual partners, or members of a 'lifestyle enclave'. It is a world in which individuals are not characters in a shared drama but the temporary occupants of roles. The concept of loyalty becomes hard to understand. But we anticipate, for with Ayer and Sartre we have begun to move beyond liberalism to libertarianism, a stage in the story we have not yet reached.

What we have seen, though, is that language has tracked the movement of the self, from embeddedness in the structures of society, to detachment from, even hostility towards them. The self of individualism speaks a radically purified language, purged of the complex attachments to family, tradition, custom and community that once allowed words to bridge the gap between 'is' and 'ought'. What was happening to these institutions meanwhile, the 'little platoons', the local birthplaces of belonging and identity, the contexts in which we become not abstract individuals but particular persons with specific histories and loves?

13

Stewart Sutherland

Education, Values and Religion: A Diagnosis

The former Bishop of Liverpool, the Rt. Rev. David Sheppard, when he was a parish minister, was once discussing the advantages and drawbacks of being both a clergyman and an opening bat for England. On the downside, the main problem seemed to be what we have now come to describe as a 'double-whammy'. If there are two things which the man on the Clapham omnibus, or the average London taxi-driver, knows about they are religion and how to open the batting for England.

The honour of the invitation to be one of the Cook Lecturers is somewhat mitigated by what I can only call the 'triple-whammy' administered by the Cook Trustees in the title given to this particular series of lectures, *Education, Values and Religion*. If there are three things upon which it seems that red-blooded Brits have red-blooded opinions, they are education, religion and the difference between right and wrong, and all the signs indicate that this is also true of blue-blooded Brits! I have to confess that I speak with both feeling and experience here. When I used to divide my time between being Vice-Chancellor of the University of London and Her Majesty's Chief Inspector of Schools, there were frequent journeys between the two offices courtesy of a London cab agency. These intrepid knights of the road had their curiosity stimulated by the fairly regular trips from one office to another — offices whose addresses and functions they knew very well. It did not take them long to work out what my respective responsibilities were and, over the two and a half years in question, I have to say that they were unstinting to the degree of generosity with their advice. I shall forego the temptation to share the minutiae of that advice with you.

All this bodes well, you might think, for in the context of plentiful widespread red-blooded opinion on these matters, we might be in for a quick summary of public opinion, an application of that to some of the issues of the day, and home for an early supper. Would that it were so straightforward! The essence of the problem is that not all the red-blooded opinions are the same. One solution might be to expect of a lecturer an early statement of the facts of the matter and a clear simple conclusion. My reservation about this is that I would then be accused of being like the politician who always prefaces his answers with the expression 'The fact of the matter is . . .' and gives you his or her opinion. However, I do not shirk the expectation of some proposed and substantiated answers, I merely suggest that they will be all the better for some interim analysis and reflection. Hence the title of this lecture *Diagnosis*.

If, for the moment, we pursue the implicit medical metaphor, what are the symptoms which suggest that there are ailments from which we suffer? These are quite evident and they all focus upon the uncertainties in our understanding of the relationships between a group of terms which are widely used in the relevant debates but which are often used in uncoordinated and imprecise ways. These terms include 'universal/comprehensive', 'diverse/elite', 'relative/ relativism', 'plural/pluralistic'. I shall try to clarify some of the relationships between these terms, because the subject of these lectures requires that. I must confess at the outset, however, that in two lectures I can at best begin to ascend some of the foothills, rather than promise to conquer all of the peaks.

It might seem a rather abstract beginning to list a series of very general and perhaps vague terms as the symptoms of a set of rather specific and concrete problems. A fair but not conclusive point. Let me put flesh on the bones by giving some examples. We hope that our schools will help pupils equip themselves for citizenship in the twenty-first century. What should be top of the agenda in such an aim: Use of the internet? The development of entrepreneurship? The green agenda? The importance of the market economy? The history of Scotland? (Whose version?) The importance of a spiritual dimension of life? (Whose version?) Or, as the London cabbies are meant to say, 'And another thing': If there is a total sum of money which the public purse can afford to spend on public services (and whatever party forms the government, there has to be such a number identified), where do the priorities lie, between say health and education; or within education, between nursery, primary, secondary, further and higher education?; or within the schools how do we weigh the claims of Jill and Jack who respectively are showing exceptional ability in mathematics and in the mastery of the violin, against those of Alex and Heather who have different forms of special educational need? 'And another thing', what do we make of the English school which, it is reported, has ignored the ruling of the 1988 Education Act which specifies that while there may well be reason for differences in balance, nonetheless religious education shall be mainly Christian in character, and is offering a form of religious education which is predominantly Muslim in character?

My point is that all of these very specific questions, some of which are part of the daily bread and butter of teachers, head teachers and local authority officials, can only begin to be tackled if we are clear about the meaning of words like 'universal', 'comprehensive', 'diverse', 'elite', 'relative', 'plural' and so on. And if that were not daunting enough, I have to start by drawing attention to the fact that there is a basic division in our society about what we think education is and can be.

The division is best exposed by asking ourselves about how we see the school. Is the school (a) a microcosm of society? or, (b) the engine of social change? (In parenthesis it is worth noting that at the moment universities are all too evidently settling into the role of reflecting the agendas set wholly from outside, rather than seeing themselves making a distinctive contribution to setting the agenda of society and in that sense accepting that they must be, if only because they are, one of the engineers of social change).

There need not necessarily be, but there is in our society a tension between these two perceptions of what a school is, and therefore of what we believe to be the wider role of education. Thus there was no doubt that in the policy of John Knox, summarised neatly in the slogan 'a school in every parish', the idea of the school as the engine of social change in Scotland was paramount. We are all still benefiting from that. It is equally plain that in Nelson Mandela's South Africa, the education system must be one of the major engines of social change. Pupil/teacher ratios of eighto to one in primary schools in poor areas of Zululand ill serve the desperate needs of South Africa. In a different century, in a different context, all of John Stuart Mill's writings on education are premised on the idea of education as the generator of social change.

In the twentieth century in our own country Butler's great 1944 Education Act (whose religious clauses were described by Churchill, variously as 'Zoroastrianism', or, 'the County Council Creed') was intended as, and indeed was a foundation stone for the fashioning of post-war Britain. Equally, when Tony Crosland in his period as Secretary of State for Education implemented plans to reform secondary-school education, there was no doubt that the intended consequences went far beyond the specifically educational. Perhaps one of the most telling examples of education as social change used to be quoted by Sir David Smith, my predecessor as Principal of Edinburgh University. He used to surprise audiences by pointing out that statistically the most important correlate of improving evidence of birth control in developing countries was the provision of education to mothers and potential mothers.

Evidence for the view of schools as resources for social engineering is significant, as well as widespread. What of the view of schools as microcosms of society — as societies 'writ small'? There, it might be said, is the rub. Schools do reflect the societies in which they are to be found. This is true for two reasons. The first is that all schools are concerned in part with the transmission of culture — the latter understood in varying degrees of breadth. Thus in conservative societies a primary role of schools will be to underline and reinforce the basic structures and values of that society. Equally in societies in which a particular form of religious belief is part of the social fabric, schools will play a part in reinforcing that pattern of religious belief. This is as true of the religiously-based schools in this country, as it is of those in the USA where strong and sometimes successful attempts were made to control the biology curriculum, and as it is of schools within some Muslim states.

The view of schools as engines of social change is not inevitably incompatible with this. It may simply reflect the view of a society which either wholly, or through the dominant political powers, is in search of social change. In that sense the schools in question are microcosms of that particular society. The society in question is different in that its prevailing posture or ideology is one of social revision. As I have just pointed out, not all societies are like that. Some differ because they take their respective forms from alternative unifying principles. Some, however, differ because there is no unifying set of principles. In such a context the school may well be — in almost all cases will be — the microcosm of a society which by lacking such a unity ensures that certain of the tasks and responsibilities normally expected of schools cannot be met.

My thesis is that our basic picture of education, and therefore of schools as one dominant aspect of that, is that schools reflect the nature of the societies to which they belong. Thus whether religion is taught in schools, and if so the manner and content of that teaching, is likely as a matter of intention, or in default of that as a matter of fact, to reflect the prevailing fortunes and standing of religion in that society. Equally, the values which inform the provision of education as well as the processes of education within the school sector, as well as within individual schools, will be drawn from the wider prevailing currents within society. Of course there are other constraints and economic performance is one of them, but my prediction is that, for example in Mandela's South Africa, the provision and nature of school education will reflect the new order, just as surely as the apartheid values and strategies of the old order did. Somewhat nearer home, geographically if not historically, the Edinburgh of Dugald Stewart in the first part of the nineteenth century, as well as in its own way the Balliol moulded by Jowett for the second half of the same century, produced the educated ruling and administrative elites essential to the direction which British society was already taking. One major point of difference was the diverse sources from which they respectively drew their students. But my basic point is that the types of education offered in these two places both reflected and served the prevailing direction of society.

What is the relevance of all of this to what I earlier described as the 'triple-whammy' of the title of these lectures? The answer to that, and therefore the beginning of the diagnosis, is quite plain. If there are as many views about what we want from our schools generally, as well as in matters of values and religion, as there are taxi-drivers, then it is not surprising that schools are in some difficulty over these questions. The face of the adolescent, whether it be bright or sullen, cheeky or submissive, is in part a mirror in which we as a society see ourselves. Of course it is not a mirror reflecting ourselves as adolescents twenty or even forty years ago, it is a mirror reflecting what we think to be important and have by our actions and decisions, or lack of them, thought to be important for the intervening twenty, thirty or forty years.

At one level, this has fairly direct implications. There is sometimes a gap between what we say about values and what we do. We expect varied and not easily compatible things from schools. We expect them to produce pupils who can ask all the difficult questions, but when they do, and we are not sure about the answers, we expect pupils who can show a bit of respect for authority. We expect schools to produce pupils who have savoured and can express their individuality, but on the other hand a bit of conformity will not go amiss from time to time. We want future generations to be sensitive to the environment in both aesthetic and 'green' terms, but equally we teach them the attractions of an economy based upon low inflation, high employment, and mass consumerism as the basis of both. We like to say that we understand the importance of religious belief, but not too much of it, and that we should like the curriculum to reflect that. Thus we want the future of our society to rest on individuals who are vigorous, thrusting, (one might even say 'aggressive') entrepreneurs: yet they must also be kind to grandmothers, animals and the environment, although probably in the reverse order. They should have the single-mindedness of the athlete, but the clubbability of the veteran Saturday afternoon cricketer. At times they should, like good girls and boys, be seen and not heard, but equally be able to strut their stuff with the attention-grabbing precociousness of a Shirley Temple. If we shout instructions as if we are inhabitants of the Tower of Babel, we should not be surprised if the desk instructions of teachers do not produce singleness and coherence of practice and outcome. And so on I could go. Sometimes the inconsistency is to be found within each one of us: sometimes it manifests itself in the diverse views of different groups within society.

There are two reflections which I should like to offer at this stage. The first is that this diversity within society is reflected in the microcosms which schools are, and which makes the task of being a teacher, or head teacher or governor of a school so difficult. In the areas of values — overall educational objectives — we make things exceptionally difficult for teachers. I am second to none in expecting the highest professional standards from teachers, and I confess to wanting pupils to be able to read, write, spell and communicate well, but when it becomes a matter of values and religion we are less than precise about what we as a society expect. These points, however, whether the difficulties for teachers or the uncertain guidance which we give them, are not the diagnosis in itself, they are the symptoms.

Any adequate diagnosis must look beyond the symptoms to try to discern underlying causes. The various symptoms to which I have drawn attention show themselves most clearly in the competing and not always compatible demands which we make of the classroom.

Not surprisingly this gives rise to dissatisfaction being expressed about the results of the educational process and usually this becomes very quickly criticism of the practitioners — the teachers. Now I have no difficulty in accepting that those of us in education are rightly held responsible for much of what happens in education. However, particularly in the context of the values which inform and are expressed in and through the educational process, some of the fault lies elsewhere.

Let us take note of a chain of connections which, I propose, are exceptionally important, but which for various reasons we have allowed to become dangerously tenuous. Educational practice, whether in school or university, depends upon well-grounded educational theory. That is to say we must have some basis for what we do and why we do it, and have the intellectual structures within which to reflect upon, modify, change and develop those practices in the light of experience. That is what a good theory should provide.

There are, however, also preconditions for what a good theory in this context should be. In what follows I shall point only to one or two of these which are particularly important for my thesis. They relate to what is essential for any theoretical basis of the practice of education. Education is in part the transmission of culture and in part the creation of the conditions of individual and communal flourishing in the future. Thus any adequate educational theory will be based upon two further sine qua nons. The first is a clear account of what the fundamental values and objectives of the relevant culture is: the second is a clear account of what it is for human beings to flourish both as individuals and as members of society.

Let me underline the argument which I am propounding, for all else that I have to say rests on this. Educational practice rests upon educational theory, and that in turn rests upon an adequate account of human fulfilment and flourishing. The latter is what theologians used in unreconstructed days to refer to as a Doctrine of Man, or philosophers more recently as a philosophical anthropology, or theory of human nature. If you are in any doubt about the sort of thing which I mean, then I can happily refer you to an excellently readable book from the philosophy stable in St. Andrews, Leslie Stevenson's *Seven Theories of Human Nature* (1974). Since education is an essentially social concept it clearly also requires an account of the nature of human society. Immediately, however, that must be qualified, for insofar as education is both a transmission of culture and the provision of the conditions of the future of society, the requirement is for more than a theory of society in general: the requirement is for a clear account of this society and its common purposes. It is because of the validity of these linkages that we can see a little more clearly why it is inevitably the case that the school is a microcosm of society. Equally it is only insofar as there is a clear picture or perhaps vision of human and societal flourishing that the school could in any worthwhile sense be the engine of social change. Unless we know what we want to change to, and can provide some worthwhile justification for wanting to do so, there is little prospect of healthy social change and development.

It may well have occurred to some of you that this is all very theoretical in itself, and I confess that it is. But I also insist that if we want to move from symptom to diagnosis then this theoretical excursion is essential. However, I can now point very clearly to the connection between cause and effect. There is uncertainty about the values which inform the construction of the curriculum, because there is uncertainty in our society about what it is for human beings and human societies to flourish. Perhaps that oversimplifies the situation. There are degrees of great certainty in parts of our society about what, again to quote earlier theological formulations, 'man's chief end' is. There are Christians, Muslims, Jews, Buddhists, Humanists, Sociobiologists, New-Ageists, Psychotherapists and so on and on, all of whom are certain about the nature of human flourishing. What's more each of these sub-divide into as many variations again. The critical point is that none of them agree with each other, and yet they are all citizens of this particular realm! What hope the education theory, or the teacher who tries to satisfy all of them?

These, however, are not the only faultlines which run through our society. There are three faultlines of a severity which dominates much of what we do and can achieve and which certainly have direct impact in our classrooms. The first is implied in the variety of examples which I have just offered of certainty in our accounts of human flourishing. Our society is increasingly pluralist in character. It is often assumed that this is a recent phenomenon, a result of immigration into Britain, particularly in the twenty years or so following the Second World War. This is at once too narrow and too diverse as an account of religious and cultural pluralism. It is too diverse in that it presupposes that pluralism only occurs when Orient meets Occident. It is too narrow in that it fails to appreciate that since the great Toleration Act of 1689 increasing provision has been made in law to provide the necessary statutory conditions of a religiously plural society. The Roman Catholic Relief Acts of 1791 and 1829, are particularly important here, as are the 1813 Unitarian Relief Act, the 1832 Roman Catholic Charities Act and the 1846 Religious Disabilities Act. This last extended rights to Jews amongst others, which earlier Acts had extended to Christian groups other than the established churches.

Our society is then, by statute, as well as custom, religiously plural in character. This is much to its credit — if, that is, religious pluralism is all right with you. There are however, many societies in which religious pluralism is not tolerated in similar fashion, and at various times in the history of these islands, that has been true here. For some, this is also thought to be a virtue. Both Jewish and Muslim friends have pointed out to me what they regard as the sad end point of such pluralism — the current state of Western society. I shall return to the implications of such a view in due course. The point to emphasise at the moment is that such pluralism raises major issues for the classroom. The first and most obvious is that in a society in which headteachers are required by law to hold assemblies and make provision for worship in schools, whose god we should worship. Or should all schools now invoice the local authority for an altar to the unknown god? There is in England a further complication in that the 1992 Education Act (Schools) made explicit what is still implicit in Scottish education. There is a requirement that in addition to the inspection of the provision made in schools for the cultural, moral and social development of children there should also be inspection of the provision made for the spiritual development of children. What is more, that will be separate from the inspection of religious education in schools. The point there is that in a school which is a religious foundation, be it Christian or Jewish, the school can insist on inspection of religious education being carried out by appropriate members of the same faith community — an option which is almost invariably taken up. However, all schools in England have the provision made for the spiritual development of children evaluated under what for shorthand reasons I shall refer to as the secular inspection teams.

This is an entrancing, or at least diverting prospect and one which preoccupied me very much when I was HMCI (Her Majesty's Chief Inspector of Schools). How would one assess such an element of the life of a school? Were there performance indicators of spirituality? Is there a scale of humility from Uriah Heep to Michael Heseltine in terms of which one could devise an output measure? Is meditation a whole class activity or for group work? More importantly, should there be streaming, or setting for classes in spirituality? As you can see the imagination began to run riot, but I absolutely deny the rumour that there was pressure from either the Government or the *Daily Telegraph* to produce spirituality league tables for schools! Of course there is room for more serious discussion of this and I shall return to the issues in the next lecture.

The second main faultline in our society which has huge implications for education, be it primary, secondary or tertiary, is what I can only refer to as the fragmentation of knowledge. The Book of Isaiah offers us the vision of the lamb lying down with the lion as a paradigm of perfection. I have more modest and interim dreams. When will the sociobiologist talk to the particle physicist? Or the chemist to the historian? Or the theologian to the molecular biologist? And so on we could go. Of course none of this is a matter of assigning blame. Equally none of this implies that what consenting historians, or consenting chemists or physicists do in private is not eminently worthwhile. But the point is that there is a sense in which much of it is 'in private'. And if that is thought to be an accusation I would hasten to point out that it does not stick equally to, for example, all historians.

The main point to note is that this is not an accusation. The benefits of the advancement of these subjects which immeasurably enhance our lives today would not have been possible without the intensity of discussion, argument, enquiry and experiment which thrives within what I am referring to as the fragmentation of knowledge. If chemists had not been singlemindedly chemists, there would be no pharmaceutical chemistry, and none of the drugs which enhance the quality of life by moderating cardio-vascular disease and blood pressure, and which have virtually banished the need for major surgery to treat ulcers. Specialisation, which is a response to fragmentation, has delivered many benefits in terms of both the advance and the application of knowledge. Indeed it has been a precondition of that advance.

The problem still remains. Some of the most intelligent people in our society cannot talk to each other about what preoccupies them in their working lives. Their immediate response, which up to a point is reasonable, is, 'So what?' They meet and talk about other things — football, the theatre, Sainsbury's wine selection, the Scott Enquiry, the choice of schools of Labour front bench members . . . Sometimes, and this is where genius is in the wings, the particle physicist talks to the computer scientist, and a new insight into the cosmos is possible.

Sometimes the physiologist talks to the pharmacologist and there is some relief in sight for those in the stranglehold of a particular disease. There are, that is to say, formal as well as informal ways to mitigate the effects of this type of fragmentation. What then is the problem? Why not simply bow to the effects of the inevitable? Not only is it the case that we can't all know everything: for the last couple of hundred years or so we have had to accept that no-one can know everything.

Before we settle down to that cosy reassurance, let us remember education. How do you educate for such a society? One problem we all know too well. Where does specialization in the curriculum begin? At the end of primary school? At the age of 14? 16? The Scots are thought to have an advantage here in the difference between the Highers and A-Levels, yet we keep pulling them up by the roots to check that they are still growing. There was a time when specialisation began after an undergraduate degree, whether in a professional qualification or in post-graduate study. Now the route to most postgraduate study is blocked to others than those who have already completed a specialist undergraduate degree (usually a single honours degree). There are messages for the Scottish universities here.

Not surprisingly this has caused detailed problems for the classroom. These have been highlighted in England by the introduction of the National Curriculum, and by its less prescriptive counterpart in Scotland. On the whole I do think that the introduction of the National Curriculum was overdue and that its benefits outweigh its disadvantages. However, after reminding ourselves that it is in itself a reflection of the fragmentation of knowledge, let us take note of just two examples of what I regard as the 'microcosm effect'. The first is that the introduction of the National Curriculum underlines rather than solves the problem of when specialisation is appropriate. It is not simply a matter of how many A-Levels or Highers a pupil should take — although the fewer they are in number the greater the problems of specialisation — it is also a question of NVQs (National Vocational Qualifications), GNVQs (General National Vocational Qualifications), SCOTVEC, (Scottish Values Educational Council) parity of esteem, and in an older style 'the problem of two cultures'. The second example to which I point is the difficulty faced in primary schools posed by one particular aspect of the National Curriculum. For the most part and to the warm endorsement of the teachers, primary schools operate on the one-teacher/one class principle. The whole curriculum is the responsibility in any one teaching year of one teacher assigned to each class. This system has much to commend it, but my own belief is that in most primary schools it is no longer sustainable. Teaching a bright eleven year old about electricity is not something which can reasonably be expected of a primary school teacher whose sole formal scientific qualification is an O-Grade in biology of twenty years standing. The teachers themselves are powerful counter voices to my proposal, but I believe that there is good evidence to show that intransigence on this is not in the interests of the children. At any rate the case was conceded for music instruction decades ago. Maths and science are no less in need of specialist skills and training at the upper end of the primary school curriculum.

Such are some of the practical difficulties for education which are a consequence of this second fault line in our society — the fragmentation of knowledge. But so far, as you will have realised, I have not answered the question of the contented specialist, 'So What?' In fact in pointing to the problem in the primary school I have implicitly accepted that the answer lies in further specialisation in the provision of teaching. In so far as I do this, I am underlining the first part of my diagnosis — the school is a microcosm of society. But the broader question still stands: What does this have to do with the problem of values and religion in education?

In concluding this lecture, let me point to a connection which Alasdair MacIntyre made in his seminal Gifford Lectures, published under the title *Three Rival Versions of Moral Enquiry*. He made, in his own interesting fashion, the point about the fragmentation of knowledge, and summarised its impact on intellect and society as follows:

> Enquiry had become finally fragmented into a series of independent, specialised and professional activities whose results could, so it seemed, find no place as parts in any whole. Such medieval and renaissance metaphors as those of a tree of knowledge or a house of knowledge had finally lost their application. (MacIntyre, 1990, p. 216).

MacIntyre drew two important further conclusions from this. The first is that at that point western society began to lose the idea of an educated public. My gloss on this, which is central to the diagnosis which I am offering you, is that the loss of the idea of an educated public was the loss of the definition of what an educated public should be educated about. Of course each subject specialist has his or her idea about this, but the ideas don't add up to a coherent realisable curriculum. The problem of the over-crowded curriculum, which we all encounter at all levels of education, is one symptom of this, and the problem of specialisation in the curriculum is another. But at root, when we try to move from symptom to diagnosis, the real difficulty is that there is no common agreement about what it is to be educated. Therefore there is no common agreement of what we expect of education in school or university. There are worries about this and some half-hearted attempts to define something called 'core' and increasingly 'transferable' skills. Now there are important issues here about the training which all might reasonably have, but this account of education as engineering social change still leaves unanswered the question of what tune the organ-grinder wants all these well-trained, core-skilled monkeys to play.

What is missing is some account of the values in terms of which we exercise these skills, choose the fragments of knowledge to be explored further or to be given priority in the curriculum. I shall return to this issue in the next lecture, but let me make the final point in this one, by reflecting on a further comment by MacIntyre from the same section of his book:

> . . . it was not merely that academic enquiry increasingly became professionalized and specialised and that formal education correspondingly became a preparation for and initiation into professionalization and specialisation but that, for the most part and increasingly, moral and theological truth ceased to be recognized as objects of substantive enquiry and instead were relegated to the realm of privatised belief (MacIntyre, 1990, p. 217).

The fragmentation of knowledge may be thought to be neutral with regard to values, and in a sense it was. But it was the neutrality bred of a redrawing of the boundaries of civilized discourse which left moral and theological truth outside the camp. Of course we do still have moral preferences, we might have religious or anti-religious beliefs but these are matters for the individual. They belong to at best the private allegiances of the individual in which my opinion is as good as your opinion and any other suggestion is outlawed as 'judgmental'. What is permissible is the creation of alliances on particular issues which are then prosecuted by the lobbying techniques pioneered in the USA by single-issue pressure groups. Such an approach may or may not be acceptable: that rather depends on the nature of the single issue. What is clear is that it is an inadequate basis for reflection within our society on what common values, if any, we now share.

The absence of such informed debate and reflection is seen in the increasing moral atomisation of our society. We are approaching a state whereby all we offer our young people by way of guidance on tackling questions of values and decisions of life, is a pair of all-purpose questions: How do you feel about it? and, How will I benefit from this?

Such questions would hardly equip an apartheid supporter — whether in the South Africa of the seventies, the Nazi Germany of the thirties, or Croatia of the nineties — for deep moral reflection and tough moral decision.This moral atomisation is the third faultline in our society which I offer as partial diagnosis of the problem of what to say and do in dealing with issues of values and religion in schools and education more generally.

In summary, my diagnosis of the problems of the triple whammy is as follows: in education generally, but in the case of schools particularly, we must never forget that schools are a microcosm of society. To build a satisfactory education system, we must base it upon a clear view of the purposes of education. This must itself be founded upon a picture of what it is for human beings to flourish. The particular problem in our society is the absence of any shared view of what that is. There are three 'faultlines' running through our society which underlie our difficulties. These are cultural pluralism, the fragmentation of knowledge and the moral atomism which has followed from this.

14

Stewart Sutherland

Education, Values and Religion: Prognosis? Cure?

As any worthwhile doctor knows, one of the great dangers of offering a diagnosis is that if the complaint is more than trivial, then the very pronouncement of the diagnosis may exacerbate the problem by adding to it the symptoms of depression. In the first lecture I offered a diagnosis of the problems of trying to relate to each other the concepts of education, values and religion. In the end I pointed beyond a number of symptoms which I had identified, to what I referred to as three fault lines within our society: pluralism, the fragmentation of knowledge, and moral atomisation.

For some this may have seemed a rather gloomy story to offer as a diagnosis, and that it was bound to be followed by an even gloomier prognosis. Most depressing of all, it might have seemed to eclipse totally the healing light of a cure. However, before succumbing completely to the temptation which Groucho Marx described as 'building dungeons in the air', we should remind ourselves of the broader context in which these social and intellectual phenomena belong.

In the first place, pluralism belongs within the legal context which I outlined, of the Great Toleration Act of 1689 and the various Acts extending rights of religious minorities over the half century from 1792 to 1846. Problems of pluralism are not new, and there have been successful sallies against them already. There are societies which have grasped the problem of living more pluralistically but yet peacefully. It must nonetheless be recognized that such gains can be lost, such visions torn to shreds. Whether in fifteenth-century Spain or in the late twentieth-century Balkans, neighbour can be turned against neighbour, and religious and cultural communities can turn the backstreets of the suburbs into the highways of persecution. However, in this country we have lived within a statutory framework expressing both the values and intent of tolerance for over three hundred years. We have the platform of accumulated experience upon which to build — albeit that the practice still has some way to go to fulfil the statutory potential.

The fragmentation of knowledge, contribute as it may to our diagnosis, has also brought great benefits to our society and age. Life expectation is now far greater than ever it was. Standards of living for all members of the community have risen steadily over the last century and more. We know and understand a great deal more about ourselves and the universe we inhabit than ever we did and the impact of the technological skill which has accompanied and accelerated this seems almost without limit.

Equally, despite what I have described as moral atomisation, there are still saints and heroes in our world. The catalogue of human achievement in the twentieth century seems not to be a diminishing return. In music, whether we think of Bartok, Britten and Shostakovitch, or Armstrong, Davis and Monk, creativity bursts forth in ways beyond forecast. In even the darkest moments of politics men emerge who lead nations out of the shadows — Churchill, Gandhi, Gorbachev and Mandela — each emerging in moments of acute need and each giving their own highly distinctive response appropriate to the hour. And so one could proceed by turning to the scientists, Einstein, Crick, Watson and Wilkins, or the writers and artists, Eliot, Beckett, Solzhenitsyn, Picasso, Sutherland and Bacon.

My point here is not to over-gild the lily, but to remind ourselves of the fact that human beings are immensely resourceful. We would not be here otherwise, as even the most aggressive Darwinian would tell us. Of course there is the other dark side of human nature — Stalin, Hitler, Saddam — but the message of this paragraph is of human possibility and creativity.

My diagnosis points to the fact of the twentieth century being one of upheaval, disruption and uncertainty in its deepest social and intellectual foundations. Yet it is an age in which in all areas of human life, individuals — and in some cases whole communities — have demonstrated beyond question that the changes which come upon us have not yet exhausted all human possibilities. Somewhere within (some) human beings the resources sufficient for the task in hand have been found. The conclusion which I draw from this is that, difficult though the diagnosis may be, its depth and seriousness does not rule out altogether the element of hope in our prognosis. That assertion, however, leaves all the running to be made in relation to the shape of the prognosis, let alone the possibility of a cure.

If a cure is to be proposed, then some account must first be taken of the connections which may or may not exist between our three faultlines of cultural pluralism, intellectual fragmentation and moral atomisation.It would be easy but oversimplistic and therefore mistaken, to assume that there is a causal relation between these three faultlines — easy but wrong, that is, to insist that there is a causal sequence from say either cultural pluralism or intellectual fragmentation to moral atomisation. It is not as clear and sharp as that. Nor would other possible permutations reveal otherwise hidden causal links.

On the other hand, it is unlikely that these phenomena are wholly unconnected. They do, I believe, have some sources in common patterns of thought and can be seen, helpfully and up to a point, as interconnecting branchlines on a common network of ideas. To the extent to which that metaphor can be pressed they do mutually confirm each other.There are two common antecedents which can help us illuminate our contemporary situation. I shall exemplify and characterise these by reference to a number of philosophers who were significant, but not alone and unaided, in developing the patterns of thought in question.

One critical thread in Western thought has been the growing dominance of different types of scientific method in the resolution of a range of intellectual issues which extend well beyond the scientific. Early and clear examples of this are to be found in Descartes' search for a single (scientific) method. He pursued this with the single-mindedness of that kind of genius through *The Regulae, The Discourses* and, pre-eminently, *The Meditations.* His search was conditioned by his perception of the evident success of the sciences in reducing to some order our picture of the universe of which we are a part, but of which we are not the physical or geometrical centre. The hope which he had was that there lay in wait of discovery an equivalently fertile method which could be used to tame the rather rugged landscape of metaphysics and theology.

Descartes model was nearer in structure to the analytical methods implicit in certain forms of mathematics. A century or more later David Hume showed equal preoccupation with the methods of empirical science, which John Locke had already applied with some success to the problems of philosophy in his *Essay Concerning Human*

Understanding. In his *Treatise of Human Nature* Hume developed a clear and empirically-based scepticism in Book I and, in Book III applied that with dramatic and lasting effect to some of the central issues of moral philosophy. The epistemological scepticism of Book I, developed rigorously from the principles of the empirical sciences, led to an extreme statement of moral scepticism:

> Tis not contrary to reason to prefer the destruction of the whole world to the scratching of my little finger (Hume, 1740, 1964).

Doubtless Nero or Caligula would have found that, at face value, a perfectly plausible view of the world. In so doing they would have misunderstood Hume, but not been alone in that. The issue here however, is not the exegesis of Hume, but rather the highlighting of the connection between the sources of empirical thought which did in due course lead to the development of the fragmentation of knowledge, and one element of moral atomisation. The connection is that in his rejection of standard rational and rationalist arguments in support of ethical beliefs, Hume simultaneously relied upon a form of radical empiricism and provided a basis for an apparently wholly subjective and therefore individualistic form for ethics. I have already hinted that this is not the whole story for Hume, but what it did is pose a problem — the foundations of ethical beliefs, to which he offered at best a partial and indirect answer.

What Descartes and Hume had in common was the belief that a single intellectual method could be the basis for the solution of problems as widely different as the composition of the physical world, the trustworthiness of our perceptions of that world, the existence of God and evil, and the basis for moral beliefs. Simultaneously the trails which led to the fragmentation of knowledge, to moral atomisation in one context, and to morally relativistic interpretations of pluralism in another had been staked out.

At this point enter, stage left, the great German philosopher Immanuel Kant — 'awakened by Hume', as he described it himself, 'from his dogmatic slumbers. Kant's great project of the second stage of his philosophical life was to find an alternative basis for the resolution of the problems of metaphysics and epistemology, to that offered by discredited forms of rationalism, or alternatively by what he intended to show was an inadequate Humean scepticism. His aspiration, by offering an account of the conditions of empirical knowledge, was in part to redefine, and in part to answer, both traditional metaphysical questions such as the nature of the self, and key epistemological ones such as what I may claim to know as distinct from believe, and what grounds there are for such a claim.

The scale of Kant's achievement is still being measured and the complexity and indeed the obscurity of some of his detailed exposition is still a torment to students of philosophy. At the heart of his intention however, is a desire central to the theme of this lecture. He states plainly that in attempting to give an account of the limits which are set to human knowledge he wished also to define the areas which should be the province of belief. This emphasis has been variously misinterpreted, minimised or even ignored. Sometimes the emphasis in question has been inappropriately raised as a standard on the flagpole of religious apologetics, but more often than not it has been set aside as a misperception by Kant of the true force of his own achievements. Neither of these responses adequately perceives the impact of Kant's work on subsequent generations. To capture something of that impact is the central focus of this part of the lecture.

In fact, the effect of Kant's limitation of knowledge to give adequate intellectual space for belief, was in the end to lead to the forms of relativism and moral atomisation which I outlined in the first lecture. The situation had, for our purposes, two key elements: the first was a further underpinning of the intellectual centrality of what in shorthand I shall call scientific method as the key to truth and knowledge; the second was what was not intended by Kant to be, but in practice and in fact was, the relegation of central questions of moral and religious belief to at best a second-rank status.

Thus Kant's rejection of Hume's religious, moral and epistemological scepticism had a price, and that price was the separation of the discussion of matters moral and religious from the domain of knowledge. God, Freedom and Immortality became at best, in Kant's terms, 'Postulates' rather than as Aquinas, or even Descartes in his own way might have argued, well-found, grounded beliefs.

The consequences of these shifts in perception and intellectual priorities have been of massive significance. If it is accepted, as it has been very widely in the West, that there is a disjunction between the realms of morality and religion and the possibility of knowledge and evidence-based certainty then the implications run very deep. In MacIntyre's words quoted earlier:

> . . . . for the most part and increasingly, moral and theological truth ceased to be recognised as objects of substantive enquiry and instead were relegated to the realm of privatised belief. (MacIntyre, 1990, p. 217)

There is of course much more to be said about this than is possible within the confines of one lecture, but I hope that I have illustrated that the development of what I have referred to as forms of both (relativistic) pluralism and moral atomisation are connected to the development of the dominance of the scientific method, which I would argue provided the launching platform for the fragmentation of knowledge.

A rather different but equally important illustration of my view that the intellectual faultlines of our contemporary sensibility run deep is to be found by reference to the work of one of Hume's contemporaries, Adam Ferguson (1723–1816). Ferguson who held successively the Chairs of Natural and Moral Philosophy in the University of Edinburgh, was one of those who provided the building blocks of the development of what we now refer to as the social sciences.

Ferguson's particular contribution was his *Essay on the History of Civil Society* (1767). It is the project itself, rather than the myriad of detailed reflections which is important. Ferguson epitomised early in the process the growing awareness of society, and indeed human beings, as best understood as part of history and social and cultural geography. He did not develop a specific sociological method, but he illustrated reflectively the possibility of contemplating the development of human ideas and self-perception as interlocked with rather than the forerunner or precondition of social institutions.

From this developed, in and beyond Ferguson's work, an approach to the understanding of human beings and human society which was based upon phenomenology and description rather than critical evaluation. There was thus a development in Ferguson and others, on a rather different basis from that of Hume and Kant's response to Hume, of a pattern of thinking which encouraged the alliance of empirical procedures to pluralistic or even relativistic approaches to moral and social questions.

The full-fledged exploration of sociological method which followed in the nineteenth century accompanied the growth of contact with a diversity of cultures and beliefs. The economic and imperial goals of the time were followed by a shift in perception in the twentieth century from difference in culture being seen as a ground for domination or exploitation, to cultural diversity being hailed as worthwhile and valuable in itself. But of course one accompaniment of that was a growth in both pluralism and relativism in cross-cultural appreciation.

We are still coming to terms with the consequences of this. I do not at this stage want to anticipate further elements of my analysis, but rather to emphasise the points of connection between the growth of our cultural fault lines. Thus by extended empirical enquiry to human institutions and values in the hope of finding an appropriate method for social *science* the intellectual basis for cross-cultural criticism or judgment had been undermined. Although the scientific method might provide the basis for the analysis and comparison of different cultures and values it could not, for all the reasons briefly sketched above, provide a basis for cultural judgment or evaluation. When two or more cultures come to live side by side, serious issues arise and may remain dangerously unresolved.

To ensure that the relevance of this is kept in mind, we should remind ourselves of the difficulties which follow from this for the classroom: for even apart from the questions of social and moral education, values and cultural norms are both implicit and explicit in organisation of school and classroom. How are these to be established in a context defined in some cases by the reality of multicultural communities? Some of the complex issues which arise here are examined with great care by Bernadette O'Keeffe (1986).

Perhaps a summary of the argument so far would be helpful. The central element of my diagnosis is that the problems faced in the classroom when education, values and religion have to come to terms with each other are much exacerbated and possibly even defined by three major intellectual faultlines which run through our culture. These are the fragmentation of knowledge, the development of pluralism, and moral atomisation. The prognosis which I believe follows from this is conditioned by two factors: the first is the good news that human beings have found themselves immensely resilient and have shown no end of ingenuity in extending the boundaries of what we believe and experience to be possible; the second is the ambiguous news that the faultlines are not superficial and the prognosis will depend upon our ability to tackle the very deep-seated issues which they denote.

What then, if anything, may be said of the possibilities of cure? In the days of boyhood, many stories were read in which, in the most desperate of straits, the hero would tear himself from the clutches of disaster and, so the text would run, 'in one single bound he was free'. To the contrary, in the real life of the adult world and in the response to my diagnosis there are no such bounders: there is no *single* simple solution or cure to the faultline ailments of our contemporary culture. However, to quote again from boyhood adventure stories, 'all is not lost'.

In so far as there is a cure, that will be established step by step, in the process of reversing the trends established as the faultlines have, now over the centuries, etched deeper gorges in our cultural and intellectual landscapes. This process begins with two questions:

1)   How do we reverse the processes of fragmentation, of relativisation and of moral trivialisation without losing the benefits which the processes of intellectual specialisation, the extension of tolerance, and the abandonmentof the aridities of a wholly rule-governed and rationalistic approach to ethics, have conferred upon us?

2)   What implications may we draw from this for the organisation of schools and their curricula?

I have to confess that my reply to these questions may initially have the shape of a version of humanism, but I would equally plead that such a view is based on a limited understanding of the possibilities of the human condition. It would, I suggest, be worthy only of a Canute-like gesture, to return to the search for a Cartesian single method which would be adequate to the whole rich tapestry of the understanding of human beings, and the world in which they live. Even if the physicists are intent upon identifying and taming an account of a single force which would unify our current physical knowledge of the world, the notion of completeness in such an account is itself deeply suspect. To elaborate such a claim would require a detailed discussion of the insights of philosophers as diverse as Kant, Gödel and Wittgenstein, and this is not the place for that. Suffice it to point out, as a holding position, that such a goal is an aspiration rather than achievement of physics.

My alternative suggestion is that rather than look for unity in method or technique, we should create a form of unity by focusing upon a common goal for all human knowledge and understanding. The first part of that goal is stated well by Pope: 'The proper study of mankind is man. . .' The second element of the focus of the human search for knowledge is an aspect of that, but one which, as I have already argued, was identified forcefully in the writings of Adam Ferguson, the study of the varieties of human society which human beings inhabit. The third element of the common focus of our need to find understanding is that of the world in which we live, and of which we are part.

That is to say, the search for a kind of unity in the fragments of knowledge which is our inheritance, is not the search for a single method, but rather the unity to be created in the common purpose of seeking a self-knowledge of what it is to be human, and an understanding of the determinants of human life — the possible structures of human society and the actual truth about the empirical world which we inhabit in all its vastness and minuteness.

This will drive us not to monolithic forms of enquiry, but to the kind of structured dialogue between the specialists and experts who probe in their various arenas the limits of our knowledge. Of particular importance will be the boundaries, not only of the outer fragments of knowledge, but of the interfaces between the chemist, the biochemist and the molecular biologist as they seek to account for the necessary and sufficient conditions of human life; or between the neuroscientist, the computer scientist and the philosopher as they attempt to give accounts of the nature of consciousness and thought.

Equally, in understanding human society and the conditions and manner of its operation, if we are to do better than partiality and tunnel vision, the economist must sit down with the social psychologist, and both must talk also to the historian, the philosopher of law, the sociologist of religion and the experts in all aspects of urban and rural environments, and many others also. *Mutatis mutandis,* comparable dialogue is essential for those whose many fragmented specialities help us to partial understandings of the empirical world.

There are clear implications to be drawn from this for the school curriculum. However, to give due warning on a point of some technicality in the design of curricula, it should not be presumed from this that I am commending a move to abandon subject-based teaching in favour of project-based learning. That smacks too much of 'one single bound'. Rather it is a matter of ensuring that between subject and project a due balance is struck, and that in all cases the limitations of focusing upon one single method is understood.

So far as concerns pluralism and its alter ego relativism, the first point to be made is that sociologically pluralism of culture, religion and values is a fact in contemporary Britain, although more so in some cities and regions and others. The faultline develops as that pluralism becomes the driving force of radical forms of relativism.

My proposal for the path from diagnosis to cure once again avoids the temptation to seek a single method or set of criteria for settling every question of value or social priority. Rather, I suggest, we should seek to identify the questions which are posed by the very realisation of the degree of pluralism which characterises our society. These questions although not elaborated by Kant, have a Kantian form:

1)   What are the conditions for the functioning of a society which is plural in character?

2)   What in such a context are the conditions of civil liberty?

In each of these enquiries the elucidation of the concept of toleration, begun interestingly by John Locke, will play a central part, but the enquiries will not be purely conceptual or philosophical in character, for they will have to draw upon the sorts of questions outlined above and the many varied and specialist contributions implicit in them to our understanding of human society. To give just one illustration, quite central to the matter is the relationship between particular forms of economic strength in a society and the prospects for the acceptance of tolerance and therefore pluralism.

There are clear implications in this for schools in relationship to shaping the curriculum — for example in identifying what depth of understanding of aspects of these interactions and also of the diversities of culture present in any specific community is a precondition of the practice of toleration by the citizens of the future. Equally important however, is how such awareness on the part of the staff and governors of schools informs the ethos, structure and institutional practice of those schools.

The main difficulty which I have with the theory implicit in what I have called moral atomisation is that it does not do justice to what human beings are, nor to the possible structures of human society. Various attempts have been made to characterise societies and human beings whose basic value structure would seem to encompass one form or another of this catch-all concept of moral atomisation. For example Huxley's *Brave New World* presumes that what moves most of the citizens of that fable is an attachment to what gives individual satisfaction. This is not a description of a form of selfishness, but rather of a value system which has no alternative priority because for most of the citizens no alternative is conceivable. The question has to be whether human beings are like the citizens of Huxley's world, or whether, as a modern Thomas Hobbes, Huxley is not simply giving us warning of the dangers of allowing such an account of moral values to inform our picture of human beings.

My point here is not to elaborate in particular on Huxley's rather bleak view, but rather to remind us that any view of what it is that human beings value can be tested at one level as an empirical question. The significant value of a Hobbesian or Huxleyan vision of what moves human beings to action is that it forces us once again to reconsider what manner of beings humans are, and whether what they value is as the vision in question suggests. This returns us to 'the proper study of mankind', and in so doing raises further questions.

If as a matter of fact the values which inform human lives extend beyond those of Hobbes and Huxley and their respective grim visions, then we must give an account of what those extended values are and to what human aspirations they give practical expression. These questions have initially the form of empirical questions, and elucidating the answers will involve many intellectual skills and techniques. But as we begin to answer them we shall find the character of our enquiries changing. From the questions of the nature of human aspirations and the expression of them in values and action, arise the further questions of whether these aspirations are most successfully expressed in this way or that, and whether the practical realisation of them is best found through this code or ethic or that.

Underlying these issues of practical morality is the more fundamental question of what it is for human beings to flourish. That in itself is not a straightforward empirical question, though the answer to it — whether single or plural in form — will require underpinning from the answers to questions such as the range of aspirations which human beings actually have, and the range of possible goals or purposes to which they do as well as might aspire.

Again, if there is a 'cure' for what I have described as 'moral atomisation', then it will be found by pursuing the question of what it is for human beings to flourish, and the implications of answers to that for setting goals and purposes. I think it unlikely that the outcome will be the accounts of human life sketched by either Hobbes or Huxley. We have once again arrived at a question which can be put in a Kantian form: What are the conditions of human flourishing? That in itself might seem too individualistic in character to embrace all of our concerns, but it will seem a much stronger contender as a 'cure' if it is accompanied by the questions of comparable form which arose implicitly in our discussion of pluralism and relativism: What are the conditions of flourishing within a pluralistic society?

To summarise this part of the argument, I hope that I have shown that the intellectual tasks set by the presence of what I have referred to as the three great faultlines in our society are in fact when analysed, both intelligible and manageable. This is not to say that the questions set which chart the way ahead are easy, but easy solutions/cures were never on offer. The implications of all of this for the school curriculum are many and varied, but must include developing in children the capacity for moral reflection, *mutatis mutandis*, along the lines suggested above. Apart from all the material in the great religious traditions of the world, Aesop's Fables and Tolstoy's short stories will each provide excellent stimulation at different stages of development.

I have one last comment. The diagnosis which I have offered of the faultlines within our society, and the subsequent outline of a cure, may seem both excessively daunting and rather abstract. To take the latter point first, I do accept that this is how the matter may well now appear, but may I remind you that the problem facing teachers is a very serious and deep one. Unless the society in which they live and work can give some coherent account of what it considers important in human life then teachers have no real framework within which to operate, and by which they and their pupils and the parents can evaluate whether the school is being successful in providing for, to quote the relevant words from the 1992 (Schools) Education Act, 'the spiritual, moral, cultural and social development' of pupils.

If the reasons for the difficulty which our society has in answering the question of what counts as 'spiritual, moral, cultural and social development' lie in deep faultlines, then superficial bridges over those faultlines will not do. There is work here for philosophers and intellectuals if only they would rise to the challenge. However, as I have suggested there is work also for the teacher and the headteacher also: for as they reflect individually and together upon what sort of community a school is and what capacities for reflection and reasoning are preconditions of the membership of a school community, then they too will be contributing to the debate. To illustrate further with one very difficult and perplexing problem faced by our schools. When a pupil is excluded from a school what is it that is lacking? Is it a capacity within the pupil? Is there a structural problem within the school community which makes it impossible for this individual to be part of that community? Or is there no conceivable educational community which could encompass this and other non-excluded pupils? The answers to these questions are no more and no less difficult than the seemingly abstract ones posed earlier in the lecture, yet they exemplify in definitive educational form aspects of what I have referred to as the faultlines in our society. Perhaps in this sense too, schools are microcosms of our society.

Part 5:

EDUCATION, VALUES AND SCIENCE

15

Mary Midgley

Science and Poetry

Is art a luxury? Is there any connection between poetry and science? Today it may not be easy for us to relate these two topics on a single map. Academic specialization usually keeps them apart. But there is one very simple map which does suggest a way of relating them, a map which is worth looking at because it still has quite an influence on our thinking today. It is the map which the distinguished chemist Peter Atkins draws in the course of arguing that science is *omnicompetent*, that is, able to supply all our intellectual needs.

Atkins notes that some people may suggest that we need other forms of thought such as poetry and philosophy as well as science, since science cannot deal with the spirit. They are mistaken he says. These other forms add nothing serious to science:

> Although poets may aspire to understanding, their talents are more akin to entertaining self-deception. They may be able to emphasise delights in the world, but they are deluded if they and their admirers believe that their identification of the delights and their use of poignant language are enough for comprehension. Philosophers too, I am afraid, have contributed to the understanding of the universe little more than poets . . . They have not contributed much that is novel until after novelty has been discovered by scientists. . ... While poetry titillates and theology obfuscates, science liberates (Atkins, 1995, p. 123).

Now though this view is not usually declared with quite Atkins's degree of outspokenness and tribal belligerence, the view itself is actually not a rare one. A lot of people today accept it, or at least can't see good reason why they should not accept it, even if they don't like it. They have a suspicion, welcome or otherwise, that the arts are mere luxuries and science is the only intellectual necessity. It seems to them that science supplies all the facts out of which we build (so to speak) the house of our beliefs. It is only after this house is built that we can — if we like — sit down inside it, turn on the CD player and listen to some Mozart or read some poetry.

This is a notion which can make things really hard for young people who are trying to decide what subjects they should specialise in at school and college. More widely, too. It has an odd effect in other aspects of education. The idea that science is a separate domain, irelevant to the arts, is liable to produce a strange kind of apartheid in the teaching of literature, a convention whereby important and powerful writings get ignored if they have a scientific subject-matter. Thus H.G. Wells and the whole vigorous science-fiction tradition which derives from him were long cold-shouldered out of the syllabus entirely and have not yet fully reached it — and this even though writers like Joseph Conrad and Henry James, whose works are central to that syllabus, admired Wells deeply and saw the great importance of his vision. Until quite lately, even *Frankenstein* was ignored. Potent ideas expressed in these writings do not get properly faced and criticised in the teaching of literature. These ideas are, of course, often ones *about* science and its relation to the rest of life, which is itself a topic of wide-ranging importance. Increasingly, too, they include ideas about the meaning of the environmental crisis.

These matters get excluded from discussion of literature because the literary theories that have been recently in favour tend to play down the importance of all reference to the outside world in the works studied, concentrating instead wholly on the mind-set of writers and readers. No doubt this is a reaction against an unduly naive, social-realist approach favoured in the past. But the reaction seems now to have gone so far that intending students are confronted with a rather bewildering choice. On the one hand they are offered a somewhat introspective and subjective approach to literature. On the other, they face a kind of science-teaching which never mentions the attitudes and background assumptions that influence scientists at all — indeed, one that often views any mention of these topics as vulgar and dangerous. Thus, they may study either the outer *or* the inner aspect of human life, but must on no account bring the two together. It seems that, despite the efforts of many both in schools and universities, Descartes still rules. Mind and body are still separated. And since this educational situation has been around for some time, it has by now produced a generation of one-eyed specialists on both sides, specialists who tend, not unnaturally, to find their respective opposite numbers puzzling and so to drift into an unprofitable warfare. Since many of these people are unhappy with this situation, I suggest that it is worth while to take a much harder look at the misleading imaginative picture out of which it arises.

Lucretius and the Vision of Atomism

This is really a very odd picture, one which does not fit the actual history of thought at all. Re-reading Atkins's words lately, I began to think about his remark that poets and philosophers 'have not contributed much that is novel [to the understanding of the universe] until after novelty has been discovered by scientists.' What struck me then was the influence that a single great philosophic poem, — Lucretius's *On The Nature Of Things (De Rerum Natura)* — has actually played in the formation of modern Western thought and especially of Western science.

That poem was the main channel through which the atomic theory of matter reached Renaissance Europe. It was forcibly stated there, all ready to be taken up by the founders of modern physics. Of course it was the Greek Atomist philosophers who had invented that theory and no doubt their work would have reached later thinkers in some form even without Lucretius's poem. But the force and fervour of the poem gave atomism a head start. It rammed the atomists' imaginative vision right home to the hearts of Renaissance readers as well as to their minds. That vision included, not just the atomic theory itself but also the startling moral conclusions which Epicurus had already drawn from it. In this way it forged a much wider strand in Enlightenment thinking.

For Lucretius did not see atomism primarily as a solution to scientific problems. Following Epicurus, he saw it as something much more central to human life. For him it was a moral crusade — the only way to free mankind from a crushing load of superstition by showing that natural causation was independent of the gods. Human beings, he said, are continually tormented by groundless fears of natural events and by useless precautions against them:

> They make propitiatory sacrifices, slaughter black cattle and dispatch offerings to the Departed Spirits . . . As children in blank darkness tremble and start at everything, so we in broad daylight are oppressed at times by fears as baseless as those horrors which children imagine coming upon them in the dark. This dread and darkness of the mind cannot be dispelled by the sunbeams, the shining shafts of day, but only by an understanding of the outward form and inner workings of nature . . . How many crimes has religion led people to commit (Lucretius, Book II, lines 50–62, Book I, line 101).

Thus Lucretius launched the notion of science as primarily a benign kind of weedkiller designed to get rid of religion, and launched it in great rolling passionate hexameters which gave it a force that it would never have had if it had been expressed in dry, unemotive prose. His work is visibly the source of the anti-religious rhetoric that is still used by later imperialistic champions of science such as Bertrand Russell and Atkins himself.

The Primacy of Visions

I am not just making a debating point here for the deplorable War of the Two Cultures which Atkins is so keen to wage. This story of the influence that Greek atomistic philosophers have had, by way of a Roman poet, on the founding of modern science is not just a meaningless historical accident. It is a prime example of the way in which our major ideas are generated, namely, through the imagination. New ideas are new imaginative visions, not just in the sense that they involve particular new images, such as Kekule's image of the serpent eating its tail etc, but in the sense that they involve changes in our larger world-pictures, in the general way in which we conceive life. These changes are so general and so vast that they affect the whole shape of our thinking. That is why something as important as science could not possibly be an isolated, self-generating thought-form arising on its own in the way that Atkins suggests. To picture it as isolated in this way — as a solitary example of rational thinking, standing out alone against a background of formless emotion — is to lose sight of its organic connection with the rest of our ideas. And that connection explains why we have to attend to it.

Changes in world-pictures are not a trivial matter. The mediaeval world-picture was static and God-centred. It called on people to admire the physical cosmos as God's creation, but it viewed that cosmos as something permanently settled on principles that were not really open to human understanding at all. By contrast, the atomists showed a physical universe in perpetual flux, a mass of atoms continually whirling around through an infinite space and occasionally combining, entirely by chance, to form worlds such as our own. In principle, this new universe was physically comprehensible because we could learn something about the atomic movements and could thus understand better what was happening to us. But it was not morally comprehensible. According to Lucretius, the attempt to comprehend the world morally had always been mistaken and was the central source of human misery. In their mistaken belief that they could reach such an understanding, anxious and confused people had taken refuge from their ignorance in superstition:

I]n handing over everything to the gods and making everything dependent on their whim....Poor humanity! to saddle the gods with suc responsibilities and throw in a vindictive temper! . . . This is not piety, this
oft-repeated show of bowing a veiled head before a stone, this bustling to
every altar, this deluging of altars with the blood of beasts.

. . . True piety lies rather in the power to contemplate the universe with
a quiet mind (Lucretius, Book V, lines 1185 and 1184–1203).

Instead of this anxious pursuit of bogus social explanations for
natural events — instead of these wild speculations about irrespon-
sible gods, people should now become calmer and look for physical
explanations which, though much slighter, would be reliable so far
as they went, and would thus quench their anxiety.

This dynamic and chilling yet ordered world-picture made physical speculation seem possible and indeed necessary. At the Renaissance, moreover, it came together with another picture which had
not been available before — namely that of the world as a machine.
The invention of real complex machines such as clocks gave the
human imagination an immensely powerful piece of new material.
Machine-imagery changes the world-view profoundly because
machines are by definition under human control. They can in a sense
be fully understood because they can be taken to pieces. And if the
world is essentially a machine, then it can be taken to pieces too. It
was the fusion of these two imaginative visions that made modern
science look possible. And it had to look possible before anybody
could actually start doing it.

This dependence of detailed thought on entirely non-detailed
visions is the main point that I want to get across. By their nature, the
originating visions are necessarily vague. When the Greek atomists
spoke of the various kinds of atoms as having their own specific
movements, they had not the remotest idea of what these movements might be or how anybody could discover them. Though it was
central to their position that the movements themselves were fixed,
definite and invariable, they could not, in the nature of the case, possibly supply definite examples. They had to convey their point
through the necessarily vague medium of imagery. What they were
supplying was much more like a Turner sketch than it was like a
photograph, and it was not in the least like an engineer's diagram.

At this imaginative stage, then, they were putting forward a theory *about* exactness — they were envisaging an ideal of exactness
comparable with that which we now think of as typical of science —
but they had not got anything like an exact theory. It is important
that, at this stage, this kind of vagueness is not a vice, any more than

it is a vice in a map of the world that it does not show the details of the small areas within it. It is natural and proper that our detailed thinking arises from imaginative roots. But it is important that we should recognise the nature of these roots — that we should not confuse the ideal of exactness with the actual achievement of it.

Impressive and influential theories do not originally gain their influence by telling us exact facts about the world. It is usually a long time before they can provide any such facts. Actual precision comes much later, if at all. What makes theories persuasive in the first place is some other quality in their vision, something in them which answers to a wider need. That need is sometimes a genuine intellectual thirst for understanding, but not always. Any theory that has a serious and widespread influence on thought owes its appeal to satisfying a number of different needs, many of which those who are influenced by it are not aware of. As the theory is used and developed, this plurality of power-sources begins to become visible, and it can result in serious conflicts.

The Meaning of Determinism

For instance, the determinism which the atomists introduced — the belief in a completely fixed, completely knowable physical order — obviously did not originally owe its appeal to being established as an empirical fact. It goes so far beyond any evidence that there is no way in which it could be established empirically. Much of this appeal was obviously due to its convenience for science — to the fact that it seemed to promise intellectual satisfaction by guaranteeing the regularity of nature. But of course, the fact that we want this satisfaction does not show that nature will always supply it. Determinism was not and could not be a conclusion proved by scientific methods. It was an assumption made in order to make the scientific enterprise look, not just plausible so far, but infinitely hopeful. And that infinite hope was not seen as optional. When, early in the twentieth century, physicists began to question this total determinism it became obvious that scientists did not view their deterministic faith merely as a dispensable matter of convenience. They saw it as a central element necessary to any scientific attitude. Einstein, when he objected to the reasonings of quantum mechanics by insisting that God does not play dice, was certainly talking metaphysics. Karl Popper, commenting on this, remarks

> Physical determinism, we might say in retrospect, was *a daydream of omniscience* [my emphasis] which seemed to become more real with

every advance of physics until it became an apparently inescapable nightmare (Popper, 1972, p. 222).

Popper is suggesting that determinism was really welcomed as much for its flattering view of ourselves as for its soothing account of the world — as much because it declared *us* infinitely capable of knowledge as because it claimed that the world itself was ordered and knowable. While both claims are unprovable, it was (he says) the first claim — our own potential omniscience — rather than the second which was really attracting theorists. (It still does). This bias towards establishing and glorifying our own status is still more obvious over mechanism — the further development of determinism which relies on machine imagery, thus producing the delightful impression that in principle we can copy all natural objects as well as understand them. Thus Julien de Lamettrie, meeting objections to mechanism based on the complexity of natural beings, replied that, with a bit more trouble, we will be able to make machines to imitate every kind of complexity;

> If more instruments, wheelwork and springs are required to show the movements of the planets than to mark and repeat the hours, if Vaucanson needed more art to make his *flute player* than his *duck*, he would need even more to make a *talker* . . . The human body is an immense clock, constructed with so much artifice and skill that if the wheel that marks the seconds stops because of rust or derailment, the minutes wheel continues turning . . . (La Mettrie, 1994, p. 69).

Fatalism and Contemplation

At this point, however, the messages from these different visions begin to divide. Lucretius and Epicurus did not promise this kind of complete knowledge at all and took no interest in the technology that might grow from it. They were much more thoroughly sceptical. They had no confidence in any practical improvements of human life. In fact, Epicurus himself despised the pursuit of theoretical knowledge for its own sake as one more distraction from the pursuit of inner peace and warned his followers against it. 'Set your sail, O happy youth' he cried, 'and flee from every form of education'. Lucretius is more interested in details about atoms, but for him too knowledge itself is not the aim. Knowledge is a means not an end and a means to inward peace, not to improved outward activity. Primarily it is a cure for anxiety, a path to *ataraxia*, peace of mind. It is in these terms that he celebrates Epicurus's achievement:

> When human life lay grovelling in all men's sight, crushed to the earth under the dead weight of superstition . . . a man of Greece was first to

raise mortal eyes in defiance, first to stand erect and brave the challenge. Fables of the gods did not crush him . . . He, first of all men, longed to smash the constraining locks of nature's doors. . . He ventured far out beyond the flaming ramparts of the world and voyaged in mind throughout infinity. Returning victorious, he proclaimed to us *what can be and what cannot; how the power of each thing is limited* . . . Therefore superstition in its turn lies crushed beneath his feet, and we by his triumph are lifted level with the skies (Lucretius, Book I, lines 62–78).

This is splendid stuff. But there is no mention here of any research programme to follow, no talk of the need to track down every kind of atom and establish its powers. It is enough for Epicurus to have shown, in principle and *a priori*, 'what can be and what cannot', that is, essentially it is enough to have proved a negative, to have shown that we need not fear the gods.

This vision of salvation through science — this hope that scientists can ensure human happiness simply by removing religion — is still familiar today. It is worth while to ask how far the people who now preach it actually share Lucretius's vision. Essentially, what the Epicureans were preaching was a fatalistic quietism. They did not think that human happiness could be increased either by political activity or by the satisfactions of love, or indeed by knowledge either. Instead, they put their faith in a stern limitation of human ambition, a concentration on what little is possible to us here and now. They thought that people who had once fully grasped that they could not change the world at all, either by sacrificing to the gods or by any other kind of effort, would cease their anxious striving, would compose their minds, would be able enjoy the satisfactions that life actually gave them in the present, and would console themselves for their sorrows by admiring the cosmos. Knowing that death would not lead to divine punishment or to a gloomy afterlife, they would no longer fear it. When they died, they would be content simply to dissolve away into their constituent atoms. And, since they knew that natural disasters — lightning, earthquakes, diseases — could not be prevented, they would concentrate on facing these things calmly, instead of dissipating their energy on fruitless efforts to influence nonexistent gods.

The Limits of Epicureanism

Things have not, of course, turned out that way. Anxiety turns out to be a much more robust and central part of human life than Lucretius supposed. We modern addicts to anxiety may be deprived of an outlet to it through sacrificing to the gods but this does not stop us worrying. We simply exhaust ourselves instead in a frantic search for success, or security, or for better life-styles or for new medicines. No doubt, the general thought that the physical world is orderly and reliable does have some reassuring effect. But we don't seem to have gained the salutary recognition of our own insignificance, the humility which Epicurus hoped would flow from his vision of the vast, formless impersonal universe — has not followed. Our knowledge of science has not stopped us living largely in the future rather than in the present. We are still continually planning crowds of incompatible schemes and continually being disappointed. Most of us still live on jam to-morrow instead of soberly enjoying what we have while we have it, as Epicurus advised.

In fact, though Epicurean morality has much to recommend it, it does not seem to be compatible, as a whole, with the nature of human striving. Historically, Epicureanism was a faith born of very brutal and unmanageable times — hopeless times during the last century of the Roman Republic when civil war and corruption made it seem that all effort to improve the world was indeed futile. And there were many such bad times in the Greco-Roman world, and during the Dark Ages. Accordingly, Epicureanism was valued throughout those eras as a spiritual refuge where people could shut themselves away when necessary and try to forget about outside distresses. When things went a little better and civic activity became possible they tended to prefer Stoicism, which left much more scope for social interests and duties.

During the Renaissance, people who were searching for new ideas found both these pagan philosophies helpful in many ways and used them both freely in forming later thought. There is much more of both in our current ideas than we usually notice. But in the early modern period there was a further special reason for welcoming the Epicurean attack on religion, namely the wars and persecutions that disgraced the name of religion in the sixteenth and seventeenth centuries. Enlightenment philosophers such as Hobbes, Hume and Voltaire who were horrified by those wars and persecutions saw a quite new force in Lucretius's invectives against religion. His exclamation, *'Quantum religio potuit suadere malorum'* ('how many crimes has religion made people commit') expressed their views exactly. I believe that this is why atomism itself was once more seen as having a profound moral significance. That is why its world-picture gained so much force and prevalence among a wide readership — a circle far

wider than just the scientists who managed to turn it into a successful physical theory.

Religion, Magic and Contemplation

Now, what am I *not* saying? I am not saying that the atomic theory
would never have emerged in science if it had not had these particular philosophical and poetic roots in Greece and Rome. I *am* saying
that, if the theory had had different roots, it would not have brought
with it this particular world-picture, this myth, this drama, this way
of accommodating science in the range of human activities, this
notion of what it is to have a scientific attitude. In particular, there
seems no reason to think that the mere advance of science itself
would necessarily have brought with it the Epicureans' undiscriminating, wholesale hostility to religion — their notion that the value of
science lay primarily in its power to make people happier by displac-
ing religion from human life.

That idea surely is peculiar because the notion of religion that it
involves is such a narrow one. Of course the anxious, insatiable business of propitiatory rituals which Lucretius describes does play a
large part among the vast range of human proceedings which we call
religious. But it clearly belongs in a special department of that range,
namely the department called Magic. Among the great religions,
Buddhism rejects this kind of magic entirely and in Judaism there
were strong protests against it as early as the Psalms. It was never
incorporated into Christian or Islamic teaching. The idea of bribing
or bullying a deity to change your destiny is quite foreign to the
spirit of these religions. Of course it has often crept into religious
practice and often become prominent there, because anxiety is such
a powerful human motive — for instance in the sale of indulgences.
But when magic has crept in in this way, reforming movements have
repeatedly been formed within these religions to get rid of it and to
point out that this is not what they are about at all.

Besides this, Pagan religions too usually contained far more admirable things than the kind of low-grade magic that Lucretius
deplores. His own tradition contained Pindar's hymns to Apollo,
Plato's myths and the Eleusinian mysteries. And indeed, Lucretius
himself furnishes an example of the splendid things that Paganism
could contain in the great opening passage of his poem *On the Nature
of Things*. This passage is a straightforward Hymn to Venus — an
invocation of her as the Spirit of Life, the generous maternal force in
nature which fills living things with delight and makes possible the

whole admirable world around us. Here is devotion to a force and an ideal which is clearly seen as spiritual as well as physical — devotion of a kind which polytheists often express very nobly towards their deities, because those deities mean something serious for them. When Lucretius mentions the Earth, too, he repeatedly has trouble in restraining himself from openly venerating it as our divine Mother (e.g. Book II line 596–600 and lines 993–8) in a way that recalls the current embarrassment of some scientists in handling the concept of Gaia.

But beyond this and more centrally, he shows an intense reverence for the vast atomic system that he portrays — a system that he sees as essentially ordered and universal although in another way it is chaotic. And it is just this reverence that he wants, above all, to arouse in his readers. He hopes that it will take the place of the useless anxiety that now drives them to make their futile sacrifices, that it will cure them of fearing death and also of entertaining idle ambitions, since it will show that earthly success is hollow, trifling and transient in the perspective of this vast impersonal universe.

There is no doubt that this is a noble vision. But it does seem to be rather a narrow one. In some ways, the Epicurean ideal is quite close to the Buddhist concept of enlightenment through non-attachment, but it is much more purely negative and asocial. There is no element of Buddhist compassion here, no suggestion of delaying one's own enlightenment to promote the salvation of other sentient beings. Epicureanism offers us a private salvation if we will only respond rationally to the physical universe. But we may want to ask, can the thought of that physical universe alone be expected to produce this degree of philosophic detachment? Can such calm acceptance be expected to follow simply from the findings of physical science? There are now many scientists in our culture who are deeply convinced of the atomic structure of matter and who know far more about it than Epicurus ever dreamed of. But it is not clear that this acceptance frees them from the fear of death, nor even that it tends to cure them of ambition. It certainly doesn't necessarily make them view Nobel Prizes with lofty contempt as mere earthly trifles. If we want to get a wider perspective within which earthly success really does appear insignificant we will probably need to turn to sages who are prepared to give us a more positive and constructive spiritual vision.

The Need for Dialogue

It is important to concede the part Lucretius got right. The exaltation of science does indeed have a philosophic point. The modern scientific vision of the world does have enormous grandeur. Contemplation of it certainly can enlarge our mental horizons, distract us from mean preoccupations, raise our aspirations, remind us of wider possibilities. This is a real benefit, for which we should not be ungrateful. The trouble about it is that, once we have this new vision, there are many different interpretations that we can put on it, many different directions in which it can lead us. It is quite hard to distinguish among those different directions and to map them in a way that lets us navigate reasonably among them. This kind of mapping is not itself scientific business, so scientists tend not to be trained in it. It calls for different ways of thinking.

For instance, many different responses are possible to the miracles of modern physics. To some people, those miracles suggest only more and better weaponry. That is why a high proportion of the world's trained physicists are now engaged on military projects. Beyond this, there is a wider circle of people to whom these miracles chiefly symbolise just an increase in power, without any special idea about how that power had best be used. Out of this fascination with new power there arises our current huge expansion of technology, much of it useful, much not, and the sheer size of it (as we now see) dangerously wasteful of resources. It is hard for us to break out of this circle of increasing needs because our age is remarkably preoccupied with the vision of continually improving means rather than saving ourselves trouble by reflecting on ends. This is the opposite bias from the fatalistic quietism of the Epicureans, who refused to think about means at all. It is not clear that our bias is any more sensible than theirs. But, at a casual glance, it is just as natural a response to the grand vision of the physical world which we derive from modern science.

The difficulty is to make that glance more than casual, to criticise properly the various visions that constantly arise in us. We need to compare those visions, to articulate them more clearly, to be aware of changes in them, to think them through so as to see what they will commit us to. This kind of criticism is not itself scientific business, though of course scientists can and do engage in it. It is necessarily philosophic business (whoever does it) because it involves analysing concepts and attending to the wider structures in which those concepts get their meaning. It starts with the fuller articulation of imaginative visions and moves on later to all kinds of more detailed thought, including scientific thought.

That is why all science grows out of philosophical thinking — out of the criticism of imaginative visions — why it takes that criticism for granted and always continues to need it. It is why Peter Atkins's vision of a free-standing, autonomous science with a monopoly of rationality — a science that does all our thinking for us — is not workable. Philosophic assumptions don't stop being influential just because they have been forgotten. They lie under the floorboards of all intellectual schemes. Like the plumbing, they are really quite complicated, they often conflict, and they can only be ignored so long as we don't happen to notice those conflicts.

When the conflicts get so bad that we do notice them, we need to call in a philosophic plumber. Of course this person need not be a paid philosopher, but he must be someone who knows that the philosophical angle matters. Rationality is not available without this kind of attention to the conflicts between our various assumptions because rationality itself is something much larger than mere exactness. Rationality itself is an ideal — one which we perceive somewhat cloudily in a vision, but towards which we can certainly move — an ideal of a just and realistic balance among our various assumptions and ideals.

The Cognitive Role of Poetry

As for poetry and the arts generally, they too play a central part in our intellectual life because they supply the language in which our imaginative visions are most immediately articulated, the medium through which we usually get our first impression of them. Shelley said that poets are the unacknowledged legislators of the world. This is strong language, but his point may really be needed in an age when literature may seem to have sublimated itself into a haze of texts bombinating above us in a metaphysical stratosphere. Shelley meant that poets — including, of course, imaginative prose writers — express, not just feelings, but crucial new ideas in a direct form that is often necessary before our intellects can grasp them, and that these ideas directly influence our life. These writers do not usually do their legislating by literally spelling out theories, as Lucretius did, but by showing forcefully (as novelists and dramatists can) how the new ideas would work out in real life. Shakespeare does this all the time. And again, the ideal of detachment from worldly affairs which the Epicureans offered is one that can take many forms and lead to many different life-styles. Plato presented one of these life-styles dramatically in the portrait of Socrates that he drew in his dialogues, There are others, ranging from the totally ascetic and solitary to the altruistic, which would lead to very different lives. In *War and Peace*, Pierre attempts this kind of detachment; the difficulties which he runs into cast a sharp light on its problems. Since we often have to make choices among paths of this kind, literature plays a vital part in life by stirring our imaginations and making us more aware of what particular choices can involve. If it is taught in a way which plays down or even suppresses this imaginative action, something vital is lost from life. And we may begin to wonder why, on these conditions, it is important to study literature at all.

It is worth noticing, too, that in this way philosophy itself is a branch of literature. Any major kind of philosophising always presents some distinctive ideal for life as well as for thought because life and thought are so closely related. The great philosophers of our tradition have usually displayed their ideals quite explicitly, as have those of other traditions, and if contemporary academic philosophers suppose that they are not doing this they are deceiving themselves. Academic narrowness is a way of life as much as any other. It is quite as easily conveyed by a style of writing, and even more easily by a style of teaching.

The Imaginative Role of Science

All of us who talk and write reveal what kind of things we think important and what we think trivial. We all communicate our particular vision of life, and those of us who deal in large visions convey them more clearly and more influentially than the rest of us. As I have been pointing out, science too incorporates these influential visions, and this is certainly not something that scientists should avoid or be ashamed of. Scientists have influenced our life profoundly and they do so increasingly today. However much they may try to be objective about particular facts their own personalities inevitably influence the general shape of their message and there is no reason why it should not do so. They influence us by their imagery, by their selection of topics, by the ways in which they explain their theories, by the views that they express about what does and what does not constitute a proper scientific attitude. In this way they contribute to the constant ferment of dialectic that goes on as we try to compare different attitudes and balance the force of various ideals.

And this is thoroughly satisfactory provided that they know that they are indeed making this kind of contribution — provided that they listen to the other contributors and grasp the general shape of the debate as Galileo and Darwin and Huxley did, rather than supposing that the particular imaginative vision espoused by current science must always prevail.

Peter Atkins is not mistaken, then, in claiming that science plays a crucial part in our intellectual life. His mistake lies in the somewhat wild suggestion that science occupies the stage alone, that it is the sole contributor of rationality to an otherwise thought-free world. This kind of illusion of omnipotence is a disease that easily afflicts people who isolate themselves from general conversation. It is strongly encouraged by today's academic specialisation, and it infects other academic tribes as well as the scientific one. We all tend to think that we know best. Today's over-exaltation of science originated as a response to the absurd over-exaltation of classical studies that ruled in the nineteenth century. At present, various kinds of rather unreal anti-science rhetoric tend to encourage this warfare by supporting the idea of a simple conflict between a single personified science and some other champion for the single position of intellectual dominance. No such position is available, so the idea of a War between Two Cultures is a futile one. Instead we all need to sit down together and exchange our visions.

16

Mary Midgley

Atoms, Memes and Individuals

In my first lecture I discussed Peter Atkins's claim that science is 'omnicompetent' — an independent, solitary intellectual citadel, the only real source of rational thought, a central government under which both poetry and philosophy are only minor agencies. As I said then, this idea is not often expressed today as confidently and brutally as Atkins puts it. Yet it deserves attention because it flows from an important element in our current beliefs, namely the mysterious isolation of science. The trouble is that modern specialization makes it so hard for us to relate the various aspects of our thought that the physical sciences tend to appear to us as somewhat cut off from the rest of our thinking. To most of us, the most obvious fact about them is simply their power. Seeing their immense successes embodied in technology, we often find it natural to exalt them, so we are not surprised by the claim that their methods ought to be extended to cover the rest of our thought. That claim — first made by Auguste Comte, founder of positivism, and repeated by many sages since — underlies many desperate attempts today in other studies — especially in the social sciences — to become, in some sense, ever more 'scientific'.

On the other hand, this mysterious isolation can just as easily produce alienation and fear. We are struck by the dangers of technology. We see how easily the power of science can be misused, and that science itself cannot correct that misuse. We despair of the scientific ideal and sometimes declare war on science itself. We oscillate between idealising science and fearing it.

In these lectures I want to say that both these attitudes are equally wrong. Both express an unreal abstraction. The sciences are *not* cut off in this way from the rest of our thought. They don't compose one solid, distinct, autonomous intellectual entity. There are many scientific ways of thinking but all of them grow out of common thought, draw on its imagery and share its motivations. Scientists do indeed aim at objective truth about the world and they sometimes achieve it. It really is true that water is made of hydrogen and oxygen and that the liver secretes bile. But scientists have to select for their investigation patterns in that world which particularly interest them. And the reasons for that selection are by no means always as obvious as they may seem.

Now I am *not* suggesting, as some sociologists of science have done, that scientists just make up their results by framing experiments to prove what they already want to believe. Extreme social constructionism is not a convincing story at all. But I do find it striking how deeply scientific thinking is pervaded by patterns from everyday thinking and, in particular, how strong an effect the imagery chosen has on what is conceived at a given time as being scientific. In order to illustrate this, I shall go on talking in this lecture about the meaning of the atomic model.

The Meaning of Atomism

As I mentioned in the previous lecture, the pioneers of modern science drew that model from the Greek atomist philosophers and more directly from the passionate Epicurean version of it given by the Roman poet Lucretius. They did not receive atomism merely as a scientific hypothesis but as part of a strong and distinctive ideology. They saw it not just as a literal truth but as a symbolic pattern suggesting meanings affecting much wider areas of life. Morally, for instance, atomism seemed to point the way, not only away from religion but also away from communal thinking and towards social atomism — that is, towards individualism. And in the matter of scientific knowledge, atomism seemed to promise a most reassuring kind of simplicity and finality — a guarantee that the world would prove intelligible in the end in relatively simple terms, once we had split it up into its ultimate elements. In fact, *understanding* the world was essentially a matter of finding those ultimate units.

Both these promises — the social reliance on individualism and the intellectual confidence in final simplicity — were central elements in Enlightenment thinking. They are both still prominent in our thought today. But both are now causing us a lot of trouble. On the physical side, scientists no longer think in terms of hard, separate, unchangeable atoms at all. Attempts to go on imposing atomistic patterns in other intellectual areas are increasingly unhelpful. And, on the social side, things really do not work well when we imagine people as separate, independent atoms of that kind. Yet we still find it very hard to reshape both these thought-patterns. These ideas, like a lot of others which we owe to the Enlightenment, have come to be accepted as necessary parts of rationality. Changes in them tend to look like attacks on Reason itself. If we want to rethink them as we now need to, I think it will help to glance back and see what made them so appealing in the first place.

The Source

Atomism arose in Greece out of a desperate attempt to find something in the world which was truly fixed and immutable. Parmenides proposed that what was real could only be a single ultimate unchangeable substance. He thought this was necessary because any plurality or change in the world would involve a void or nothingness, and nothingness cannot be real. It does not exist. Both change and plurality were therefore only illusions. It followed that all the things which we actually experience are unreal. For, as Heraclitus had pointed out, these everyday things are many and are in constant flux, they change as constantly as if they were made of fire. As he said, you can't get into the same river twice . . .

So, putting Parmenides's insight together with that of Heraclitus, it seemed that the world around us was indeed unreal, that reality must be a mysterious eternal something lying behind it, a realm which was altogether hidden from us. This was not a satisfactory situation. Democritus and Leucippus therefore did everybody a service by breaking the deadlock by introducing atoms. They suggested that the changing world consists of innumerable tiny units which genuinely are changeless — ultimately real in just the way Parmenides demanded — and which really do cause the changes which we see. They called these units *atoms*, which simply means indivisible objects.

An infinite number of these atoms, then, swirl around randomly through infinite space and infinite time, colliding and combining now and then by chance to form temporary universes, of which there are many besides our own. There is no purpose anywhere in this process and the gods, who have been formed by it just as much as humans have, do not try to control it. Nor do they interfere in human life. They simply live serenely on their own in the space between the universes. As for mind, it is real enough but it too consists of atoms — very fine, spherical atoms which can move freely through the coarser forms of matter. At death, this mind-stuff dissolves away into its component atoms just like the rest of the body and is lost in the vast cosmic chaos.

Now this is an extremely impressive vision. In my first lecture I said something about its moral and social consequences. I mentioned its usefulness in resisting superstition and also its thinness as a total philosophy for life. Here I want to look rather at its consequences for science and for our notion of what it is to be scientific. We can see at once that some of these consequences are good. The sheer vastness of the perspective — the sense of infinite space and time surrounding us — is most impressive. And the central insight that visible processes can sometimes be explained by finding smaller, invisible processes going on inside them is of course hugely powerful. It has been immensely fertile for science. Yet there is an unbalance in the scheme which is bound to lead to trouble. It concentrates so strongly on the atoms themselves that it has little to say about how they are related.

We naturally ask what forces are making the atoms move. But on this point the Atomists were parsimonious to the point of being miserly. They thought that nearly all the movement was simply caused by collisions. They did add the idea of a *clinamen* or bend — a kind of native, original tendency in the atoms to move slantwise. But that seems only to have been a defence against the objection that otherwise they might never meet at all, merely falling in parallel like rain. No reason was given for the slant, and since the atoms have no working parts it is hard to see how there could be any such reason. The atoms collided and sometimes got hooked together, but they never truly interacted. Nor, of course, was the slanting motion of any actual use in explaining in any detail why they behaved as they did, still less how they came to be moving in the first place. Change itself had not really been explained at all.

Trouble with Time

This difficulty is part of a twist in the original model which has caused lasting trouble — namely, that it is essentially static rather than dynamic. The Greek atomists' notion was that the mere shape and size of the atoms would explain their workings fully without reference to any forces at work or to the kind of whole within which they were working. Their pattern was still that of Parmenides, a timeless pattern requiring an inert whole incapable either of change or relation. The Atomists had not got rid of this pattern, they had merely repeated it indefinitely on a smaller scale. Their atoms are tiny Parmenidean universes.

As we know, however, later developments in physics have not borne out their insight. Since Faraday's time particle physics has steadily moved away from this static model. Forces and fields are now the main players in the game and mass is interchangeable with energy. Particles are defined in terms of their capacities for action, which naturally vary with the contexts in which they are placed. There is genuine interaction. But this scientific development was delayed for a long time by the imaginative grip of the static model — by the belief that impact was indeed the only possible source of movement, the only force that reason could recognise. In particular, the notion of gravitation was long thought to be irrational because it involved action at a distance, not caused by any collision.

Underlying these difficulties, there was a real and lasting reluctance to admit that change itself could be real. Werner Heisenberg, in his profound little book *Physics and Philosophy*, remarks on how far modern physics has now moved away from this Parmenidean obsession with the static. As he says,

> Modern physics is in some ways extremely near to the doctrines of Heraclitus. If we replace the word 'fire' by the word 'energy' we can almost repeat his statements word for word from our modern point of view. Energy is in fact the substance from which all elementary particles, all atoms and therefore all things are made, and energy is that which moves. Energy is a substance, since its total amount does not change . . . Energy may be called the fundamental cause for all change in the world . . .
>
> In the philosophy of Democritus the atoms are eternal and indestructible units of matter, they can never be transformed into each other. With regard to this question modern physics takes a definite stand against the materialism of Democritus and for Plato and the Pythagoreans. The elementary particles are certainly not eternal; they can actually be transformed into each other (Heisenberg, 1989, pp. 51, 59).

As Heisenberg explains, after these collisions the resulting fragments again become elementary particles on their own — protons, neutrons, electrons, mesons — making up their lost mass from their kinetic energy. So it is this energy itself which can be defined as 'the primary substance of the world' if anything can. As he puts it,

> The modern interpretation of events has very little resemblance to genuine materialistic philosophy; in fact, one may say that atomic physics has turned science away from the materialistic trend it had during the nineteenth century (Heisenberg, 1989, p. 47).

Reality and Intelligibility

What *materialism* means here we will consider in a moment. The first thing to notice is that this shift calls for a deep change in our traditional notion of reality, a change which we have by no means fully made yet. We are free now from the metaphysics which seemed to go with the old physics, from the notion that only the unchanging is real. We don't any longer need to posit a static terminus to explanation, treating all explanations as provisional until they reach that terminus.

Change, in fact, is *not* unreal, it is a fundamental aspect of reality. The reason why Parmenides thought that changeable, interacting things were unreal was that he thought they were unintelligible. But this idea flows from a special notion of what intelligibility is, of what it means to understand something. Certainly there are some forms of understanding which abstract from time and change, notably in mathematics. And this timelessness does give these explanations a specially satisfying kind of completeness. But for other problems, such as when we want to understand fire or explosions, time and change are part of the subject-matter. And there are other situations again, notably ones involving living organisms, where a whole range of different changes are going on at the same time. Yet we do gain some understanding of these matters. Thermodynamics and biology and climatology are not just a string of lies and delusions. Their explanations are in a way less complete, less final than those of mathematics, but this is because, being less abstract, they do so much more work. Their greater concreteness allows them to apply more directly to the actual world around us and that world is what we need to explain. That world is (we must insist) not an illusion. It is not a flimsy shell covering a true reality. It is the standard from which our notions of reality are drawn.

We need to disentangle the physics here from the metaphysics. The physical question *what stuff things are made of* is quite distinct from the much more mysterious question of *what reality lies behind the whole world of everyday experience*. Physics itself is of course part of that everyday world. The ontological question about a presumed reality behind appearance implies a sweeping distrust of *all* experience — including the observations reported in science. And that distrust needs some special kind of justification.

In the passages just cited, Heisenberg is not just doing physics. He is not just telling us that modern science finds Heraclitus's conceptual scheme more convenient than that of Democritus. He is also pointing out how misleading Democritus's scheme is metaphysically, how it can distort our notion of reality, leading to the notion that mind or consciousness itself is in some sense *not* real. The trouble is not just that Democritus's proposal of fitting mind into the atomic scheme by supplying it with smooth round atoms turned out not to work because there were no such atoms. Even if there had been those atoms, they still would not have furnished a usable way of thinking about mind or consciousness. In order to do that we have to have a language for the subjective. We have to take seriously what happens at the first-person point of view. And there is no way of doing this inside the atomic scheme, which is irredeemably an external, third-person one.

This is why atomistic thinking led people to metaphysical materialism, to the idea that *only matter is real*. The Greek atomists were the first people who seriously made this striking claim, the first real materialists. Unlike their Ionian predecessors such as Thales, they did not simply take it for granted that life and spirit were included as properties of their primal substance. Instead they seriously tried to show how life and consciousness could emerge from a world consisting only of static, inert atoms.

I am suggesting that they failed resoundingly, and that this failure is enormously instructive and fertile once we understand it. We are, I think, only now beginning to get it in focus. As Heisenberg says, during the nineteenth century materialism became hugely popular and, in spite of the efforts of modern physicists, on the whole it still remains so. It became an ideology, a creed expressed in a whole stream of devout pronouncements such as that of Karl Vogt that 'The brain secretes thought as the liver secretes bile'. But what do we mean by *reality* if we deny that our own experiences are a part of it? The point can't just be that experience is misleading or unreliable; it has to be that it doesn't happen at all. After all, a brain that has finished thinking doesn't deposit any tangible, measurable residue of thought in the experimenter's petri dish. Perhaps, then, conscious thought is just an illusion which can vanish from the equation entirely?

Metaphysical behaviourists such as Watson did sometimes try to take up this startling position but they never managed to make much sense of it. Modern exponents of materialism usually take the more modest line that experience does happen but doesn't matter much, that it is somehow *less* real, more superficial than physical processes.

This means that accounts of events involving consciousness are legitimate at their own level but they are not complete or fundamental. They are only provisional. In order to be made fully intelligible they must be reduced, by way of the biological and chemical accounts, down to the ground floor of physics which is the only fundamental level, the terminus that alone provides true understanding.

Explanations

In this form, the creed doesn't necessarily mention the notion of *reality*, so it is less obviously metaphysical. Instead it appears in more modern guise as a view about explanation and what can make it complete. But the trouble here is that clearly no explanation ever *is* complete, and, in so far as we do demand completeness, contributions from physics don't necessarily help it. When we ask someone to complete an explanation, what we normally want is something visibly relevant. For instance, if an explanation of a historical phenomenon such as anti-Semitism seems to have gaps in it we ask for material that will fill them. But that material will primarily be historical or psychological because that is the field we are dealing with. There is no obvious reason why physical details about neurones in the brains of anti-Semites could ever be relevant to the problem.

This makes a great difference to what we mean by calling an explanation *fundamental*. If we say that a certain explanation has indeed managed to be a fundamental one it won't be because it involves physics. It will be because it answers the central historical and psychological questions that it set out to answer. Some physicalist philosophers believe that in the future, when we know enough about brains, we shall discover quite new kinds of explanation which will displace all these existing forms of thought on the matter and will show that they were just superficial 'folk-psychology'. But this is simply a confusion about what different kinds of explanation do. Examining the neurological causes at work in anti-Semitic brains would do nothing at all to explain the ideas involved, any more than examining the brains of mathematicians can explain the mathematics that they are working on. Nobody has yet suggested studying mathematics in this way and it is no more plausible to propose relying on it for explaining the rest of conduct.

Why Materialism?

Metaphysical materialism got into European thought in the first place as a weapon used, first by the early atomists and then by political campaigners such as Hobbes, against the dominance of religion. In modern times the prime motivation behind it was horror and indignation at the religious wars and persecutions of the sixteenth and seventeenth centuries and its main target was the notion of the soul as a distinct entity capable of surviving death. As I mentioned earlier, this social and political motivation was very close to that of the ancient atomists, especially of Epicurus and Lucretius who were also moved by outrage at disastrous religious practices.

This motivation was a very suitable one for forging a doctrine which could be used as an effective weapon against these religious practices. But it was much less able to forge one that could serve as a balanced foundation for the whole of science, let alone for a general understanding of life. For that wider understanding, change and interaction needed to be seen as intelligible in their own terms and the first-person aspect of life had to be taken seriously as well as the objective one. Descartes notoriously saw this last problem and made a magnificent attempt to deal with it by making Mind or consciousness the startingpoint for his systematic doubt. He did succeed in getting subjectivity finally onto the philosophers' agenda, but for a long time there continued to be radical puzzlement about what to do with it.

Descartes still described Mind ontologically, not as a first-person-aspect or point of view but as a substance, something parallel to physical matter but separate from it and not intelligibly connected with it. This dualism had the fatal effect of making Mind look to many scientists like an extra kind of stuff, not like one aspect (among many) of the real world but like a rival substance demanding to compete with Matter for the narrow throne of Reality. This vision inclined scientifically-minded people to sign up for an ideology called Materialism, meaning by that not just allegiance to Matter but in some sense disbelief in Mind. The idea of the two as rivals for the status of Reality persisted. Mind was seen as an awkward non-material entity which ought perhaps to be removed with Occam's Razor and one which was certainly too exotic meanwhile to deserve serious scientific attention. And alarm about it was particularly deep in the social sciences, which were becoming increasingly sensitive about their scientific status.

That is why, in English-speaking countries through much of the twentieth century, scientists, whether social or physical, avoided so far as possible any mention of subjectivity and particularly of consciousness. In psychology this avoidance was particularly strong and was expressed as behaviourism, a ruling that the proper study of man is simply overt human behaviour. After Watson, behaviourists did not usually treat this approach as a metaphysical one. They did not claim that mind was unreal. They said their choice was simply a methodological one based on convenience. Outside behaviour (they said) was easy to observe while inner motives were occult and unobservable. So it was obvious that psychologists should confine themselves to studying behaviour.

In truth, however, such a choice of method is never likely to be separate from metaphysics. Selection of subject-matter depends on what one thinks important, and judgments about importance are part of one's general vision of the world. As I said in my first lecture, both the method and the metaphysics flow from background presuppositions of which we are often unconscious, presuppositions that are part of our picture of life as a whole. About behaviourism this dependence quickly became obvious because, before long, strict behaviourist methods were found not to be at all convenient for psychology and had to be abandoned. The attempt to study behaviour without considering the motives behind it proved hopelessly artificial because it is not really possible to observe and describe behaviour at all (apart from the very simplest actions) without referring to the motives that it expresses. And since we are social animals, we actually know a great deal about those motives.

It was not convenience, then, which had recommended this method in the first place. The attraction had been a quite different one — namely, that it *looked scientific* if one defined scientific method in devoutly materialist terms, in a manner derived from the old atomistic vision, as a method that dispensed with the concept of mind. During the last thirty years, however, notions of mind and consciousness have rather suddenly escaped from this taboo that so long suppressed them. It has been interesting to watch how they have now become matters of lively debate among a wide variety of academics. The *Journal of Consciousness Studies*, founded in 1994, thrives and prospers, supplying a place for many vigorous controversies. Much of what goes on there is metaphysics though it is often supposed only to be science. The main point of the enterprise must surely be to forge a new vision that can heal the Cartesian rift between mind and body, showing them, not as warring rivals but as complementary aspects of a larger whole. Physicists like Heisenberg saw the need for that long ago and we need now to get on with this difficult business.

Atomistic Influences

So far, I have been outlining certain rather general ways in which primitive forms of atomism survive and do unrecognised harm to present-day habits of thought. But the only example of this that I have yet given is the case of behaviourism in psychology. In order to show the force of the whole phenomenon I should, I think, probably add some others.

Behaviourism itself is quite a striking example because it has been such a powerful influence throughout the social sciences and, in spite of some changes within psychology, it still remains so today. Another striking example of quite a different kind does not concern materialism but simply the atomistic habit of breaking up wholes into ultimate units. It is the social atomism that lies at the heart of individualism — the idea that human beings are essentially separate items who only come together in groups for contingent reasons of convenience. This is the idea expressed by saying that the state is a logical construction out of its members, or that really there is no such thing as society. A social contract based on calculations of self-interest is then supposed to account for the strange fact that such things as societies do actually exist.

As I say, this social atomism does not involve materialism. But the curious pattern which it traces of unrelated human units milling around in a social vacuum does seem to me to echo very closely the equally strange pattern of unrelated Democritean atoms spinning in the void. The two patterns developed in European thinking at the same time during the seventeenth century and I suspect that they may well have reinforced each other. The physical theory conferred a reassuring scientific flavour on the social one, and the social one, when it began to operate in everyday life, made the physical theory look reassuringly familiar. The language of 'one man one vote' and 'each to count for one and nobody for more than one' sounded not only rational but scientific. At the present day I think that the idea of the Selfish Gene owes much of its appeal to recent revivals of this individualistic pattern. Actual genes are not really individualistic in this way; they are elements in a whole within which they need to co-operate quite closely.

I don't want to say much here about the drawbacks of social contract thinking, and of excessive individualism generally, because I have written about them, and about the way in which they distort gene-talk, in a number of other places. So indeed have plenty of other people. I think that my best course for now is simply to quote what one of these people says about it. So here is a piece on the subject from Michael Frayn's excellent little book *Constructions*:

> In some moods, at any rate, it seems to us that Robinson Crusoe is the human archetype. Just as philosophers thought that the thick stew of human discourse, with all its lumpy inaccuracies and indigestible assumptions, could in theory be refined down to pure white crystals — atomic propositions embodying atomic fragments of experience — so we feel that human society, with all its compromises and relativities, is a construction from the series of atomic individuals, each of them sovereign and entire unto himself. We feel that we are Crusoes who have been set down in sight of one another, so that the difficulties of communication and co-operation have been *added* to those of our isolation. As if we are what we are and *then* we enter into relations with the people around us.
>
> But man is the child of man. He comes from the belly of another human creature, seeded there by a third. He can become conscious of his thoughts and feelings only by articulating them in a language developed by communication with his fellows. Even in his inmost nature he is defined by interaction with other beings around him (Frayn, 1974, p. 67).

Memes

Well, that is one kind of social atomism. Do we want more kinds of it? If we do, these days we can have cultural atomism as well, the theory that culture too has an atomic structure, being composed of units known as *memes*.

This idea was originally proposed by Richard Dawkins in the last chapter of his book *The Selfish Gene* and it has since been taken up by a number of other sages, most recently by the sociobiologist Edward O. Wilson in his book *Consilience*. Wilson hopes that, by positing these units, he can provide a means of reconciling the humanities and social sciences with physical science by bringing them finally within its province. Memes (he says) will form 'the conceptual keystone of the bridge between science and the humanities'.

But is culture the sort of thing that can be understood by dividing it up into ultimate units? It must be, says Wilson, because atomising is the way in which we naturally think. 'The descent to minutissima, the search for ultimate smallness in entities such as electrons, is a driving impulse of Western natural science. It is a kind of instinct' (p. 50) We need, he says, to search for the basic unit of culture. . . Such a focus may seem at first contrived and artificial, but it has many worthy precedents. The great success of the natural sciences has been achieved substantially by the reduction of each physical phenomenon to its constituent elements followed by the use of the elements to reconstitute the holistic properties of the phenomenon (Wilson, 1998, p. 134).

In fact (says Wilson) it has worked in science so it is surely bound to work for the humanities.

The only way of testing this idea is to see how the pattern works out in practice. But the various meme-fanciers propose several quite different ways in which they might use it. Wilson himself seems at first to keep quite close to the pattern set by the discovery of ultimate physical particles. He wants *minutissima* – ultimate units of thought comparable to fundamental particles in physics, and he thinks these units can eventually be linked to particular brain-states so as to provide a kind of alphabet for a universal brain-language underlying all thought. This is a very ambitious project. At other times, however, Wilson forgets it and describes his particles just as readily as units of culture – obviously a quite different concept.

Most of the examples that other memologists give are closer to this cultural pattern. Dawkins himself calls his memes 'units of cultural transmission' giving as examples 'tunes, ideas, catch-phrases, clothes-fashions, ways of making pots or building arches' to which he later adds popular songs, stiletto heels, the idea of God and Darwinism. These are remarkably miscellaneous and they are plainly not the kind of things which could possibly figure as Wilsonian ultimate atoms of thought.

Dawkins insists, however, that they are not just convenient, arbitrary divisions either. They are natural units not conventional ones, fixed, distinct and lasting. Daniel Dennett is still more emphatic on this point. He gives a long list which is even more mixed than Dawkins's, a list which includes *deconstructionism,* the *Odyssey* and *wearing clothes*, and he insists that these are not just conventional divisions.

> Intuitively we see these as more or less identifiable cultural units, but we can say something more precise about how we draw the boundaries. . . the units are *the smallest elements that replicate themselves with reliability and fecundity.* We can compare them, in this regard, to genes and their components (Dennett, 1995).

If that's right, we might ask why it is that the *Odyssey* (for instance) contains within it several stories which are well-known in their own right – for instance the story of Polyphemus and that of Scylla and

Charybdis? *Wearing clothes* seems to be a general term covering a vast range of customs. *Deconstructionism* is a loose name used to describe an indefinite jumble of minor theories and *the idea of God* is also a very wide and ambiguous one.

Moreover, as Dennett himself points out, none of these items is immutable, which genes (of course) are supposed to be. Customs and traditional items of the kind he lists change and develop constantly, unless we deliberately fix them, as we do the *Odyssey*, by devices such as printing them. This constant change and development means that cultural items behave in a way quite like that of whole organisms such as plants or animals but quite unlike the behaviour of genes. Sometimes, indeed, the memologists do seem to be comparing these cultural items to whole organisms — to phenotypes — and the memes to hidden entities, unseen 'replicators' which are the occult means by which those phenotypes leap from mind to mind. This is the model on which they offer to build a science of memetics, parallel to genetics, as the right means for understanding culture. Memetics is then supposed to instruct us about the devious strategies by which these imagined entities go about their business of reproduction, the ways in which they manage to infest us. But it can't do so because there is simply no room for such entities. We already know how human beings communicate. Occult causes are not needed to explain this process . . . The pseudo-genes serve no function and they need to be cut off with Occam's Razor.

In short, cultural items like these are not ultimate, immutable fundamental particles, atoms of culture, nor are they genes which might transmit it. They are patterns within culture. Understanding them is not a matter of splitting culture into its ultimate particles because culture is not a substance, a solid stuff of the kind which might be expected to consist of particles. Instead, culture is a complex of patterns, a set of ways in which people behave. And ways of behaving are not the kind of thing which breaks down into ultimate units at all.

When we want to understand some aspect of culture, such as deconstructionism or the idea of God, we do indeed often analyse it into distinct elements, sub-patterns that compose it. But just as certainly we also need to look for the wider context of ideas out of which these patterns arise, the background which is needed to make sense of them. *Explaining* such things is primarily placing them on a wider map of other ideas and habits, relating the patterns within them to the larger patterns outside. In ordinary life that is what we do when we want to understand these patterns. And people who want to understand them more precisely — people such as historians, anthropologists, philosophers, social psychologists, novelists, poets and literary critics — have developed, over time, many subtle and skilful methods of carrying this mapping process further.

That kind of cultural mapping is, in fact, the main business of the humanities. The proposal to use the meme pattern as a means of understanding culture cannot therefore be used as a way by which the sciences can liaise with this huge range of humanistic methods, as Wilson wants. Instead, it is simply a way of ignoring those methods and offering a meaningless pattern of atomic entities as a substitute. Memetics is phlogiston and, what's more it's unnecessary phlogiston. The idea of phlogiston did at least mark a blank on the map, an empty place which needed to be filled by a proper theory of combustion. But there is no such blank on the humanistic map waiting to be filled by a new, quite general, proposal for how to start understanding culture. Of course the methods that we now use are grossly imperfect, often terribly faulty. But this is because of particular faults which we must work to correct, not a case where we haven't started to see how to proceed at all.

These, of course, are alarming words. Can it (you ask) really be true that these very intelligent, high-minded and highly-qualified people are trying to sell us phlogiston? Can it be true that they themselves have bought it? I'm afraid it is, and of course I have to explain why I think that such a surprising thing is possible.

The explanation lies in the point that I have been trying to make throughout these lectures — namely the tremendous influence of imaginative visions in general and the atomistic vision in particular, on our thought-patterns. This atomistic picture has always had enormous appeal because of its seductive finality. It seems to provide ultimate simplicity and completeness and even a kind of stability, since the atoms at least last for ever even if we don't. When we are trying to understand the shifting chaos of human affairs, the idea of simplifying them in this way is hugely attractive, especially to people who have grown up thinking of the atomic pattern as the archetype of all scientific method. In the nineteenth century all scientists thought in this way. Since then the physicists — the original owners of the pattern — have seen reason to drop this seductive vision and to recognise that the world is actually more complex. Many biologists, however, still cling to the atomic model and hope to extend its empire so as to bring order into the muddled rain-forest of human society. But that hope really is mistaken. We need to recognise the atomic vision for what it is — just one possible interpretative pattern among many — and to look for our understandings of human culture elsewhere.

Conclusion

Throughout these lectures I have been emphasising the imaginative continuity between the physical sciences and the rest of our thought. I have been pointing out the imaginative visions which underlie those sciences in an attempt to break the habit of polarization that separates them radically from the humanities — a polarization which produces a hopeless 'war of the two cultures' that no-one can win. As I said at the outset, this feud saddles schoolchildren with a painful and quite unnecessary dilemma, forcing them to specialise on one side or the other of this divide — a choice which they must make much earlier and much more completely in English-speaking countries than they do in European ones.

I hope it is obvious that, in trying to close this culture-gap, I am emphasising the importance of science in our culture, not attacking it. The reason why I have drawn attention to the imaginative and metaphysical background of our scientific tradition is that this background deeply affects the rest of our thought, contributing strongly to the shape of our moral attitudes and our value-system. The reason why science cannot be viewed as an isolated, autonomous, omnicompetent castle is that it is an organic part of our total world-view. And for that reason we all need to be conscious of it. The visions that underly science ought therefore, as I believe, to get far more attention than they presently do in the teaching of both literature and the physical sciences. I suspect, too, that both these subjects will become far more interesting to students if they are taught with a clear awareness of this background than they are when it is ignored.

17

Bryan Appleyard

Science Versus the Citizen I

The Threat of Scientism

My title for these two lectures — Science versus the Citizen — is a
reversal of the title of a book published in 1938 by Lancelot Hogben.
Hogben's *Science for the Citizen* was sub-titled 'a self-educator based
on the background of scientific discovery'. It was a fat book clad in a
strange, wallpaper-like cover that sat, throughout my childhood, on
my father's bookshelves.

Then I did no more than look at the pictures — they were thrilling
illustrations of the state of science at the time. I did not read it, but the
memory of the title stayed with me. Childishly I was puzzled by the
word 'citizen' and wondered who this person was for whom science
was being done.

Finally, I have now read it, having found an identical wallpaper-
clad edition in the London Library. I admit I have still not read it all
— I omitted the very lengthy descriptions of the state of science in
the late thirties. But Hogben's justifications for his title — even his
use of that mysterious word 'citizen' — are intriguing. The book, he
says, is written:

> [F]or the large and growing number of adolescents, who realize that they
> will be the first victims of the new destructive powers of science misap-
> plied (Hogben, 1938, p. 9).

This, remember, was 1938, when Stalin was already rampant, the
war was a year away and Hiroshima only seven years in the future. It
is also written, says Hogben, because:

[N]atural science is an essential part of the education of a citizen, because scientific discoveries affect the everyday lives of everyone. Hence science for the citizen must be science as a record of past, and as an inventory for future, human achievements. (Hogben, *op. cit.*)

The citizen was not someone to be patronised. Hogben launches a savage attack on the popular science writers of the day whose work he describes as 'weak-kneed and clownish apologetics' that show contempt for the common man. And he remembers a golden age of science writing:

The key to the eloquent literature which the pens of Faraday and Huxley produced is their firm faith in the educability of mankind (Hogben, *op. cit.*).

Science, for Hogben, was in danger of losing touch with reality. He was a utopian socialist who believed in the practical application of science. He wrote:

If the physicist capitulates to the frozen patents of monopolistic capitalism and seeks refuge from reality in speculations about the future of the universe five million million years hence, if the geneticist accepts the lop-sided mechanical technology of today and is content to culture his fruit flies in the laboratory, cut off from the urgent problems of crop and stock, if our biologists use their knowledge to concoct ingenious excuses to defend educational privileges and imperialistic exploitation of backward cultures, physics and biology will lose the driving force which science has always derived from living contact with the world's productive work, and the satisfactions of man's common needs (Hogben, 1938, p. 1081).

Science's job was to assert the common cause:

The revolt against the beehive city of competitive industrialism has already become a retreat into barbarism; and the retreat will continue unless science can foster a lively recognition of the positive achievements of civilisation by reinstating faith in a form of constructive effort (Hogben, 1938, p. 1086).

The past, as is often said, is another country, they do things differently there. Hogben's idealism sounds quaint to our ears. And so, for obvious reasons, it should. After Hiroshima, after Chernobyl, after the murderous quasi-science of communism and the industrialised slaughter of Nazism, after the bloodiest and most scientific century in human history, the dream of a scientific-technological utopia sounds like the delirium of a madman.

Yet, in fairness to Hogben, we could say he was right — bad science triumphed at the expense of good. Totalitarian and capitalist science prevailed. Good, humane, communal science never happened. Perhaps Hogben was right and we should try again.

But this, in truth, is like the argument of those old Marxists who insist that real communism has never been tried. Or like those crazed free marketeers who blame the gangster economy of postcommunist Russia on the failure to impose full-blooded capitalism. Maybe they have a point, but who would dare to let them have another go? Would we really want to give Marx another chance in the vague hope that, this time, millions might not die? Would we really wish to start work on any scientific utopia on the off chance that, this time, it might just work? The risk is too great and, anyway, the benign nature of the reward is far from obvious.

And yet science, if not in the idealised form proposed by Hogben, is still triumphant. First physics and now biology have made and are making promises of a new world so potent and so radical that they reduce the mouthings of politicians and non-scientific commentators such as myself to meaningless, marginalised babble. Physics, in the form of information technology, and biology, in the form of genetics, are telling us how our lives must be. Bill Gates called his book on the future of computing *The Road Ahead* as if there were no other. And even the supposedly neutral British Medical Association entitled its book on developments in biology *Our Genetic Future* – again as if there were no other.

So we may think that the scientific idealism of the thirties sounds quaint. But we do so while mutely accepting the scientific fatalism, the technological determinism, of our own time. We may no longer believe in science in quite the way that Hogben did, but we certainly don't believe in the power of anything else to order our world, our lives and our experiences.

It is this ideology of scientific fatalism that is the target of these lectures and, for one reason or another, of most of what I seem to write these days. It is not sufficiently understood as an ideology and it is certainly not appreciated how pervasive it has become. In this first lecture, therefore, I will say something about the philosophical nature of this ideology and, in the second lecture, I shall say something about its effect on the world.

Science, it is said, is the only human activity in which progress is truly made. Philosophy is still struggling with problems posed by Plato and nobody can seriously argue that Damien Hirst is a greater artist than Titian. But our aeronautics is certainly better than Leonardo da Vinci's and our physics seems to work better than Aristotle's.

This is a common assertion. Indeed, it underpins much of the prevailing wisdom about liberal democracy. Francis Fukuyama's End of History argument, for example, hinges on the cumulative and progressive nature of scientific knowledge. And it is probably fair to say that the contemporary idea of progress is entirely constructed on the perception of the scientific method as a series of ever more accurate descriptions of the physical world. The body of evidence for the truth of this idea seems obvious — we no longer die of smallpox and we can travel to New York in the time it would have taken Caesar's or Napoleon's armies to travel less than a hundred miles. If progress is health and speed, then we, undoubtedly, progress.

Here I do not wish to deny this idea — though there are, I think, ways in which it must be severely modified — but rather to question the way in which we have come to assume the validity of its application in all areas of human life. It is one thing to say science progresses, quite another to say that *therefore* human societies or lives progress or must progress. The first uses the word 'progress' in a technical sense; the second uses the word in moral, economic, social, political and philosophical senses. Clearly the extrapolation of the scientific idea of progress into the human realm is not a simple or innocent act. Rather it is an act that makes enormous and, you might think as I do, quite incredible claims.

And yet these claims are now commonplace. Let me suggest one rather cynical theory as to why this has happened. The recent success of scientific publishing for the layman has been based on a number of spectacular marketing triumphs. Most obviously there was Stephen Hawking's *A Brief History of Time* which was a bestseller for a decade. In addition, there have been hugely successful books from Steven Pinker, Richard Dawkins and many many others.

I think one can fairly easily imagine the marketing processes at work here. On the one hand there are scientists offering publishers these extraordinary stories, strange tales of the cosmos and the living realm. On the other hand there are the publishers wishing to make sense of these stories in terms the book buyer will understand or find appealing.

The result of this partnership is that the stories invariably have a moral. 'Then we shall know the mind of God,' says Hawking at the end of *A Brief History*. And Richard Dawkins never misses an opportunity to insist that evolution does away with the need for religion.

These may appear to be saying different things, but, in fact, they are saying the same thing. They are saying science has the answers, *all* the answers. And note also that Dawkins called one of his books *The Selfish Gene* in spite of the fact that the word 'selfish' is, in his own terms, quite meaningless. A gene can be neither selfish nor altruistic, it just does what it does. The title is an act of anthropomorphism that subverts the hard science of the book itself.

But 'Selfish' in the title or 'God' in the conclusion are good marketing devices. Here are a couple of other examples — Daniel Dennett's *Consciousness Explained* and Steven Pinker's *How the Mind Works*. The first did not explain consciousness and the second did not explain how the mind worked. Never mind, they are good selling titles. But they also extend the claims of science into the moral, religious, philosophical and psychological realms. This is exactly what the publishers wanted because it made the science seem more relevant, more urgent to the lay reader.

It also launched a kind of arms race in which ever larger claims must be made for your science if you are to compete in the book shops. So now we have *Consilience* by the Harvard biologist E.O.Wilson which promises the unification of all knowledge and Frank Tipler's *The Physics of Immortality* which guarantees us an afterlife. There are dozens more. Dimly aware that I write about science — though not *what* I write about science — publishers now deluge me with ever fatter, ever grander sounding books that announce the impending, glorious resolution of all humanity's problems on the basis of the latest science. I don't read any of them unless I must and then I give them bad reviews. It is a point of principle.

This rather eccentric and probably now declining publishing phenomenon may not be the heart of the matter, but it is a clear example of the process I am trying to describe. It is a process whereby the doctrine of scientism — the belief in the ultimate competence of science in all areas — has made a dramatic come back, in this case largely because of the competitive demands of the marketplace.

Now, to go back to Lancelot Hogben, one of the striking aspects of *Science for the Citizen* is its insistence on the linkage between science and technology. Indeed, he thinks science becomes more futile the more 'pure' it gets. For Hogben the whole point of science is its application to human society and politics. The very title makes the point: science is *for* the citizen. And the implication of that is that science is the servant of society. There are two distinct realms — science and non-science and the former is subservient to the latter.

It would be difficult, if not impossible, for any of these contemporary science writers to say this in quite these terms. First, they would have the problem of the scientific catastrophes that have occured since 1938 — nuclear weapons, ecological destruction, Chernobyl, numerous misguided attempts to bring the 'soft' human sciences into the realm of 'hard' science and so on. Secondly, they don't believe it anyway. The new scientism is far more radical than Hogben and it certainly doesn't accept the idea that science is subservient to anything.

When, for example, I appeared on a television discussion with Lewis Wolpert about my book *Understanding the Present*, his opening gambit was to insist, with embarrassing passion, that I had no right or qualifications to criticise science. No layman, apparently, had. It was, in fact, a gambit that misfired because it alienated his supposed ally in that discussion, the geneticist Steve Jones. But all Wolpert was doing was making explicit an assumption that was implicit in the writings of himself and many others — we, the scientists, are not like teachers, doctors, lawyers or journalists. We, unlike them, cannot be criticised. We are different. So much for the idea of science *for* the citizen. Science is now for itself and any benefits are incidental.

While I am on the subject of Wolpert, I would like to turn to his book *The Unnatural Nature of Science*. This is not a very good book — you would expect me to say that — but it does illustrate the kind of contortions necessary to make some kind of sense of the new scientism. Wolpert writes:

> I would almost contend that if something fits in with common sense it almost certainly isn't science. The reason, again, is that the way in which the universe works is not the way in which common sense works: the two are not congruent (Wolpert, 1992, p. 11).

This is, I think, an essentially rhetorical point designed to overcome a certain kind of lay scepticism. When, for example, a physicist talks of time going backwards or the phenomenon of nonlocality or a biologist talks of the beginning of life in replicating molecules, he may dazzle the layman but he also might provoke the response: 'So what?' These things do not obviously impinge on our sense of our selves or the world, they amaze and then leave us unchanged. The clear danger here is that such scepticism would lead to science becoming marginalised, a form of arcane knowledge that had little to do with the real world and, therefore, was undeserving of public support and respect.

Wolpert, being somewhat power mad about the place of science in society, cannot tolerate this possibility. So his tactic is, first, to make it clear that science does offend against common sense. That's just the way it is and, if you want the benefits of science, you had better accept it. Science is not made less credible by this fact. Secondly, he insists on the moral and political primacy of the scientific method. Because science works by free and open discussion, by a commitment to the truth as opposed to the partisan claims of any particular individual or group, it represents a model of human organisation.

Rather startlingly, he then enlists the American philosopher Richard Rorty in this argument. Rorty has, indeed, said something like this. But he has also said some things that Wolpert would find very unpalatable indeed.

In his essay *Science as Solidarity* Rorty writes:

> Worries about 'cognitive status' and 'objectivity' are characteristic of a secularized culture in which the scientist replaces the priest. The scientist is now seen as the person who keeps humanity in touch with something beyond itself (Rorty, 1991, p. 35).

And he adds:

> So truth is now thought of as the only point at which human beings are responsible to something nonhuman.

Rorty admires the institution of science, but not as the priesthood of truth in which Wolpert believes. Indeed, he sees the truth as a damaging metaphysical delusion. What counts is the movement towards something else — something, we hope, better — not the movement towards truth. Except in a superficial sense, Rorty is, in fact, utterly opposed to Wolpert. Nevertheless, Wolpert uses this idea to leap to his conclusion:

> The main reason is that the better understanding we have of the world, the better the chance we have to make a just society (Wolpert, 1992, p. 164).

This is an entirely unsupported assertion and it is, in fact, meaningless. Why just? Healthier maybe. Richer maybe. Faster, smarter maybe. But more just? Why? Say, for example, we found, as some claim we already have, that blacks are genetically predisposed to be less intelligent and more prone to anti-social behaviour than whites. What conception of justice would that serve? In fact, only by accepting the non-scientific proposition that all men are created equal could we combat the injustice of the scientific proposition. Only, in short, by having a pre- or extra-scientific culture would we hope to deal with the power of science.

The absurdity of Wolpert's position becomes clear when he then reverses Hogben's argument. Where Hogben sees science and technology as inseparable, Wolpert insists they are two quite different things. Technology is, like politics, the way in which science is used by the non-scientific world. He writes: 'It is with technology and politics that the real responsibility lies.' (Hogben, 1938, p. 171).

Science pursues its pure truth and it is up to the rest of us not to make a mess of its findings. So science is the only way of making a just society; on the other hand the making of society is nothing to do with science. This is having your cake and eating it on a grand scale.

Wolpert is not an isolated absurdity. Something like this argument appears in the work of most of the new advocates of scientism. Biology in particular, because of its new status as the most exciting and relevant science, is prone to combining a statement of its own purity and its ability to explain and improve the human realm. Edward O.Wilson is the most eloquent defender of the possibility of a truly scientific understanding of the realms of psychology and sociology and of the idea of science as a new unifying myth which, he points out, has the advantage over previous myths of being true. And Richard Dawkins is repeatedly blurring the lines between scientific and cultural insight, most obviously in his idea of memes — cultural ideas that propagate by essentially Darwinian methods.

These scientists are, in fact, committing the precise sin that Rorty warned against — they are turning themselves into a priesthood of the truth. And they are doing so successfully because of science's apparently limitless powers of mystification.

Let me give you an example. Recently Channel 4 ran a rather daft television series in which various supposedly authoritative types, led by the ex-Labour minister Roy Hattersley, were charged with listing the 300 most powerful people in the land. Science, it was agreed, must be represented in such a list. So the scientist Susan Greenfield presented a filmed argument for including the Oxford physicist Roger Penrose. The film said almost nothing about Penrose's work on the possibility of machine replication of human consciousness except that it was somehow significant. It did not, most importantly, point out that Penrose is, as far as mainstream science in this area is concerned, a dissident. And it did not deal with the strange ambiguities in his ideas which are essential to understanding the significance of what he is saying. Yet, sagely, the committee nodded, agreed this was science and, therefore, tremendously important. There was no attempt to challenge Greenfield's assertions nor even to ask what they meant.

It was a grotesque spectacle. Here were these grand, sober representatives of our culture who were incapable of engaging in any kind of debate about science, the most powerful force in that culture. More to the point, they did not even want to engage in debate. They even took a perverse pride in their inability to do so. Paralysed by some malign combination of class-consciousness, prissy amateurism, anti-intellectualism and downright stupidity, they wallowed in their ignorance.

Now I suspect that, if seriously challenged about their complacency, their defence would have gone something like this: we don't pretend to understand these ideas because we can't and, anyway, they are not really that important. They are unlikely to change our lives significantly, they are too abstract. It is the kind of thing most people say. It represents an implicit acceptance of Wolpert's division between science and technology because it creates a realm of incomprehensible 'pure' science which will only be worth discussing once the technological applications appear. If, for example, Susan Greenfield had produced a film about a scientist who had found a way of making robots that would decide which babies should be aborted and which old people terminated — an entirely plausible scenario — then there would have been a lively discussion. But, of course, that discussion would, by then, be too late to make any difference. If science is to be subordinate to human culture — as I think it must be — then it must be prevented from escaping into these purist mystifications. Penrose's ideas are no more difficult than those of Marx and considerably less difficult than the novels of James Joyce or the poetry of T.S.Eliot. Yet it is socially desirable to be ignorant of the former and socially disastrous to be ignorant of the latter. What a strange and dangerous state of affairs.

I need now to provide a cliffhanger to prepare you for the next lecture. Let me try this. There is, as I have tried to show, a new scientism abroad which is preying on a weak and deracinated culture. This scientism claims the capacity for complete knowledge of human affairs and yet refuses any responsibility. It provides a superficially convincing narrative for a civilisation that has lost the plot. So the cliffhanger is: how much worse can the twenty-first century be than the twentieth and who will be its Marx?

18

Bryan Appleyard

Science Versus the Citizen II

The New Marx

I would like to start with another quotation from the American philosopher Richard Rorty. I apologise for its length and slightly technical air. Its meaning is, in fact, quite simple. He writes:

> The fact that human beings can be aware of their psychological states is not, on this view, any more mysterious than that they can be trained to report on the presence of adrenalin in their bloodstreams, or on their body temperature, or on a lack of blood flow in their extremities. Ability to report is not a matter of 'presence to consciousness' but simply of teaching the use of words. The use of sentences like 'I believe that p' is taught in the same way as that of sentences like 'I have a fever'. So there is no special reason to cut off 'meant' states from 'physical' states as having a metaphysically intimate relation to an entity called 'consciousness'. To take this view is, at one stroke, to eliminate most of the problematic of post-Kantian philosophy (Rorty, 1991, p. 121).

This is a commonly advanced idea of immense significance, as Rorty indicates by that last sentence. Rorty is addressing the belief that there is something odd about human consciousness. He is saying that this apparent oddity is really no more than a social construction. It is not mysterious, it is merely the way we use language. Once we understand this, he says, we free ourselves of many of the complications of contemporary philosophy. This is an idea that liberates us from metaphysics.

A broadly similar, though not identical, argument appears in the works of Daniel Dennett and others. Rorty wants to free us from a baffling technicality. But, in the hands of Dennett, the argument is a calculated act of demystification designed to show that there can be nothing beyond the reach of science. Those who disagree or find the idea inadequate are usually dismissed as 'mysterions', lovers of the comforting complexities of mystery rather than the hard simplicity of truth.

Rorty's attempt to eliminate metaphysics and Dennett's attempt to eliminate the possibility of a realm beyond the capacity of science may be the same thing, but the intentions are somewhat different. Rorty does not intend to establish a realist conception of truth, quite the opposite, he wishes to free us into a realm where truth is unnecessary. But Dennett wants realism. He wishes to say that the truth of the world is, in essence, physics *and nothing else*. Consciousness, therefore, cannot be a mystery, it must be part of the same legible narrative of cause and effect which is the subject matter of science.

Dennett must argue this in philosophical terms because, so far, it has not been proved scientifically. The problem with human consciousness is that it has so far evaded scientific analysis. The human sciences — sociology and psychology — have attained nothing like the exactitude of physics and suffer from persistent conceptual problems. Meanwhile, computer science has been promising us artificial intelligence for fifty years or more and has, so far, achieved almost nothing. Much was made of the fact that the IBM chess computer Big Blue finally beat Garry Kasparov, arguably the greatest ever human chess player. But, in truth, that minimal achievement did more to draw attention to the broken promises of artificial intelligence than to its triumphs. Chess, in spite of the claims of its fans, is not remotely like life.

Clearly these failures represent a serious problem for the ideology of scientism. Science has so successfully dispersed so many mysteries that it is routinely assumed that dispersing any few that remained was just a matter of time. Indeed, it *had* to be just a matter of time if science is, as claimed, omnicompetent.

But the argument suffers from a conceptual problem of its own. For what would we mean when we say we have 'explained' human consciousness? We may account for its evolutionary function, we may even account for its biochemistry. But what would that mean? My answer is: nothing and that the arguments of both Rorty and Dennett are simplistic. I am, I suppose, a mysterion.

But, really, I am not being that mysterious. For the argument that human consciousness is different is not necessarily some hangover of vitalism or the residue of the Christian doctrine of the soul —

though it can be both of these things — rather it is an entirely legitimate logical proposition. It is put most famously by Thomas Nagel in his book *The View from Nowhere*. At its simplest — I don't think I am qualified to put it any other way — this states that the experience of being me is not definable, describable or explicable in physicalist terms. The question was originally put in the form: what is it like to be a bat? The answer is that it is clearly like something but that something is not something we can know. It is a different type of thing to the structure of the atomic nucleus or the sequence of DNA. Consciousness is *of* the world but it is not *in* the world in the same way that rocks, trees and quarks are. It is not a fact like any other.

Denying this argument is very important to scientistic thinkers like Dennett because consciousness is a very big thing. Indeed, it is, arguably, the only thing. If this escapes our science, then there is a big hole in the structure of scientism.

Their current favourite solution to the problem is to appeal to biology. Consciousness is merely an epiphenomenon of our evolutionary legacy. It provided Cro-Magnon man with an evolutionary advantage that helped him defeat the Neanderthals. But consciousness proved too much for that simple purpose. As well as helping us hunt and produce stable social groups, it enables us to compose symphonies, write novels and build civilisations. But, the evolutionists insist, we should not be fooled by the grandeur of the latter into disregarding the evidence of the former. The phenomenon is natural selection, the epiphenomena are symphonies and civilisations.

This, I have to say, is pretty rich. As far as I am concerned, my consciousness may be an epiphenomenon to you, but it is a phenomenon to me. The very thing that is said to be incidental is, by any rational standards, absolutely central and any attempt to claim otherwise is bound to be inherently implausible.

The key point here is that merely explaining consciousness in general in evolutionary terms — or, indeed, in mathematical or biochemical terms — is not the same as including consciousness in particular in a scientific description of the world. However complete your explanation, I, to myself, will remain unviolated. And I will be driven to agree with Wittgenstein when he says:

> We feel that even when all possible scientific questions have been answered, the problems of life remain completely untouched (Wittgenstein, 1951, p. 187).

In other words, science can describe everything except the one thing that really matters.

This is not a philosophical technicality. And it is not a matter of life and death. It is, as a Liverpool manager once said of football, much more important than that. For the opposing beliefs that science can account for everything and that it can account for nothing of ultimate human significance are the fundamental components of world views that have profound and far-reaching implications in every conceivable area of human life. Which we accept will determine who we are going to be.

At the moment, I have to say, the signs are not good. Some time ago the physicist Steven Weinberg wrote an article in the *New York Times* claiming that once physics had its Theory of Everything then people would stop reading their horoscopes. He was, basically, trying to get $8 billion out of the Clinton administration to build the Super-Conducting Super-Collider in Texas, a machine that, he believed, would give us our theory. In an *NYT* article in response I lampooned this idea — how could a set of equations change such a casual and consoling habit as horoscope reading?

Since then the Theory of Everything has receded far into the distant future. The current physical model is, apparently, seriously flawed. Clinton was wise not to build the collider. Physicists are disconsolate and, as I have said, biology has taken over as the big science of the day. I'm sorry but I take some satisfaction from this.

But, in one important sense, Weinberg has been proved right and me wrong. For biology, not physics, has indeed drawn us away from astrology. Where people used to explain some personal habit or failing by saying, 'It's in my stars', now they say, 'It's in my genes'. An anatomical determinism has replaced an astronomical. And this, I think, reflects a wider and deeper, though largely unconscious acceptance of scientism throughout society. This has happened in parallel with the triumphs of biology. And it has happened because those triumphs are so much more persuasive and intimate than the equivalent triumphs of physics. The reason why a Theory of Everything wouldn't alter people's superstitions is that it is so absurdly remote in every sense. They wouldn't understand the equations and, in any case, the causal chain that linked those equations to their experience would be so long as to be utterly ignorable. And — perhaps Weinberg hadn't thought of this — since those causal chains were so long, nobody could be sure they did not, at some point, establish the truth of astrology.

But biology is different. The principle of evolution through natural selection is easily grasped. The idea of heredity is a commonplace of everybody's experience. And the fact that we are influenced by chemical events within our body is ingrained within all of us — why else would we take aspirin for a headache? As a result, though physicists may thrill with their insights, biologists get personal. People accept their findings and conclusions simply because they are so intimate and easily graspable. And what they accept is scientism.

What is or will be the effect of this acceptance? Well, let me say what I take scientism to be as an attitude rather than a philosophy. It is, essentially, bone rattling. The scientist stands before us with his skeleton or his molecules and says triumphantly: 'Look this is all you are, a bag of bones, a chance assembly of chemicals.' He is like Hamlet peering obsessively at Yorick's skull except that, unlike Hamlet, he sees no problem. Indeed, he is delighted with his deathly insight.

This bone rattling can be found in all the big popularisers of science. Daniel Dennett is particularly fond of producing big books designed to prove simply that there is nothing but a bag of bones. Richard Dawkins is a thrilling writer, but it's still just bone rattling. And Peter Atkins positively wallows in the sheer boniness of it all.

The point here is not the insight, for that is familiar. Everybody, from time to time, is struck by the irony of the fact that all that we are seems dependent on a few bones and a tub of guts. What is important is, first, the idea that the bag of bones is *all* there is and, second, the pleasure these people take in announcing the fact.

The first idea is, as I have indicated, simply wrong. You do not have to be a vitalist to know that the realm of our minds is not explained away by these insights. However much we may discover about the physical nature of this realm, we will discover nothing about its ultimate nature which is the freedom and creativity of my experience of myself. The point is simply that we do not live among molecules, we live where we appear to live — in the real world of things and people as we perceive them. We live in a totality of which the story of physical causes and effects is one small part. This totality is scientifically untestable because, as Isaiah Berlin put it: '[T]he total texture is what we begin and end with' (Berlin, 1978, p. 114).

What we really are is really irreducible. And, as for the pleasure the bone rattlers take in rattling, well, that is a kind of morbid delight in destroying what they believe to be our illusions. It indicates that they believe there is a moral force in the insistence on the blank amorality of our being. They think it proves something more than a mere causal system. It proves that there really is nothing more than bones and guts.

If this is generally accepted — and, as I have said, it already has been to a large extent — then it will tend to encourage certain obvious attitudes. Most obviously it will encourage nihilism. All culture, value and civilisation will be seen to be based on the meaningless void of physical causation. We will be seen simply as part of a process. Nothing will be of value in itself, only as a passing incident in that process. There will be nothing worth retaining or conserving, there will only be the road ahead, leading nowhere.

People have said such things about science before. Aldous Huxley's *Brave New World* is one obvious example — it portrays a world in which the technological control of reproduction has rendered all previous values redundant. When, in that book, The Savage confronts Mustapha Mond with his need for the old feelings and values, Mond simply asks: why, they cause only suffering? And, of course, he has a point. It is difficult to defend suffering *as such*.

But such anxious visions have always previously been based on what might happen. I think now we have to face the fact that it is happening. In the case of the advance of reproductive technology, we are now entering the brave new world. The old feelings and values associated with sex and reproduction are fast fading. Why should we bother with them when the new ways are so much more convenient? What precisely is the value of the suffering associated with reproduction?

Some see a brave new scientific world as merely improbable. We needn't be pessimistic — there is no reason why science and culture should not co-exist. This, I think, is the view of Stephen Jay Gould, perhaps the best of contemporary science writers. In his superb essays he evokes a warm, humane culture of science and values living in harmony. And he goes out of his way to refute those hard, bone rattling Darwinists who insist that they have the solution to everything. For Gould there is no such solution and, anyway, it is not desirable. He wants science to be the same as poetry or art, a form of continuous and complex human expression, rather than a race to a final theory.

But his vision is utopian. He assumes that people will not be persuaded by the hard scientific radicals. But they are being persuaded. How can they not be when nobody else is trying to persuade them of anything? All that is set against science are various forms of utilitarianism. We may recoil from some process in, say genetics, but the only way we can justify our revulsion is by setting up an ethics committee that invariably ends up applying a simple utilitarian calculus. There seems to be no other way in a radically plural society such as ours. Pluralism, libertarianism and the elevation of the economic principle of the free market to the level of a universal moral panacea all create a vacuum of values in which the certainty of science seems to be the only certainty. We are, in this sense, already a fully scientific culture, the world is already brave and new.

And let me be clear about my belief that a scientific culture is really no culture at all. As Roger Scruton has put it:

> [T]here can no more be a scientific culture than there can be a scientific religion; culture, like religion, addresses the question which science leaves unanswered: the question what to feel (Scruton, 1998, p. 16).

A culture consists not of a network of causalities but of understanding. We know who we are by imaginative acts of sympathy with others, not through experiment and observation.

The truth of science is a simple statement about the natural world; the truth of ourselves is an irreducible awareness. It is this kind of truth which G.K.Chesterton evoked when he said: 'You can only find truth with logic if you have already found truth without it.' In other words: we must be who we are prior to and beyond the reach of any logical, causal explanation.

It seems to me obvious, therefore, that in ceding control — or even according too much respect — to the bone rattlers, we are courting the destruction of our humanity. And, in the wake of that destruction, there will be no safeguard against new moral catastrophes to match the old ones of Nazism and communism. So to resolve the first part of the cliffhanger at the end of my first lecture: how much worse can the twenty first century be than the twentieth? Well, it can at least be just as bad.

And, to resolve the second part: who will be the next century's Marx? Simple: Charles Darwin. For it is his thought that is now proving most effective at creating both a popular and metropolitan, bien-pensant form of scientism. It is now routine to hear the best and the brightest — Ian McEwan is one of the latest converts — speak of the possibility of a totality of explanation arising from evolutionary theory. Over the past decade Darwin has been raised to the level of cultural icon. He became the most influential figure of the nineties and continued as such into the new century. His is the face of scientism. I hope it does not become the face of tyranny in the twenty-first century.

At this point I am usually asked: what, then, is to be done? You have shown us the problem, what is the solution? In general this means what should we do about some specific issue — should, for example, human cloning be banned? And, in general, this is the sort of debate in which I find myself engaged. People, these days, want soundbites.

However, I'm not sure questions like that are the point. Inevitably we end up trying to balance the demands of irreconcilably absolute positions and, therefore, we are driven back to some form of utilitarian calculus. But my concern — and, I think, my task — is not to indulge in such banalities, but to defend certain forms of language that would raise all such arguments above the quotidian effort of making ever more feeble compromises with pluralism. And, since these lectures are supposed to be about science and education, let me put my case in those terms.

The problem of a technophiliac society is that it is all means and no ends. We know how to do many things but we do not know why we should do them. The process becomes everything. But this is only a movement towards the next movement. Insofar as there is an end, it is an end defined by its role as an aspect of the process. Where does The Road Ahead of Bill Gates lead? To the Information Superhighway. And where does that lead? And so on. There is no resting place, a point at which we can say we have arrived.

The only ethic of such a system is change. The power of this ethic is already clear. Some while ago I saw Jamie Lee Curtis being interviewed on leaving her seat in the House of Lords at the state opening of Parliament. Asked about the impending dissolution of the house, she said: 'I believe in change.' Politicians — particularly in our present government — routinely say the same kind of thing. Change is seen as an absolute good. Obviously such an idea is mad. How can change of itself be good? Bad change is just as likely as good change.

But the reason people spout such nonsense is clear — the whole culture has now accepted the Gatesian idea of the highway into the future, the continuous construction of which is the only human project on which we can all agree. This is a quite fantastic piece of reductionism that is, I believe, exactly co-extensive with the reductionist ambitions of scientism. It is the most glaring piece of evidence that we have, indeed, entered the brave new world in which the past has become simply a realm of irrational and unnecessary suffering.

This is a terrifying ideology in which people's lives are constantly devalued simply by the passage of time. If change is so good, then what we are at any given moment is doomed to imminent annihilation by what we are told to be at the next moment. And it is, of course, the ideology of consumption because it makes us as temporary and unreal as the objects we are these days required to consume. People believe in change because they have been told by Microsoft how necessary it is to change their computer or their operating system at regular intervals. If we are computers, as the advocates of artificial intelligence say we are, then, like computers, we are disposable.

The way to combat this in educational terms is to teach the possibility of inherent value rather than the value of mere process. Things must be shown to be worth having in themselves rather than as contributors to a perpetual movement forward. This may be difficult because it amounts to a moral affront to the ideal of constant becoming that is so characteristic of our age. It challenges the basis of every powerful force in the world today from multinationals to Peter Mandelson. It does so because it says that we are not simply slaves of the future and our pasts are not be as lightly discarded as last year's version of Windows.

It is also difficult because it involves taking a metaphysical step in a world that is resolutely anti-metaphysical. But, if that step is not taken, then I see no hope whatsoever. The ethic of change — which is, as I say, the ethic of scientism — is the ethic of oblivion. It is a suicidal superstition. Science is now indeed *versus* the citizen. I suggest it is time for a very quiet, very gentle and very patient citizens' revolt.

Bibliography

Abrahams, I. (1976) *Hebrew Ethical Wills* (Philadelphia: Jewish Publication Society).

Aristotle, *Politics* (Cambridge: Cambridge University Press, 1988).

Aristotle, *Nicomachean Ethics* (Oxford: Oxford University Press, 1980).

Atkins, P. (1995) 'The Limitless Power of Science', in *Nature's Imagination*, ed. John Cornwell (Oxford: Oxford University Press).

Bellow, S. (1982) *The Dean's December* (London: Secker & Warburg).

Berlin, I. (1978) *Concepts and Categories: Philosophical Essays* (London: Hogarth Press).

Bodin, J. *The Six Bookes of a Commonweale*, trans. Richard Knolles, London 1606, quoted in Robert Nisbet, (1954) *The Quest for Community* (Oxford: Oxford University Press).

Cavanagh, F. A. (ed.) (1931) *James and John Stuart Mill on Education* (Cambridge: Cambridge University Press).

Cooper, D.E. (1983) *Authenticity and Learning* (London: Routledge & Kegan Paul).

Cowling, M. (1990) *Mill and Liberalism* (Cambridge: Cambridge University Press).

Crisp, R. (1991) 'Aristotle on Dialectic', *Philosophy*, 66 (4).

Dawkins, R. (1976) *The Selfish Gene* (Oxford: Oxford University Press).

Dearing Report (1994) *The National Curriculum and its Assessment* (London: SCAA.).

Dennett, D. (1995) *Darwin's Dangerous Idea* (London: Penguin).

Department of Education and Science (1991), *International Statistical Comparisons in Higher Education: Working Report*, (London: Department of Education and Science).

Derrida, J. (1988) *Limited Inc.*, trs. S. Weber & J. Mehlman, ed. Graff, G. (Evanston, Northwestern University Press).

Dewey, J. (1916) *Democracy and Education* (New York: The Free Press).

Didi-Huberman, G. (1987) *October: The First Decade*, ed. Michelson et al., (Cambridge, MA: MIT Press).

Elazar, E. (1989) *People and Polity*, (Detroit: Wayne State University Press).

Elazar, D. and Cohen, S. (1985) *The Jewish Polity*, (Bloomington: Indiana University Press).

Ellis, J. M. (1989) *Against Deconstruction* (Princeton: Princeton University Press).

Engels, F. (1902) *The Origin of The Family* (Chicago: Charles Kerr).

Frayn, M. (1974) *Constructions* (London: Wildwood House).

Gray, J. (1992) *The Moral Foundation of Market Institutions* (London: IEA Health and Welfare Unit).

Heidegger. (1971) 'What Are Poets For?' in *Poetry, Language, Thought,* (New York: Harper and Row).

Heisenberg, W. (1989) *Physics and Philosophy* (Harmondsworth: Penguin Books).

Hirst, P.H. (1965) 'Liberal Education and the Nature of Knowledge', in Archambault, R.D. *Philosophical Analysis and Education* (London: Routledge & Kegan Paul).

Hobbes, T. (1651, 1991) *Leviathan* (Cambridge: Cambridge University Press).

Hogben, L. (1938) *Science for the Citizen: a self-educator based on the social background of scientific discovery* (London: George Allen and Unwin).

Howie Report (1992) *Upper Secondary Education in Scotland*, Report of a Committee of the Scottish Office Education Department (Edinburgh: HMSO).

Hume, D. (1740, 1964), *A Treatise of Human Nature* ed. Selby-Bigge, L. A. (Oxford: Oxford University Press).

Hume, D. (1751, 1951) *Inquiry concerning Principles of Morals,* ed. L.A. Selby-Bigge (Oxford: Clarendon Press),

Hume, D. (1757, 1965) 'Of the Standard of Taste', in J.W. Lenz, ed. *Of The Standard of Taste and Other Essays* (Indianapolis: Bobbs-Merrill)

Kermode, F. (1992) *New York Times,* 23 February.

Kimball, R. (1990) *Tenured Radicals* (New York: Harper & Row).

Kuhn, T. (1962) *The Structure of Scientific Revolutions* (Chicago: Chicago University Press).

Lawrence, D.H. (1923) *Kangaroo* (London: Martin Secker).

Lucretius, *De Rerum Natura* – various translations and editions.

MacIntyre, A. (1987) 'The Idea of an Educated Public' in Haydon, G. (ed.) *Education and Values* (London: University of London Institute of Education).

MacIntyre, A. (1990) *Three Rival Versions of Moral Enquiry* (London: Duckworth).

Maimonides, *The Guide of the Perplexed,* trans. Schlomo Pines, (Chicago: University of Chicago Press, 1963).

Mann, T. (1947, 1968) *Doctor Faustus,* translated by H.T. Lowe-Porter (Harmondsworth: Penguin Books).

Marks, J. (1991) *Standards in Schools* (London: Social Market Foundation).

Mettrie, J. de La (1748, 1994) *Man a Machine* trans. Watson and Rybalka (Indianapolis/Cambridge: Hackett Publishing Company).

Midgley, M. (2001) *Science and Poetry* (London: Routledge).

Mill, J.S. (1867, 1931) Inaugural Lecture at the University of St Andrews, printed in Cavanagh, F. A. (ed.) *James and John Stuart Mill on Education* (Cambridge: Cambridge University Press).

Mill, J.S. (1859, 1991) *On Liberty* (Oxford: Oxford University Press).

Morrell, D. (1966) *Education and Change*, Lecture 1, The Annual Joseph Payne Memorial Lectures, 1965-66 (London: College of Preceptors).

Moser, Sir Claus (1990) *Our Need for an Informed Society* (London: The British Association).

Murdoch, I. (1961) 'Against Dryness', *Encounter*, 16 (1).

Murdoch, I. (1970) *The Sovereignty of the Good* (London: Routledge & Kegan Paul).

Murdoch, I. (1977) *The Fire and the Sun* (Oxford: Oxford University Press).

Nagel, T. (1991) *Equality and Partiality* (Oxford: Oxford University Press).

National Commission on Education, (1994) *Learning to Succeed*, London: Cassell).

Newman, J.H. (1852, 1919) *The Idea of a University* (London: Longmans, Green and Co.).

Nietzsche, F. (1886, 1973) *Beyond Good and Evil* (Harmondsworth: Penguin).

Nietzsche, F. (1878, 1996) 'Undervalued Effect of Grammar-School Teaching' in *Human, All Too Human* Edited by R. J. Hollingdale, (Cambridge: Cambridge University Press)

Oakeshott, M. (1972) 'Education: the Engagement and its Frustration', in Fuller, T. (1989) *Michael Oakeshott on Education* (New Haven: Yale University Press).

Oakeshott, M. (1975) 'Learning and Teaching', in Fuller, T. (1989) *Michael Oakeshott on Education* (New Haven: Yale University Press).

O'Hear, A. (1991) *Education and Democracy* (London: The Claridge Press)

O'Keeffe, B. (1986) *Faith, Culture and the Dual System* (London: RoutledgeFalmer).

Orwell, G. (1940) *Inside the Whale and Other Essays* (London: Gollancz).

Peters, R.S. (1965) *Ethics and Education* (London: Methuen).

Peirce, C.S. (1958) *Collected Works* (Cambridge, MA: Harvard University Press)

Pilkington, P. (1991) *End Egalitarian Delusion* (London: Centre for Policy Studies).

Pring, R.A. (1989) 'Child-centred and Subject-centred Curriculum: a False Dichotomy', in *Applied Philosophy* 6 (2).

Popper, K. (1972) 'Of Clouds and Clocks', in *Objective Knowledge* (Oxford: Oxford University Press).

Ranson, S. (1984) 'Towards Tertiary Tripartism', in Broadfoot, P. (1984) *Selection, Certification and Control: Social Issues in Educational Assessing* (London: Falmer).

Rilke, R.M. (1936) *Briefe aus Muzot* (Leipzig: Insel Verlag).

Rorty, R. (1991) *Objectivity, Relativism and Truth: Philosophical Papers.Volume I* (Cambridge: Cambridge University Press).

Royal Society of Arts (1980) 'Education for Capability', *RSA Journal*.

Ruse, M. and Wilson, E. O. (1985) 'The Evolution of Ethics', *New Scientist*, October 1985.

Rutter, M., Maugham, B., Gortiman, P., and Oughton, J., *Fifteen Thousand Hours: Secondary Schools and their effects on Children* (Open Books, 1970).

Sacks, J. (1997) *The Politics of Hope* (London: Jonathan Cape).

Sartre, J-P, (1959) *Existentialism and Humanism* (London: Methuen).

Schlesinger, A. (1992) *The Disuniting of America* (New York: W.W. Norton and Company).

Scruton, R. (1998) *An Intelligent Person's Guide to Modern Culture* (London: Duckworth).

Slee, P.R.H. (1986) *Learning and a Liberal Education* (Manchester: Manchester University Press).

Stevenson, L. (1988) *Seven Theories of Human Nature* (Oxford: Oxford University Press).

Taylor, C. (1989) *Sources of the Self: the Making of the Modern Identity* (Cambridge: Cambridge University Press).

Wake, R. (1988) 'Research as the Hall-mark of the Professional: Scottish Teachers and Research in the Early 1920s', in *Scottish Educational Review*, 20 (1).

Walzer, M. (1983) *Spheres of Justice* (Oxford: Blackwell).

White, R. (1986) 'The Anatomy of a Victorian Debate', in *British Journal of Educational Studies* 34 (1).

Wiener, M. (1981) *English Culture and the Decline of the Industrial Spirit 1850 to 1980* (Cambridge University Press).

Wilson, E. O. (1998) *Consilience* (New York: Knopf).

Wittgenstein, L. (1951) *Tractatus Logico-Philosophicus* (London: Routledge & Kegan Paul).

Wolpert, L. (1992) *The Unnatural Nature of Science* (London: Faber & Faber).

Index

Abrahams, Israel 183
Aesop's Fables 216
Appleyard, Bryan xii
Atkins, Peter 219f, 231f, 234
Aristophanes 81
Aristotle, 6, 38, 81-2
Arnold, Matthew 23, 37, 41, 110, 112-3, 123, 127, 173-4
Auden, W.H. 41
Augustine, 41
Ayer, A.J. 189-90

Bacon, Francis 77, 82
Bacon, Francis (artist) 206
Beckett, Samuel 206
Bellow, Saul 95
Bentham, Jeremy 78, 185-6
Bergson, Henri 43
Berlin, Isaiah 263
Bodin, Jean 173

Callaghan, James 106, 148
Carr, David ix
Cézanne, Paul 75
Chesterton, G.K. 89, 265
Choice and Diversity 135
Churchill, Winston 206
Cicero, 30
Coleridge, Samuel Taylor 56, 123
Compte, Auguste 234
Confucius, 65
Conrad, Joseph 220
Cook, Victor x-xi.
Copleston, Edward 103, 107, 109
Cowling, Maurice 79
Crick, Francis 206

Darwin, Charles 68, 186, 233, 265
Dawkins, Richard 245f, 253, 257

Dearing Report 113
Democritus 236
Dennett, Daniel 246f, 259f, 263
Derrida, Jacques 35, 44-8, 50, 61, 65
Descartes, René 69, 207f, 242
Dewey, John 19, 104, 117, 129, 158
Dickens, Charles 55, 57
Diderot, Denis 78, 82
Dryden, John 55

Edinburgh Review 103
Editions de la Pléiade 55
Einstein, Albert 206
Eleazar 182-3, 189
Eliot, T.S. 37, 96, 206, 258
Ellis, John 44,
Engels, Friedrich 187
Epic of Gilgamesh 55
Epicurus 221, 225f
Erasmus, Desiderius 41
Everyman's Library 55
Euthyphro, 8

Fanon, Franz, 43
Ferguson, Adam 186, 210
Fermat, Pierre de 90
Feyerabend, Paul 35
Fish, Stanley 47,
Fitzgerald, Edward 51
Forster, E.M. 55
Foucault, Michel 35, 44f, 72
Frayn, Michael 245
Freud, Sigmund, 46, 187f
Fukuyama, Francis 253

(Galilei) Galileo, 233
Galsworthy, John 57
Gates, Bill 252, 266
Gatherer, William ix

Genesis, 66, 174-5, 178
Ghandi, Mahatma 206
Gide, Andre 55
Gilbert & George 90
Godel, Kurt 212
Goethe, Johann 51
Good Food Guide, 64
Goodman, Fred 20
Gorbachev, Mikhail 206
Gould, Stephen Jay 264
Gray, John 137
Gray, Thomas, 41
Great Debate in Education 106, 148-51, 159
Green, T.H. 123-4
Greenfield, Susan 257

Haldane, John ix, 14
Halpern, Ralph 57
Hardy, Thomas 42, 56
Hare, Richard 78
Hawking, Stephen 253
Heidegger, Martin 35, 44, 75
Heisenberg, Werner 238f
Heraclitus 236
Hitler, Adolf 206
Hobbes, Thomas 175-7, 179, 185, 214-5, 227
Hogben, Lancelot 250-2, 254
Holbach, Paul-Henri 78
Homer, 38, 55,
Hopkins, Gerard Manley, 41
Housman, A.E. 41
Howie Report 113
Hume, David 9-10, 71, 89, 184-5, 188-9, 207f
Huxley, Thomas 110, 233
Huxley, Aldous 214, 264

Illich, Ivan 20,

Jackson, Rev. Jesse 34
James, Henry 57, 220
Joad, C.E.M. 67
Johnson, Samuel, 39, 41
Jones, William 51

Kant, Immanuel, 4, 24, 43, 78-9, 185, 188-9, 208f
Kermode, Frank 95
Kimball, Roger 67
Knox, John 193
Koran 70
Kuhn, Thomas, 35, 46, 88

La Mettrie, Julien de 225
Lawrence, D.H. 182
Leavis, F.R. Mrs 56
Leucippus 236
Lloyd Weber, Andrew 90
Locke, John 207
Lodge, David 47
Lucretius 221f, 235

McEwan, Ian 265
MacIntyre, Alasdair, xiii, 202-3, 209
Mandela, Nelson 193, 195, 206,
Mandelson, Peter 263
Mann, Thomas 86
Mannheim, 61
Marks, John 96, 98
Marlowe, Christopher, 41
Marx, Karl, 20, 46, 187f, 252
Maude, John137
Midgley, Mary xii
Mill, John Stuart 11, 22, 43, 77, 79, 81, 103-4, 107f, 123, 140, 143, 150, 186
Moore, Henry 75
Morrell, Derek 108-9
Morant, Robert 124
Moser, Claus 96-8
Mozart, 94, 95
Murdoch, I. 74-5, 79

Nagel, Thomas 95
Neill, A.S. 21
Newman, John Henry 70, 88, 93, 104, 107, 109f, 123
Nietzsche, Friedrich 46, 71-2, 74, 80-1, 84, 187f
Nozick, Robert 177

Oakeshott, Michael 78, 89, 91-3, 112, 124
O'Hear, Anthony x, 104-5, 112, 138
O'Keefe, Bernadette 211
Orwell, George 51, 77, 81

Parmenides 236f
Pascal, Blaise 41
Peirce, Charles S. 73, 89
Penrose, Roger 257
Peters, Richard 111
Picasso, Pablo 206
Pilkington, Peter 97, 121
Pinker, Steven 253
Plato, 8, 30, 38, 41, 91, 162, 187
Pope, Alexander 212
Popper, Karl 224-5
Pound, Ezra 55
Pring, Richard x
Proust 57, 75,

Quinton, Anthony x, 72, 77, 89, 104-5, 112, 138, 142, 159

Reimer, 20
Rhys, Ernest, 39,
Rieff, Philip 188
Rilke, 75-6,
Rousseau, 19, 21
Rorty, Richard 35, 41, 46-8, 61-3, 256, 259f
Royal Society of Arts 92, 112,
Ruse, Michael, 187
Ruskin, William 94
Rutter, Michael 160

Sacks, Jonathan xi-xii
Saddam Hussein 206
Sadler, Michael 124
Sartre, Jean-Paul, 44-5, 189-990
Schlesinger, Arthur 94-5
Scott, Walter 57
Scruton, Roger 265
Shakespeare, William 42, 95
Shelley, Percy 57
Sheppard, David 191

Sidgwick, Henry, 110
Smith, David 194
Socialist Education Association, 92
Socrates 80-1
Solzhenitsyn, Alexander 206
Spart, David 50
Sputnik, 52
Stalin, Joseph 54, 206
Stevenson, Leslie 197
Suslov, Mikhail 54
Sutherland, Graham 206
Sutherland, Stewart xi-xii

Taylor, Charles 71-3, 76, 78
Temple, Shirley 196
Thackeray, 55
Tipler, Francis 254
Tolstoy, 43, 56, 58, 94
Trilling, Lionel 59

Verdi, Giuseppe 94
Virgil, 55
Victor Cook Lectures viii, 104-5, 117, 138, 142, 191
Vogt, Karl 240
Voltaire, 227

Waley, Arthur 51
Warhol, Andy 90
Warnock, Mary x
Watson, James 206
Watson, John 240, 243
Waugh, Evelyn 57
Weinberg, Steven 262
Wells, H.G. 220
White, Lord 57
White, Ralph 109
Whitman, Walt 41
Wilkins, 206
Williams, Raymond 50
Williams, Shirley 150
Wilson, E.O. 72, 187, 254f
Wittgenstein, Ludwig 212, 261
Wolpert, Lewis 255f

Young, Michael 159